Maimonides' Cure of Souls

MAIMONIDES' CURE OF SOULS

Medieval Precursor of Psychoanalysis

DAVID BAKAN
DAN MERKUR
and
DAVID S. WEISS

Published by
STATE UNIVERSITY OF NEW YORK PRESS, ALBANY

© 2009 State University of New York

All rights reserved

Printed in the United States of America

No part of this book may be used or reproduced in any manner whatsoever without written permission. No part of this book may be stored in a retrieval system or transmitted in any form or by any means including electronic, electrostatic, magnetic tape, mechanical, photocopying, recording, or otherwise without the prior permission in writing of the publisher.

For information, contact State University of New York Press, Albany, NY
www.sunypress.edu

Production by Kelli W. LeRoux
Marketing by Michael Campochiaro

Library of Congress Cataloging-in-Publication Data

Bakan, David.
  Maimonides' cure of souls : medieval precursor of psychoanalysis /
David Bakan, Dan Merkur and David S. Weiss.
    p. cm.
  Includes bibliographical references and index.
  ISBN 978-1-4384-2745-4 (hardcover : alk. paper)
  ISBN 978-1-4384-2746-1 (pbk. : alk. paper)
1. Judaism and psychoanalysis. 2. Maimonides, Moses, 1135–1204. Thamaniyat fusul.
3. Psychotherapy—Religious aspects—Judaism. 4. Soul—Judaism. 5. Meditation—Judaism.
6. Prophecy—Judaism. I. Merkur, Daniel. II. Weiss, David S. (David Solomon), 1953–
III. Title.
  BM538.P68B35 2009
  296.3'71—dc22

2008048483

10 9 8 7 6 5 4 3 2 1

Contents

PREFACE		vii
ACKNOWLEDGMENTS		xv
LIST OF ABBREVIATIONS		xvii
ONE	The Will to Illness	1

Aristotelian Premises of Maimonides' Psychology, Aristotelian Forms, Actualization, Al-Farabi's Political Philosophy, Maimonides' Behavioral Therapy, Sin Causes Ignorance, Repentance, Conclusions

TWO	Worship of the Heart	25

The Commandments of Monotheistic Beliefs and Affects, Maimonides' Curriculum, Maimonides' Intellectualist Mysticism, The Rational Character of Maimonides' Intellectualist Mysticism, The Mystical Character of Maimonides' Rationalism, Maimonides' Practice of the Presence of God, The Therapeutic Effects of Meditation, Conclusions

THREE	Imagination and the Interpretation of Prophecy	49

Imagination and Anthropomorphism, Intellectualist Mysticism and Prophecy, Dreams and Visions of Prophecy, The Psychology of Imagination, The Place of Imagination in the Interpretation of Scripture, The Prophecies of Abraham, Confirmation from Ezekiel, Conclusions

| Four | Perplexity and the World to Come | 73 |

Maimonides' Esotericism, The World to Come, The Thirteen Foundational Principles of the Law, The Four Who Entered Paradise, Monistic Mystical Union, Conclusions

| Five | Secrets of the Law | 97 |

Arayot, The Account of the Beginning, Maimonides on Sexuality, The Account of the Chariot, Conclusions

| Six | Maimonides' Psychotherapy Client Population | 127 |

| Seven | Convergences of Maimonides and Freud | 137 |

Freud's Access to Maimonides, Dream Interpretation, The Privileged Place of Sexuality, Sociocultural Conflict Model, Theories of Pathology and Therapy, Psychic Reality, Understanding on One's Own, The Unconscious, Views of Judaism, Prophetic Ambition, Conclusions

| References | 167 |

| Index | 179 |

Preface

My father's father was a *sofer*, a scribe, who lived in Poland. He would send my father packages of inscriptions for door posts (mezuzahs) and phylacteries (tefillin), and once a Torah scroll, for sale to the Jewish religious goods stores in Manhattan's Lower East Side. I can remember my father coming home and asking if the *sechoirah* (merchandise) had arrived, referring to the package of tefillin and mezuzahs. He awaited it eagerly. Then he would take this merchandise and sell it to the stores on Delancy Street in New York. One of my very earliest memories is the smell of shellac in my house, because the very last stage in the production of tefillin was its shellacking. My father would take the kitchen table, cover it with newspaper, and shellac tefillin. The tefillin would dry overnight and I remember seeing in the morning a table full of shiny tefillin. I associate that memory with the first time I ever heard the story of the legend of Abraham. The story is that Abraham's father, Terah, was an idol maker. One day when Abraham's father was gone, Abraham smashed the idols. I remember that the first time I heard the story I had a twinge, and the twinge was that these tefillin for my father had nothing to do with holiness—they were completely *sechoirah*, completely merchandise. They were things for buying and selling and making money. I remember thinking how I was like Abraham, who lived in the house of his father who was a maker of idols.

My maternal grandfather knew barely a word of Hebrew. He had learned nothing but how to *davan*, recite prayers. But he was very devout. I would ask him how he could *davan* when he did not understand a word of it, and he would answer that it was enough that God understood.

As a child, I learned Hebrew and Zionism, Torah, Mishnah and Talmud, all infused with a rational spirit. And one day the *sechoirah*, the merchandise, led to my introduction to Maimonides. It was during the depression, and one of the things that was difficult for my father was to sell and to collect the money for the merchandise. He had a routine of collecting money every Sunday. A Jewish bookstore, according to my father, was not very financially responsible, and the owner was reluctant to pay for merchandise. One Sunday, my father went to that bookstore and the owner gave my father a copy of a book instead of payment. He pushed the book at my father and said, "Here, take it. It is a wonderful book in English. Take it home and give it to one of your children." The book that he gave him was the *Guide of the Perplexed*, written by Moses Maimonides and translated by Friedländer into English. My father gave it to me, although he found it strange that anyone would ever think of translating Maimonides into English. Some years later I told my father that the *Guide of the Perplexed* was originally written in Arabic and not in Hebrew. He did not believe me and told me that that was just nonsense.

That book has been with me physically, as well as psychologically, ever since. The exposure to the book has played an important role in my intellectual life consciously and, I am sure, unconsciously. I made my life as a psychologist, but I returned at intervals to study Maimonides. I had a lifetime friendship with Marvin Fox. We were colleagues in the late 1940s at Ohio State University. I was introduced to thinking about Maimonides in a scholarly manner from him. Further insight into Maimonides occurred when I read Leo Strauss's important introductory commentary to the Pines translation of the *Guide of the Perplexed*. Strauss emphasizes over and over that the *Guide of the Perplexed* is a book that has two layers: the manifest content and the latent content. Underneath the manifest, there is a whole secret text. When I was teaching at the University of Chicago, I spoke with Leo Strauss and he explained that he sees the *Guide of the Perplexed* as a book that is a riddle. But he missed one point: the genuineness of Maimonides' understanding of the relationship between Judaism and philosophy. I was also acquainted with Isadore Twersky and Alexander Altmann, two more of the finest students of Maimonides in my generation.

Now let me take up another thread of my life. When I began teaching at the University of Missouri in 1949, I arrived as a young professor and there was a course that nobody had taught for a number of years on the history of psychology. I was quite enthusiastic about it and I worked hard preparing the course. In gathering the materials for the different lines that converged in contemporary psychology, I had a very interesting experience. I found that it was mostly time that was the main barrier to discovery. It was relatively easy to go to the library and trace the history of the identifiable trends in psychology; the main limitations were time and energy. The history of psychology is an open story. However, when I came to one kind of psychology, the psychoanalysis of Freud, I drew only blanks. There was no history. If you read Freud's *History of the Psychoanalytic Movement* (1914b), you expect to find some history there and you do not. All that he wrote was how he heard jokes in a corridor once or how he had a dream and great revelations came to him. He claimed complete originality. His claim that psychoanalysis was his great personal insight was unacceptable to me. I had studied enough history to be very skeptical of claims of single authorship. My judgment was that the body of ideas that Freud put forth, seemingly as his own, simply could not be the work of a single individual, in the sense that his writing might lead one to believe. The main and strong ideas were, I felt, the product of transindividual and transgenerational work and gestation. But where does psychoanalysis link with history before Freud?

For a while, I entertained the hypothesis that Freud's psychoanalysis could and should be traced to Romanticism, particularly German Romanticism, as, say, expressed in Goethe. Then I read somewhere that Goethe had, when he was young, been involved with a group that was studying Jewish kabbalah. The puzzle started to unravel when I read the wonderful book by Gershom Scholem, *Major Trends in Jewish Mysticism* (1954). Eventually, I became persuaded that the appropriate historical backdrop for psychoanalysis was to be found in Jewish mysticism and I made the case in my book *Sigmund Freud and the Jewish Mystical Tradition* (1958). Its two major claims have both stood the test of time. The Talmud, redacted in the fifth century, but incorporating material as old as the first century, contains detailed discussions of dream interpretations that treat their latent content as their intended message and include explicit sexual concerns among the latent contents. Second, the kabbalah, from its inception in the late twelfth century, sexualized the cosmos, seeing all things as manifestations of divine hypostases that were masculine, feminine, or conjunctions of the two. Two of Freud's most important theses, the interpretation of dreams and the extension of the concept of sexuality, both had antecedents in the Jewish mystical tradition.

The book was rightly criticized, however, for not supplying the details of the connection. By what route or routes did Freud have access to Jewish mysticism? What school or schools of thought within Jewish mysticism influenced Freud? Capps (1971) noted that Freud cited writings by Eduard von Hartmann, who wrote explicitly of the Christian cabala. Merkur (1994) found two details—the therapeutic significance of interpreting manifestly sexual fantasies, and the interpretation of parapraxes—in the teachings of Hasidism, the ultraorthodox Jewish sect in which Freud's father Jacob was raised. Drob (2000a, 2000b) suggested that Rabbi Isaac Luria, a sixteenth century kabbalist, was a connecting figure.

Deepened understanding of the teachings of Maimonides has convinced me, however, that the convergences with the thought of Maimonides are dramatically more plentiful (Bakan, 1989). The particular version of Jewish mysticism that influenced Freud came out of Maimonides. Altmann (1936) demonstrated that the kabbalistic writings that had traditionally been attributed to Maimonides were pseudonymous works produced generations after his death. Maimonides was a contemporary of the origins of the kabbalah. He wrote, it would seem, in opposition to the Platonizing, "proto-kabbalistic" views of Judah ha-Levi and other medieval authors who were his contemporaries or immediate predecessors (Kellner, 2007). The earliest unequivocal evidence that we possess of the kabbalah, involving the figures of Rabbi Abraham ben David (Rabad), his son Rabbi Isaac the Blind, and the anonymous *Sefer Ha-Bahir*, "the Book of Radiance," dates to the last quarter of the twelfth century (Scholem, 1954), the very years when Maimonides published his *Commentary on the Mishnah*, the *Mishneh Torah*, and the *Guide of the Perplexed*. Maimonides' mysticism constituted an alternative to the early kabbalah that had formative impact on the kabbalah's subsequent development. Moshe Idel (1990, 2004) argues that Maimonides' publications provoked the first kabbalists to publish their views in order to defend their position against him. Scholem (1954) established that Maimonides' writings were major influences on both Moses de Leon and Abraham Abulafia. De Leon was the probable author of the pseudonymous *Sefer Ha-Zohar*, "the Book of Splendor," the late thirteenth century sourcebook of the "theosophical" school of kabbalah; while de Leon's contemporary Abulafia founded the minority rival tradition that Idel (1988) terms the "ecstatic" kabbalah. Abulafia claimed no less than that the *Guide* and *Sefer Yetsirah* were the only guides to esoteric wisdom (Heschel, 1996, pp. 125–126).

Blumenthal (1977) argued that the mysticism of Maimonides was an instance of philosophic mysticism that was devoted to the *nous*, "Intellect." As Aristotle's concept of *nous* was developed in the Neoaristotelian and Neoplatonic traditions of late antiquity, early medieval Christianity, and the Islamicate, it was often called the "Active Intellect," the technical term that Maimonides used. Maimonides' approach to intellectualist mysticism may profitably be compared with the versions of his Muslim predecessors and contemporaries, al-Farabi, Ibn Sina (Avicenna), Ibn Bajjah (Avempace), and Ibn Rushd (Averroes). All agreed that the Active Intellect produces knowledge of the universals by acting on the rational faculty of the human soul. They differed, however, regarding the role and nature of imagination.

I had been trying to work out the riddle of Maimonides for years when it became apparent to me that Freud's understanding of dreams was the key to understanding Maimonides' *Guide of the Perplexed*. For Maimonides, prophets apprehend prophecy through visions and dreams quite in the same way that Freud described dreams. From this point of entrance into Maimonides' secrets, I began to decode the passages in his texts that were composed as sealed writings. In the coded portions of the *Guide*, I found that Maimonides' subtext goes beyond the public discussion among the Muslim philosophers to integrate the secret teachings of the Rabbis concerning the sexual symbolism of dreams and visions. In this way, Maimonides presents an exquisitely Jewish version of intellectualist mysticism. For Maimonides, much more than philosophic truth and ethical conduct were at stake. Maimonides was concerned, above all, with "the healing of the soul and its activities" (*Eight Chapters*, p. 38), and Freud was indebted to Maimonides' distinctively psychological version of intellectualist mysticism.

A few years ago I presented my first findings on Maimonides in a book called *Maimonides on Prophecy* (1991). I now find that there is much more to say on Maimonides' therapy of the soul and its convergence with the psychoanalysis of Freud.

DAVID BAKAN

I knew David Bakan as his student, colleague, and friend for a quarter century. When, due to advancing years, David found himself unable to continue working for extended periods of time, he asked me to assemble his notes on Maimonides into a book. The assembly was done in two phases. I produced an initial draft in 2000, and in the months preceding David's death in 2004 I created a second draft by incorporating new materials that David had written in the interval. The individual passages that David composed varied in length from fifty to a thousand words. Many existed in multiple variants that had to be synthesized before the individual units could be organized into a coherent exposition. David assigned me the task of creating the overall design and structure of the book, which of course revealed unanticipated gaps in his arguments and necessitated further study of Maimonides.

At the time that I began the second draft of the manuscript, David asked me to see the book through to publication and invited me as co-author. David lived to see the second draft, but neither to review nor complete it. Following his death, Rabbi David S. Weiss, with whom David had met regularly for many years to study Maimonides, read the draft and provided many useful comments and suggestions. He also composed a few original passages that included views that David Bakan had expressed orally during their meetings. I then undertook what eventually became a series of further drafts of the book, with David Weiss's help, reading and commenting on each version. Early in the process of posthumous collaboration, I was uncertain whether to remain within the scope of David Bakan's notes or to exercise greater license in order to fulfill David's ambitions for the project, and I had a dream one night in which I saw David saying to me, "Keep on going." I counted David's acquired intellect among the angelic intelligences and wrote accordingly. Later, after a publisher's readers agreed that the manuscript was insufficiently advanced, I decided, in consultation with David's children, to undertake further research and to redesign the manuscript so that David's vision of Maimonides and Freud could find a public audience. The result has been a true collaboration—a book that is as much mine as David's. David's notes and oral comments to David Weiss account for perhaps 80% of the close readings of Maimonides' *Guide*, perhaps 20% of the readings of *Eight Chapters*, and almost all of the final chapter's comparisons of Maimonides and Freud. I bear responsibility for occasional readings of Maimonides, together with placing David's readings of Maimonides in the context of medieval Aristotelianism, the kabbalah, and the history and theory of psychotherapy.

I would like to thank David S. Weiss for his collaboration in this project. I am indebted also to David R. Blumenthal and Dereck Daschke, whose comments on an earlier draft were invaluable to my redesign of the text. I thank the Bakan family, and especially Danny and Jacob Bakan, for their support in bringing this book to completion. Lastly, I thank my children Matthew, Jeremy, Kira, and Isaiah, for their love.

DAN MERKUR

Many Jews today have a tremendous thirst for knowledge and mysticism and are searching for direction. Unfortunately, that direction is often explored outside the Jewish tradition and thought. One important contribution of this book, *Maimonides' Cure of Souls*, is an integrated response to that need. The book leverages the extensive writings of Maimonides on law, ethics, philosophy, prophecy, and psychology and delivers an integrated approach to Jewish spirituality. The challenge to readers is to use the knowledge of this book to unleash a deeper and more meaningful apprehension of what Judaism and life are all about.

This book, *Maimonides' Cure of Souls*, has been the product of over twenty-five years of study and work. My journey began in 1981 at an Ontario Psychological Association Conference. I sat in on a lecture by David Bakan who presented on the topic of "The Cloak and the Couch"—the intersection of religion and psychology. One of his messages was that the most pressing problem for Judaism today is that "we have to stop telling children's stories to adults." He argued that Judaism must be more than simple stories of Abraham smashing his father's idols, and of miraculous redemptions after hundreds of years of slavery. After his presentation, I approached David and told him that I was an ordained rabbi and psychologist and that I was very interested in his ideas. He asked me what I thought of *The Guide of the Perplexed* by Maimonides, and I gave him the common answer that after studying it I was even more perplexed than before. He then said excitedly that he was looking for someone like me, a perplexed rabbi-psychologist, to be his study partner and explore the wisdom and insights of the *Guide* with him. We began to meet at his home to study the *Guide*, which quickly became a regular study partner "*chavruta*" relationship that continued until his death on October 18, 2004 (Weizmann & Weiss, 2005).

In 1991, David published a book, *Maimonides on Prophecy*, which was an ad locum commentary on selected chapters of *The Guide of the Perplexed*, but we felt that we still needed to respond to the widespread perplexity today that necessitated an integrated and meaningful "adult" story for Jewish adults. The result is this book, *Maimonides' Cure of Souls*. My hope is that it will create a meaningful and unified understanding of Jewish spirituality and provide the multitude of perplexed Jews with the foundational insights to help them out of their perplexity.

It has been an invigorating and spiritually uplifting experience to co-develop the thoughts in this book. I want to express my deep gratitude to my co-authors. To David Bakan, my mentor, study partner, and friend—thank you for exposing me to your mind and including me in your life. I dedicate my work on this book to you. To Dan Merkur—thank you for your commitment, insights, and tireless work throughout this writing process. Finally, to my wife, Dr. Nora Gold, and my son, Joseph Weissgold—thank you for your constant love and support throughout the many years of this work.

DAVID S. WEISS

Acknowledgments

Quotations from *Guide of the Perplexed* by Moses Maimonides, translated by Shlomo Pines, with an Introduction and Notes by Shlomo Pines, Vols. 1 and 2 published by the University of Chicago Press, 1963. © The University of Chicago. Used courtesy of the University of Chicago Press.

Abbreviations

Commentary on Aboth	Maimonides, Moses. (1983), *Maimonides' Commentary on Pirkey Avoth: The Mishna of Avoth with the Commentary and Selected Other Chapters of Maimonides.* Trans. Paul Forchheimer. Jerusalem & New York: Feldheim Publishers.
BK	Maimonides, Moses. (1937), *Mishneh Torah: The Book of Knowledge.* [Volume 1 of Maimonides' Code.] Trans. Moses Hyamson. New York: Bloch Publishing; reprinted Jerusalem: Feldheim Publishers, 1971.
BT	Babylonian Talmud
Eight Chapters	Maimonides, Moses. (1912), *The Eight Chapters of Maimonides on Ethics (Shemonah Perakim): A Psychological and Ethical Treatise.* Trans. Joseph I. Gorfinkle. New York: Columbia University Press; reprinted New York: AMS Press, 1966.
Guide	Maimonides, Moses. (1963), *The Guide of the Perplexed.* Trans. Shlomo Pines, 2 vols. Chicago: University of Chicago Press.
Guide, trans. Friedländer	Maimonides, Moses. (1904), *The Guide for the Perplexed.* Trans. M. Friedländer, 2nd ed. New York: Dover, 1956.
Helek	Maimonides, Moses. (1966), "Maimonides on Immortality and the Principles of Judaism," trans. Arnold Jacob Wolf, *Judaism* 15:95–101, 211–216, 337–342.

JT   Jerusalem Talmud

Letters   Maimonides, Moses. (1977), *Letters of Maimonides*. Trans. Leon D. Stitskin. New York: Yeshiva University Press.

Resurrection   Maimonides, Moses. (2000), Treatise on the Resurrection. Trans. Hillel G. Fradkin, pp. 154–177. In Ralph Lerner, *Maimonides' Empire of Light: Popular Enlightenment in an Age of Belief*. Chicago & London: University of Chicago Press, 2000.

ONE

The Will to Illness

RABBI MOSHE BEN MAIMON (c. 1136–38 to 1204), who was known in Latin as Moses Maimonides, is famed for his contributions on Jewish law, philosophy, and medicine. His extant legal writings include several letters, surviving portions of youthful commentaries on Talmudic tractates, a *Commentary on the Mishnah*, a list of biblical laws entitled *Book of the Commandments*, and the *Mishneh Torah*, literally "Second Law," a codification of rabbinical law that is also called the *Code* and the *Compendium*. Maimonides' legal writings coincided with his activities as a religious community leader, an international authority on rabbinical law, and the author of the first systematic codification of the Jewish legal tradition. His formulations of Jewish philosophy, both in the opening volumes of the *Mishneh Torah* and especially in *Guide of the Perplexed*, used medieval Aristotelianism to promote science and rationalism, shaped the course of all later Jewish philosophy, and also influenced European thinkers from Thomas Aquinas (Burrell, 1988) and Meister Eckhart to Isaac Newton (Popkin, 1988, 1990). Maimonides is also remembered for medical treatises that included important minor contributions that arose out of his private practice as a physician. This book is the first to address the comparatively little known topic of his program of psychotherapy.

Shemoneh Perakim, "*Eight Chapters*," is a self-contained treatise on faculty psychology and psychotherapy that is contained within Maimonides' multivolume, running ad locum *Commentary on the Mishnah*. It is today discussed chiefly from perspectives in the histories of philosophy and psychology that scarcely know what to make of Maimonides' self-presentation as a physician of the soul. He wrote:

> You know that the improvement of the moral qualities is brought about by the healing of the soul and its activities. Therefore, just as the physician, who endeavors to cure the human body, must have a perfect knowledge of it in its

entirety and its individual parts, just as he must know what causes sickness that it may be avoided, and must also be acquainted with the means by which a patient may be cured, so, likewise, he who tries to cure the soul, wishing to improve the moral qualities, must have a knowledge of the soul in its totality and its parts, must know how to prevent it from becoming diseased, and how to maintain its health. (*Eight Chapters* i; p. 38)

In Maimonides' view, moral behavior, the implicit concern of his exhaustive legal writings, has its foundation in the health of the soul. Maimonides wrote: "The soul's healthful state is due to its condition, and that of its faculties, by which it constantly does what is right, and performs what is proper, while the illness of the soul is occasioned by its condition, and that of its faculties, which results in its constantly doing wrong, and performing actions that are improper" (*Eight Chapters* iii; p. 51). Because Maimonides regarded virtue as healthy and vice as an illness, he maintained that a moral educator had to be a physician of the soul, who possessed a philosophical—we might today say theoretical—understanding of the soul, its makeup, activities, and vicissitudes. Conversely, the diseases of the soul were moral in character, and people afflicted with illness of the soul were advised to seek the help of moral physicians.

> Those whose souls become ill should consult the sages, the moral physicians, who will advise them against indulging in those evils which they (the morally ill) think are good, so that they may be healed by that art ... through which the moral qualities are restored to their normal condition. (*Eight Chapters* iii; p. 52)

The location of the *Eight Chapters* within the *Commentary on the Mishnah* reflects the integral relation that Maimonides saw between psychotherapy and ethics. The *Eight Chapters* is located immediately before and serves as an introduction to Maimonides' commentary on *Pirke Avoth*, "Chapter of the Fathers," the section of the Mishnah that concerns ethics.

ARISTOTELIAN PREMISES OF MAIMONIDES' PSYCHOLOGY

Contemporary writers on the *Eight Chapters* stress its historical position as an instance of medieval Aristotelian faculty psychology. Aristotle began with a very broad definition of soul that applied to plants, animals, and people: soul was the whole of the difference between a living being and its corpse. "Soul [is that] by which primarily we live, perceive, and think" (Aristotle, *On the Soul* 414^a 12). Soul was integral to the functions of a living body and could not exist in its absence. "Soul is an actuality or account of something that possesses a potentiality of being such" (414^a 28–29). Aristotle used the term "form" in reference to soul, but he did not refer to shape or image. The body's "matter is potentiality, form actuality" (414ª 16), in the sense that a corpse has the matter but not the form of a living body. By "form" Aristotle meant something that included activity, function, and purpose. An example that he provided claimed that the form of a hand included holding, grasping, manipulating, touching, feeling pleasure, pain, heat, cold, softness, hardness, and so on. The hand of a corpse, like the hand of a statue, was a hand in name only because neither a corpse nor a statue could do what a living hand could do; it was what a hand did that constituted it as a hand, warranting its designation as a hand rather than as inert flesh, or marble, or whatever (Robinson, 1989, pp. 44, 51, 91).

Maimonides distinguished five faculties of the soul. (1) The nutritive faculty, which was common to vegetable and animal life, had the power of attracting nourishment and retaining it, along with digestion, repulsion, growth, procreation, and differentiation of the nutritive juices for sustenance from those to be expelled. (2) The sensitive faculty, which distinguished animal life, accomplished seeing, hearing, tasting, smelling, and touch. (3) The appetitive faculty was responsible for desiring and loathing things, leading to pursuit or flight, inclination or avoidance, anger and affection, fear and courage, cruelty and compassion, love and hate, and so on. (4) The imaginative faculty accomplished two things. The first was the retention of what had been perceived by the senses. The second activity of imagination was the construction of things themselves not directly perceived by the senses by separating and recombining the retained impressions. (5) The fifth of the soul's faculties was uniquely human. Unlike the souls of vegetation and animals, the human soul had the function of conceptualizing forms. The rational faculty, the capacity for abstract conceptual thought, was consequently the special and distinguishing faculty of human souls. Aristotle had written, "the intellect more than anything else is man" (*Nicomachean Ethics* 1178ª 7–8); Maimonides echoed, "Reason, that faculty peculiar to man, enables him to understand, reflect, acquire knowledge of the sciences, and to discriminate between proper and improper actions" (*Eight Chapters* i; p. 43).

When Maimonides emphasized that "the human soul is one," he was rejecting the idea, favored by Platonists, that people have multiple souls. Maimonides recommended that physicians who wrote of three souls, the vegetable, animal, and human, should be reinterpreted to refer to different faculties of a soul that was single and unified (*Eight Chapters* i; pp. 37–38). The question of the soul's unity had profound implications for the practice of psychotherapy. Consider, for example, the *Spiritual Physick* of Rhazes (864–925), a Muslim physician who was widely regarded as one of the greatest medical authorities of the Middle Ages. Rhazes provided naturalistic language for the Platonic perspective whose theological expressions were normative for both Christian monasticism and Muslim Sufism. Working with a Platonic dualism of intellect and matter, Rhazes aimed at freeing "the rational and divine soul" from both "the choleric and animal [soul], and . . .

the vegetative, incremental, and appetitive soul" (Rhazes, 1950, p. 29). The rational soul's freedom was to be achieved through "the suppression of passion, the opposing of natural inclinations in most circumstances, and the gradual training of the soul to that end" (p. 22). Rhazes pursued what Christian monasticism termed *apatheia*, an emotional indifference that freed "the rational soul that is the true man" (p. 41) for a life of pure intellectualism. The reduction of the human soul to its capacity for rationality meant that all else was viewed as an impingement on the well-being of the rational soul. Emotion, desire, and passion were all counted as illness. "Of all the appetites," Rhazes considered "sexual enjoyment . . . [as] the foulest and most disreputable" (p. 41). The soul was said to be cured when efforts at self-control successfully achieved involuntary inhibition and anhedonia (lack of emotions).

In proposing asceticism as a corrective for the evil of passion, Rhazes advocated a comparatively moderate approach to Platonic psychotherapy. Other techniques that similarly aimed at reducing a human being to a purely rational soul were more extreme. Exorcism sought to expel the effects of demons who produced the evils of passion and imagination within the soul, while Platonic mystics aspired to avoid contaminants by achieving states of pure intellectualism, devoid of affect, when the soul communed or united with a pure spirituality that they attributed to God.

Aristotelians proceeded differently. Because they regarded soul as the form of the body in all of its vegetative, animal, and rational aspects, Aristotelians conceptualized the soul's health with similar complexity. Both the body and the soul's vegetative processes might be either healthy or diseased. Neither emotions, nor imagination, nor any other functions of the animal faculty was intrinsically evil; each function might be either wholesome or sick. Conversely, the purity of abstract conceptualization was no guarantee of its sanity. Making a virtue of prudence and an ideal of the golden mean, the Aristotelian perspective aspired to a healthy harmony among the soul's vegetative, animal, and rational faculties. Our modern concepts of mental integration, conflict reduction, and wholeness derive from the Aristotelian legacy.

Modern scholars have made much of medieval philosophers' routine quibbling over the details of the soul's faculties (Wolfson, 1935a). For example, Aristotle's *On the Soul* enumerated the faculties as nutritive, sensitive, motor, appetitive, and rational. Maimonides agreed with Aristotle in counting nutritive processes as a vegetative component within soul, but he followed the Muslim philosopher al-Farabi (c. 870–950) in substituting imagination where Aristotle had listed motion (*Eight Chapters* i; p. 39 n. 1). His formulation disagreed with Aristotle's statement, "the faculty of imagination is identical with that of sense-perception" (*On Dreams* 459^a 15–16), and conformed instead with the formulation of the Muslim philosopher Ibn Sina (980–1037) that the common sense, which brings the five senses together in a unified perception, is a discrete function that occurs before unified sense impressions are conveyed to the imagination (Wolfson, 1935b, p. 349).

Their differences notwithstanding, the Muslim and Jewish philosophers of the medieval Islamicate commonly understood philosophy to be transformative. Medieval philosophy was not, as philosophy is today, an exercise of logic for its own sake. Medieval philosophy continued the classical and Hellenistic project of personal transformation. Hadot (2002) explained:

> Whether or not they laid claim to the Socratic heritage, all Hellenistic philosophers agreed with Socrates that human beings are plunged in misery, anguish, and evil because they exist in ignorance. Evil is to be found not within things, but in the value judgments which people bring to bear *upon* things. People can therefore be cured of their ills only if they are persuaded to change their value judgments, and in this sense all these philosophies wanted to be therapeutic. In order to change our value judgments, however, we must make a radical choice to change our entire way of thinking and way of being. This choice is the choice of philosophy, and it is thanks to it that we may obtain inner tranquillity and peace of mind. (p. 102)

Regardless of the differences among their schools, ancient, late antique, and medieval philosophers proceeded by identifying and confronting illogicality not merely in order to gain intellectual understanding of reason or truth, as is the modern practice, but specifically as a means to the further end of bringing the soul toward wholeness through its conformance with the assumed rationality of the world. Their goal was not only to think about truths, but also to know them existentially. Among contemporary practices, it is not philosophy but insight-oriented psychotherapy that continues the ancient philosophic project of identifying and resolving mental conflict through systematic talk about inconsistency and reality-testing.

ARISTOTELIAN FORMS

A portion of Maimonides' cure of souls—the portion that contemporary scholars appreciate best—followed the Aristotelian program. In his *Nicomachean Ethics*, Aristotle had recommended contemplation as the consummate activity of human beings. Having defined the rational faculty as the portion of the soul that was distinctively human, Aristotle regarded the perfection of reason during contemplative experience as the purpose and end of human existence. Because animals are logical in their pursuits of their appetites, it was not logic that made the rational faculty distinctively human. What Plato and Aristotle had considered uniquely human was the soul's capacity to entertain abstract concepts. Contemplation, the consummate activity of the rational faculty, consisted above all in the attainment of abstract concepts in moments of understanding, insight, inspiration, or intuition.

Maimonides adopted Aristotle's view in his characteristic manner as an exegete of biblical and rabbinic teachings. Maimonides cited Onqelos, who translated the Bible into Aramaic in late antiquity, as a rabbinic precedent for his own adoption of the Aristotelian distinction between matter and form. "The things that in his opinion, I mean that of *Onqelos*, can be grasped in their true reality are . . . endowed with matter and form" (*Guide* I:37; p. 86). For Maimonides, form was not a shape that can be pictured by the imagination, but an abstract concept that is conceptualized by the mind.

> You can never see matter without form, or form without matter. But the human mind divides in thought an existing body into its constituents and recognises that it is made up of matter and form. . . . The forms that are devoid of body cannot be perceived with the physical eye, but only with the mind's eye; in the same way as we are conscious of the Lord of the Universe, without physical vision. (*BK, Laws on the Basic Principles of the Torah* IV:7; p. 39a)

Mathematics provided Maimonides with examples of the category of "forms that are devoid of body." He wrote: "The mathematical sciences have taught . . . that there are things that a man, if he considers them with his imagination, is unable to represent to himself in any respect . . . something that the imagination cannot imagine or apprehend and that is impossible from its point of view, can exist" (*Guide* I:73; pp. 210–211).

Consider the example of a triangle. It is possible to apprehend a triangle in the mind in a way that could never be apprehended by the senses. A triangle is a figure with three sides and three angles, each angle adjoining two sides. The form of the triangle by itself is never apprehended by the senses except with additional particularity. A sensible triangle must be one with no equal angles, with two equal angles, or with three equal angles. The triangle as such, without one of these particularities, is only apprehended by the mind, never by the senses. The *general* triangle has never been seen with the physical eyes, although we certainly can see it with the "mind's eye." The concept of color will provide a second example. Red, yellow, blue, and their many combinations are visible to the eye, but the concept of color is evident only to the mind, as an abstraction.

Commenting on the biblical teaching that human beings are made in the image of God (Gen 1:26–27), Maimonides explained the text in keeping with Aristotelian psychology. He wrote: "It is the intellect which is the human soul's specific form. And to this specific form of the soul, the Scriptural phrase 'in our image, after our likeness' alludes" (*BK, Laws Concerning the Basic Principles of the Torah* IV:8; p. 39a). According to Maimonides, when Scripture stated that human beings were made in the image of God, it alluded to the rational faculty.

Maimonides interpreted the biblical notion of the image of God in parallel. Aristotle had contended, and Maimonides agreed, that the same forms that exist in the external world of sense perception may also exist in the soul.

They reasoned that form was conceptual in its very nature. Not only is it comprehended through its abstraction from perceptible phenomena, but it is conceptual in its objective actuality. Aristotle sometimes referred to forms as "abstract objects," meaning that they are abstractions that have objective existence because they inform objective events in the external world. Their objective existence is perhaps most easily appreciated with reference to processes. Life and death, the presence and absence of soul, are highly complex processes at work within organic chemistry. Again, the Darwinian principle of "survival of the most fit" is a process, a form, that shapes highly complex interactions among individual life forms. More generally, laws of nature are patterns of interaction among physical quiddities that arise from the intersections of their properties. The laws are not intrinsic to the properties of any individual quiddity alone. When the quiddities are in isolation, there are no interactions, no processes, and, in an empirical sense, no laws. The laws of nature describe regularities in the interactions of physical quiddities. They too are a category of forms in Aristotle's sense of the term.

In the human mind, just as in the perceptible world, form was both passively and actively intelligent. It was passively intelligent in the sense that any piece of information embodies intelligence. However, form was also actively intelligent in the sense that form is intelligence in functional action. A form in the mind is not simply a thought. It is a thought that exerts agency. It produces thinking by making associations and constraining conclusions, feelings, and behavior to which the associations lead. A form in the mind is intelligible, but it is also an active agency, an intelligence or intellect. Small or large, a form is regularly formative—or, in contemporary jargon, performative.

Maimonides interpreted references to the formative activities of forms in commenting on the plurality of the biblical phrases "our image . . . our likeness." Rabbinical tradition conventionally understood the plurality to refer to God and his angels.

> All that the Holy God, blessed be He, created in His universe falls into three divisions. Some are creatures consisting of substance and form, continuously coming into being and decaying. Such are bodies of human creatures and other animals, plants and minerals. Others are creatures consisting of substance and form which do not . . . change, from one body to another or from one form to another, but retain their form permanently in their substance. . . . Such are the heavenly spheres and the stars placed in them. Their substance is not like other substances nor are their forms like other forms. Others again are creatures that consist of form without substance. These are the angels. For the angels are not material bodies, but only forms distinguished from each other. (*BK, Laws Concerning the Basic Principles of the Torah*, II:3; p. 35b)

Working with a conventional Aristotelian cosmology that contrasted the ethereal heavens with the sublunar world of the four elements, Maimonides divided forms into three categories. He claimed that the Bible had discussed incorporeal forms under the term *malakhim*, "angels." "The notion of an *angel* is that of a certain act" (*Guide* II:6; p. 265). Conversely, "all forces are angels" (*Guide* II:6; p. 263). As actions, forces, or processes, the incorporeal forms are objective parts of the created universe made by God that exist objectively, independently of whether they are apprehended or not. For example, as an abstract concept, the triangle has objective characteristics. Its three angles equal the angle at any point on a straight line, and a triangle imparts these characteristics to any physical object that is triangular.

The further categories of forms were forms that were permanently united with matter in the heavens, and still others that were impermanently joined with matter on earth. Human souls were instances of the latter.

Maimonides explained the singular phrasing, "God created man in his own image (*zelem*)" (Gen 1:27) with reference to a further Aristotelian concept. No different from any other incorporeal form, the particular form that was the singular *zelem* of God was an angel. The term *zelem* has generally been translated as "image," but according to Maimonides, image, in the sense of sensory image, was precisely what *zelem* did not mean. Maimonides wrote: "People have thought that in the Hebrew language [*zelem*] denotes the shape and configuration of a thing." Doing so led to error. "This supposition led them to the pure doctrine of the corporeality of God" (*Guide* I:1; p. 21). He went on to say that "the proper term designating the form that is well known ... the shape and configuration of a thing is *to'ar*." The word *zelem* differed. It "is applied ... to the notion in virtue of which a thing is constituted as a substance and becomes what it is. It is the true reality of the thing in so far as the latter is that particular being" (*Guide* I:1; p. 22). In this way, Maimonides invested the word *zelem* with the technical sense that "form" had in Aristotelian philosophy. It was a formative form, an intelligible intelligence engaging in intellection.

What was the "form" of God? For Aristotle, form as such, the totality of all forms in the universe, comprised *nous*, "Intellect" or "Mind." Our modern concept of natural law, a single, self-consistent set of rational concepts that are everywhere at work in the cosmos, is an impoverished derivative of Aristotle's concept. *Nous* consisted of objectively existing, abstractly conceivable, natural processes, as distinct from the laws that people formulate in order to describe the processes and their functions. In addition, Aristotle included within the scope of knowledge or science not only mathematics, physics, astronomy, and biology, but also metaphysics, ethics, psychology, and the social and political sciences. *Nous* referred to the rationality, coherence, or intelligibility of all that exists and occurs. The soul's rational faculty reflected *nous*. Aristotle likened the rational faculty to sealing wax on which a signet ring impressed its shape. *Nous* was an active source of forms, an Agent or Active Intellect as the medieval Aristotelians called it. The human soul, by contrast, was a passive intellect that was capable of receiving forms. For Maimonides, Active Intellect was the *zelem*, created by God, that the rational faculty has a capacity to know.

This Aristotelian approach to epistemology was an instance of philosophic realism. The objects in the world, the products of God's creation, exist. They are real and not illusory. Some people may understand them rightly and others wrongly, but they are objectively real in both events. Reality includes both material and nonmaterial things. As an example of nonmaterial things, consider the essential feature of philosophy: the recognition that meaning is, in and of itself, real. This is the meaning of Brentano's immanent object of thought. This is the meaning of Aristotle's God thinking Himself, or Parmenides' to think is to be, or Sextus Empiricus indicating the meaning of a word as a third thing, the *lekton*, "saying," after the word itself and the sensory thing referred to by the word. It is also Plato's distinction between the sensory and nonsensory apprehension, that which is apprehended in the latter's being real. It is the thing that becomes evident in mathematics when the enterprise is that of finding the theorem implicit in the axiom. Materialism affirms, however, that there is nothing outside of the material, the material that impinges on the senses. Idealism affirms the opposite extreme—that there is nothing outside of the ideal. All that exists is apprehended by the mind, including the apparent apprehension of things by the senses. Idealism consequently holds that the ideals exist whether or not a human mind exists to think them. Realism, the position common to Aristotle and Maimonides, holds that both matter and meaning exist.

Realism is obliged to acknowledge both the objective reality of things that are knowable and the subjective nature of knowing them. Maimonides discussed the problem explicitly in his *Commentary on the Mishnah*, when he pondered the relationships among knowledge, reasons, and intelligence. He began the passage by treating knowledge as objective and reasons, by which he meant motives, as subjective. Presently, however, knowledge and reasons dissolved into each other.

> The knowledge which comes to us and which we acquire in turn lets us understand the reasons to which it leads, if the whole idea is analysed in detail and understood, or we can understand the separate reasons in their essence without applying them as knowledge. But the reasons themselves constitute essentially items of knowledge. This understanding is called intelligence, and it constitutes knowledge in itself, while knowledge is a medium for intelligence in that it makes it possible for us to understand whatever we do understand. It is like saying that if we do not understand the reason, we have no real knowledge, while, if we have no knowledge, we do not understand the reason, because we understand it only based on our knowledge. To understand this idea is very difficult. (*Commentary on Aboth* III:20; p. 105)

Maimonides was grappling here with the problem of the subjectivity and objectivity of knowledge. He defined reasons as subjective, and knowledge as objective. Knowledge leads to reasons, and reasons cannot be understood in the absence of knowledge. However, people may have reasons without being able to conceptualize the knowledge that the reasons presuppose, and knowledge cannot be known in the absence of reasons. Knowledge, insofar as we can know it, is mediated by reasons. Accordingly, knowledge, like reason, is subjective; reasons are "essentially items of knowledge." Forced in this way to concede that knowledge is inalienably subjective, Maimonides nevertheless maintained a realist position in philosophy. He postulated that "intelligence" "constitutes knowledge in itself" and exists objectively. Subjective as knowledge may be, the rational faculty attained objectivity when it considered, for example, arithmeticals, geometricals, scientific laws, and so forth.

In Maimonides' view, it was only because intelligence existed objectively in the world that people were able to understand it. In this sense, the intelligence in the world might be said to overflow into the intelligence of the person who understands it. As Maimonides explained: "*In Thy light do we see light* [Ps 36:10] has the . . . meaning . . . that through the overflow of the intellect that has overflowed from Thee, we intellectually cognize, and consequently we receive correct guidance, we draw inferences, and we apprehend the intellect" (*Guide* II:12; p. 280). For a person to apprehend an intellect subjectively is for that person to acquire the objectively existing intellect as a subjective intellect.

The conjunction of the subjectivity of the soul with the objectivity of knowledge is intrinsically mystical and was understood as such by the Aristotelian tradition. Aristotle had maintained that the process of thinking and the content of what is thought are two aspects of a single phenomenon. "In the case of objects which involve no matter, what thinks and what is thought are identical; for speculative knowledge and its object are identical" (*On the Soul* 430ª 3–5). Maimonides added that the distinction between the intellecting subject and the intellectual object exists only as long as the subject is only potentially intellectual. The distinction vanishes when the intellect is actualized because the intellectual object then exists within the intellecting subject and is part of it.

> The intellect in actu is nothing but that which has been intellectually cognized and made abstract, that thing being the intellectually cognizing subject, is also indubitably identical with the intellect realized in actu. For in the case of every intellect, its act is identical in essence; for intellect in actu is not one thing and its act another thing; for the true reality and quiddity of the intellect is apprehension . . . the act of the intellect, which is its apprehension, is the true reality and the essence of the intellect. (*Guide* I:68; p. 163)

For Aristotelians, rationality was potential—unformulated, unthought, unconscious—until the process of philosophizing actualized rationality in consciousness. Rationality is a knowledge about things that has only potential existence until it is actualized through its mental construction. Neoplatonists instead maintained that rationality exists objectively in a discrete realm of existence, a world of ideas, and is accessed through its perception—implicitly, through its extrasensory perception by the rational human soul. For example, Plato famously maintained that the idea of a circle exists eternally and is perceived in the moment of its apprehension, but an Aristotelian would contend that in seeing any round object, our intellects have the potential to abstract the concept of a circle, even if no true or perfect circle exists anywhere. The distinction between extrasensory perception, on the one hand, and an exercise of logical abstraction, on the other, committed Neoplatonists to metaphysics and Aristotelians to psychology. The Aristotelian understanding of the unity or identity of the subjective and objective nevertheless remained intrinsically mystical. Interestingly, the inalienable paradoxicality of philosophic realism is integral to the British psychoanalyst D. W. Winnicott's (1971) discussions of "transitional phenomena" that are midway between subjective and objective, can neither be proved nor refuted, and are best handled playfully (see also Pruyser, 1983).

ACTUALIZATION

Robinson (1989, p. 105) remarked that "Aristotle's human Psychology ... is a *self-actualizing* Psychology, though more rigorous and reasoned than the latter-day 'humanistic' versions." It was simultaneously a depth psychology, in that Aristotle's concept of intellect, the potential that was optimally to be actualized, was implicitly a concept of the unconscious (Brentano, 1977).

For Maimonides, the Active Intellect—the Arabic term *'aql* translated Greek *nous*—was the particular incorporeal form that causes the potentiality of the rational faculty to turn into actuality. The Active Intellect causes potential to become actual both in the mind and in nature.

> The Active Intellect['s] . . . existence is indicated by the facts that our intellects pass from potentiality to actuality and that the forms of the existents that are subject to generation and corruption are actualized after they have been in their matter only in potentia. Now everything that passes from potentiality to actuality must have necessarily something that causes it to pass and that is outside it. And this cause must belong to the species of that which it causes to pass from potentiality to actuality. (*Guide* II:4; p. 257)

In Maimonides' view, the Active Intellect causes ideas that do not exist within the human mind, whose existence is only potential, to become actual by existing within a person's rational faculty. "That which brings intellect into existence is an intellect, namely, the Active Intellect" (*Guide* II:4; p. 258). Maimonides understood the Active Intellect as a *process* that is to be distinguished from the material forms of the ideas whose existence it causes. "The Active Intellect . . . is separate from matter; and . . . it acts at a certain time and does not act at another time" (*Guide* II:18; p. 299).

Maimonides followed Aristotle in treating intellect not only as the unique possession but also as the primary purpose of the human being. The major project of human life was precisely the cultivation of the rational faculty in order to actualize its potential. Aristotle wrote: "That which is best and most pleasant for each creature is that which is proper to the nature of each; accordingly the life of the intellect is the best and pleasantest life for man" (*Nicomachean Ethics* 1178ª 5–7).

In Maimonides' view, life has two goals: "a first perfection, which is the perfection of the body, and an ultimate perfection, which is the perfection of the soul" (*Guide* III:27; p. 511). Because the capacity for knowledge is inborn, knowledge always exists in potentiality. The ultimate perfection and major project of life is the fulfillment of one's rational nature through the actualization of its potential—a project that Maimonides regarded as an obligation. Maimonides wrote that "being a rational animal is the essence and true reality of man. . . . A man . . . should take as his end that which is the end of man qua man: namely, solely the mental representation of the intelligibles" (*Guide* I:51; p. 113; III:8; p. 432).

Because the intrinsic nature of the human being is to be a rational animal, possessing intellect, the perfection of a human being qua human being is to be perfectly rational, that is, to be rational in actuality and not only in potential.

> The true human perfection . . . consists in the acquisition of the rational virtues—I refer to the conception of intelligibles, which teach true opinions concerning the divine things. This is in true reality the ultimate end; this is what gives the individual true perfection, a perfection belonging to him alone; and it gives him permanent perdurance; through it man is man. (*Guide* III:54; p. 635)

Maimonides' phrasing should not be taken in a Platonic sense, as advocating a pure intellectualism that was devoid of emotion. Although Maimonides advocated the intellectual life as a religious devotion, he made explicit reference to its ecstasy. He repeatedly stated that *hesheq*, "passionate love," and *simchah*, "bliss," attended the consummation of human life in the worship of God (Blumenthal, 1988, pp. 4–5). In this assertion, Maimonides echoed Aristotle's claim that *eudaimonia*, "bliss," "felicity," or "happiness," arises out of goodness and is the most desirable form of life (Robinson, 1989, pp. 97–101).

AL-FARABI'S POLITICAL PHILOSOPHY

The classical understanding of philosophy as a transformative or therapeutic endeavor, that reconciled the soul with objectively existing ideas (*logoi*) or mind (*nous*) in evidence throughout nature, has left its stamp on Jewish, Christian, and Muslim practices of mysticism. It was, however, only a first step in the history of psychotherapy. The function of psychology in Aristotelian philosophy underwent important changes at the hands of both al-Farabi and Maimonides. Aristotle had offered a pedagogical psychology. He endeavored to understand the soul with the goal of knowing how to design a curriculum that would cultivate ethics; he sought ethics, in both the individual and the state, as the means to *eudaimonia* (Robinson, 1989). Believing that "moral excellence comes about as a result of habit" (*Nicomachean Ethics* 1103^a 16–17), Aristotle wrote about the pedagogical cultivation of good moral habits.

> Moral excellence is concerned with pleasures and pains: it is on account of pleasure that we do bad things, and on account of pain that we abstain from noble ones. Hence we ought to have been brought up in a particular way from our very youth, as Plato says, so as both to delight in and to be pained by the things that we ought; for this is the right education. (*Nicomachean Ethics* 1104^b 9–13)

Aristotle discussed good habits and the excellence or perfection that was to be obtained through knowledge, but he wrote not a word about the correction of bad habits. His oversight was consistent with Socrates' simplistic claim that vice is always a product of ignorance. If education to truth was all that needed to be done, the contemplative actualization of reason was a complete program of transformation.

Al-Farabi, whom Islamicate philosophers called the "Second Master" after Aristotle, integrated Aristotle's psychology of ethics within his own program of political science. In his *Fusul al-Madani*, "Aphorisms of the Statesman," al-Farabi revived Plato's concept of the philosopher king and made metaphoric use of Plato's concept of the physician of the soul (Davidson, 1963). Al-Farabi (1961) wrote: "He who treats souls is the statesman, who is also called the king" (p. 27). In this treatise, the soul's health and illness were metaphors that concerned good and evil. "The health of the soul is that its states and the states of its parts are those by which it always does good and noble deeds and fair actions. Its sickness is that its states and the states of its parts are those by which it always does wicked and evil deeds and ugly actions" (p. 27). Psychology was an applied science. A king was obliged to know psychology, "but it is requisite for him to know about the soul only as much as he needs in his art" (p. 28).

Although al-Farabi's political theory was Platonic, his account of the soul belonged to the Aristotelian tradition. He divided the soul into five parts: the nutritive, sensory, imaginative, appetitive, and rational faculties (al-Farabi, 1961, p. 29). He attributed different virtues to rational and appetitive faculties. Rational virtues included "wisdom, intellect, cleverness, readiness of wit, excellence of understanding." The appetitive faculty was instead concerned with ethical virtues, "such as temperance, bravery, generosity, justice" (p. 31). Both virtues and their corresponding vices were inculcated through habit. "The ethical virtues and vices result and are established in the soul, simply by repeating the actions which proceed from a particular disposition many times over a certain period and becoming accustomed thereto" (p. 31). In some cases a natural disposition toward a virtue or vice might be completely replaced by habit; in other cases only partially; yet in still other cases not at all. They may nevertheless "be opposed by resisting and restraining the soul from their actions and by contending and striving" (p. 33). Virtue was the condition of happiness. "Happiness is an end such that it is attained by virtuous actions, as knowledge results from learning and study, and the arts result from learning them and persevering in their actions" (p. 61).

Also Aristotelian was al-Farabi's (1961) doctrine of the mean. "Actions which are good deeds are the moderate, mean actions between two extremes, both of which are bad, the one excess and the other defect. And similarly the virtues, for they are mean states and qualities of the soul between two other states, both of which are vices, the one excessive and the other defective" (p. 34). Good and evil vary with circumstances. "Just as the mean in foods and medicines is a mean and moderate for most men most of the time, is sometimes moderate for one group to the exclusion of another at a particular time, and sometimes moderate for individual bodies at individual times, long or short, similarly the mean and moderate in actions is sometimes moderate for all or most men most or all of the time, sometimes moderate for one group to the exclusion of another at a particular time and sometimes moderate for a man at one time and not at another" (p. 36).

From these premises al-Farabi derived the conclusion that authoritarian government accomplishes a healing of souls.

> He who brings out and produces the mean and moderate of whatever kind in foods and medicines in the doctor. The art by which he brings it out is medicine. He who produces the mean and moderate in morals and actions is the ruler of the city and the king. The art by which he brings it out is the political art and the kingly craft. (al-Farabi, 1961, p. 36)

Al-Farabi advised that kings aim at the common good without troubling over the personal health of individuals who are incapable of virtue.

> It is not the business of the ideal governor and the first chief to perfect the virtues of one the nature and substance of whose soul are such that it does not receive the virtues. His end is simply to bring souls like these as far as possible for them, and to a point of virtue consistent with the advantage of the people of that city, just as it is not the duty of the ideal doctor to bring the bodies whose condition is as we have described to the most perfect grades and highest levels of health. It is his business merely to bring them, as regards

health, as far as possible with their nature and substance, and consistent with the actions of the soul. For the body is for the sake of the soul and the soul for the sake of the last perfection, viz. happiness, which is virtue, hence the soul is for the sake of wisdom and virtue. (al-Farabi, 1961, pp.75–76)

From these foundations in Aristotelian pedagogy and al-Farabi's political ideology, Maimonides fashioned a psychotherapy.

MAIMONIDES' BEHAVIORAL THERAPY

Maimonides' *Eight Chapters* embraced al-Farabi's concept of healing souls by correcting evil habits (Davidson, 2005, pp. 93, 155), but he systematically ignored al-Farabi's political concerns (Davidson, 1963, p. 42). For Maimonides, the cure of souls was not a metaphor that pertained to ethics, but a concept that pertained literally to a medical undertaking. Maimonides advised that when the "soul becomes diseased . . . it is proper . . . to resort to a cure" (*Eight Chapters* iv; p. 58). The cure aimed at undoing or reversing the extremism of the vice in order that the educational process might be able to take effect. The practitioners of the cure of souls were not statesmen but Torah sages. "The wise who are physicians of the soul" prescribe emotional correctives that are appropriate to an individual's moral disposition. They "heal their maladies by instructing them in the dispositions which they should acquire till they are restored to the right path" (*BK, Laws Relating to Moral Dispositions and to Ethical Conduct* II:1; p. 48a).

In other respects, Maimonides followed the views of Aristotle and al-Farabi. Maimonides adhered to the Aristotelian principle of the mean or middle way: "It is man's duty to aim at performing acts that observe the proper mean" (*Eight Chapters* iv; p. 66). "The right way is the mean in each group of dispositions" (*BK, Laws Relating to Moral Dispositions and to Ethical Conduct* I:4; p. 47b). Maimonides followed both Aristotle and al-Farabi when he wrote:

> Virtues are psychic conditions and dispositions which are mid-way between two reprehensible extremes, one of which is characterized by exaggeration, the other by deficiency. To illustrate, abstemiousness is a disposition which adopts a mid-course between inordinate passion and total insensibility to pleasure. . . . The psychic dispositions, from which these two extremes, inordinate passion and insensibility, result—the one being an exaggeration, the other a deficiency—are alike classed among moral imperfections.
>
> Likewise . . . Gentleness is the mean between irascibility and insensibility to shame and disgrace; and modest, between impudence and shamefacedness. . . . So it is with the other qualities. (*Eight Chapters* iv; pp. 55–57)

Maimonides similarly followed both Aristotle and al-Farabi in treating moral education as a matter of behavior.

> Know . . . that these moral excellences or defects cannot be acquired, or implanted in the soul, except by means of the frequent repetition of acts resulting from these qualities, which, practised during a long period of time, accustoms us to them. If these acts performed are good ones, then we shall have gained a virtue; but if they are bad, we shall have acquired a vice. (*Eight Chapters* iv; p. 58)

Davidson (1963, p. 41) noted that Maimonides failed to cite Aristotle on ethics, as though he had neither a translation nor a summary of the *Nicomachean Ethics* and instead depended on al-Farabi's account of Aristotle's views. Maimonides agreed with al-Farabi in recognizing that the premises of Aristotelian pedagogy required modification before they could be applied to the correction of established vices. Moral virtues can be cultivated in the young through education, as Aristotle had taught, but habituation in virtuous conduct does not suffice to correct a prior habituation in vice. Al-Farabi urged the legislation and enforcement of the mean, and he advised statesmen to be content with the public good. Maimonides was instead concerned with the cure of individuals. Working differently with the Aristotelian concept of the mean, Maimonides' cure of vice aimed at restoring the mean through behavior that was equal but opposite to the illness.

> If one is irascible, he is directed to govern himself that even if he is assaulted or reviled, he should not feel affronted. And in this course he is to persevere for a long time till the choleric temperament has been eradicated. If one is arrogant, he should accustom himself to endure much contumely, sit below every one, and wear old and ragged garments that bring the wearer into contempt, and so forth, till arrogance is eradicated from his heart and he has regained the middle path, which is the right way. And when he has returned to this path, he should walk in it the rest of his days. On similar lines, he should treat all his dispositions. If, in any of them, he is at one extreme, he should move to the opposite extreme, and keep to it for a long time till he has regained the right path which is the normal mean in every class of dispositions. (*BK, Laws Relating to Moral Dispositions and to Ethical Conduct* II:2; p. 48b)

The technique that Maimonides described in Aristotelian terms is today called desensitization in the context of cognitive-behavioral therapy (Wolpe, 1958, pp. 139–165). Like Maimonides' program, the modern technique has its basis in learning theory and is useful in reducing the severity of symptoms of anxiety. Although it neither ends the anxiety nor addresses its sources, it increases the effectiveness of defenses against anxiety and can sometimes make crippling anxiety manageable. Unlike modern cognitive-behavioral therapy, Maimonides' technique also included the converse of desensitization. For example, Maimonides recommended generosity in order to desensitize an avaricious person, but he also recommended frugality in order to inculcate sensitivity in a squanderer (*Eight Chapters* iv; pp. 58–59).

Maimonides remarked that inordinate passion was more easily cured than insensibility to pleasure. "It is easier for a man of profuse habits to moderate them to generosity, than it is for a miser to become generous" (*Eight Chapters* iv; p. 60). His observation that the depraved are more easily brought to repentance than the overly scrupulous is often corroborated in psychotherapy today. Noting the same phenomenon, the psychoanalyst Ella Freeman Sharpe (1930) explained: "The so-called normal person has often a longer and stubborn task before him in reaching the deepest levels of the mind."

SIN CAUSES IGNORANCE

Moral behaviorism was only the beginning of Maimonides' cure of souls. He also offered an original theory of mental illness that he developed by applying Aristotelian categories to the understanding of selected biblical and rabbinical passages. Maimonides began with Socrates' theory that all wrongdoing was a product of ignorance. Ignorance produced profound error in understanding the condition of human beings and the world in which human beings exist. Error in understanding, leading to error in conduct, was the vehicle of all evil. Maimonides wrote:

> These great evils that come about between the human individuals who inflict them upon one another . . . derive from ignorance. Just as a blind man, because of the absence of sight, does not cease stumbling, being wounded, and also wounding others, because he has no one to guide him on the way [so does] every individual according to his ignorance [do] to himself and to others great evils. . . . If there were knowledge . . . they would refrain from doing any harm to themselves and to others. For through cognition of the truth, enmity and hatred are removed and the inflicting of harm by people on one another is abolished. (*Guide* III:11, 440–441)

Because Maimonides defined evildoing as counterproductive behavior, his use of the language of ethics formulated the same phenomena that Freud articulated by reference to self-sabotage. As well, Maimonides' phrase, "doing . . . harm to themselves and to others," reflected his view that the welfare of the individual coincides with the welfare of the group. Maimonides believed that it is in the objective nature of reality that doing harm to others coincides with doing harm to oneself, and that sin against others is always also a sin against oneself. He also believed that it is in the objective nature of reality that benefit to oneself coincides with benefit toward others, that it is possible to "love your neighbor as yourself" (Lev 19:18) and not possible to do otherwise. To love only oneself or to love only others are both impossible (Fromm, 1939), both forms of ignorance, both damaging, and both sin. Maimonides' phrasing used ethical discourse in order to express an insight into human nature to which clinical experience has brought psychoanalysis. Masochistic self-damage and sadistic harm to others never occur separately, but always occur in tandem, whether simultaneously or serially.

Socrates' attribution of wrongdoing to ignorance led Plato and Aristotle to formulate psychologies of pedagogy. If the soul needed nothing more than to know the good in order to choose to do it, then the soul had only to be taught. Aristotle had been aware, however, that Socrates' attribution of evil to ignorance was simplistic. Aristotle recognized that doing harm involuntarily, as, for example, through ignorance, was no vice. To constitute evildoing, harm had to be willful. "Not only are the vices of the soul voluntary, but those of the body also" (*Nicomachean Ethics* 1114a 22–24). Aristotle never reconciled his ethical voluntarism with the naturalism that otherwise informed his philosophical thinking. In the end, he could not sustain his own belief in will and instead followed his predecessors in promoting a deterministic model of wrongdoing. Aristotle wrote of *akrasia*, "weakness of will," by which a person might voluntarily corrupt knowledge and become ignorant. Akrasia might be produced through distraction, error in logic, or physical incapacitation by sleep, diseases, or conflicting desires (Robinson, 1989, pp. 105–109).

Al-Farabi (1961) did not significantly advance the problem. He explicitly associated virtue with knowledge when he suggested that "a deed is only right and a virtue when a man rightly knows the virtues which are thought to be virtues" (p. 72). The phrasing implies ethical voluntarism. Unless virtue involves knowing choice, what does it matter whether a virtue is or is not known to be a virtue? Al-Farabi did not develop the implication.

Maimonides unequivocally challenged determinism in the contexts of both astrology (*Eight Chapters* viii; pp. 86–87) and Aristotle's deification of nature (*Guide* II:25; p. 328). Maimonides maintained that freedom of will is consistent with the lawfulness of nature.

> When [the Rabbis] said that man rises and sits down in accordance with the will of God, their meaning was that, when man was first created, his nature was so determined that rising up and sitting down were to be optional to him; [not] that God wills at any special moment that man should or should not get up. . . . Just as God willed that man should . . . have fingers, likewise did He will that man should move or rest of his own accord. (*Eight Chapters* viii; p. 91)

Maimonides insisted, moreover, that a theory of ethics must include the doctrine of freedom of will. Unless will is free, doing benefit and doing harm can have no ethical qualities. If all actions are caused in a rigidly determined way, all actions are compelled, and individual responsibility does not exist. Unless alternative actions are possible, benefits and harms cannot be good and evil, nor their performance virtues and vices; God would be doing injustice in rewarding good and punishing evil.

Maimonides appreciated that a theory of mental illness—defined in terms of counterproductive behavior—must take serious account of the freedom of will. He allowed a place to conventional moral education when he stated that ignorance that arises through inadequate education has its remedy in learning. He drew attention, however, to the problem of ignorance that arises through the will to do wrong. Temporary corruptions of knowledge may result, as Aristotle maintained, in weakness of will, but it is also the case that a strong will may freely commit sin. Maimonides allowed that sin is not possible without self-deception, the willful choice to believe that an evil is not punished but is instead rewarded. However, Maimonides did not limit himself to cases of akrasia when, for one reason or another, people contrive to behave as though they were ignorant of what they very well know. He also addressed the further circumstance that once a person willfully becomes ignorant, the person may no longer be in a position to reconsider. The person may then no longer have the knowledge that is needed to choose the good and must instead persist in the sin. In these cases, ignorance is an inhibition that is *consequent* of sin. Maimonides explained:

> God has, moreover, expressly stated through Isaiah that He punishes some transgressors by making it impossible for them to repent, which He does by the suspension of their free will. . . . Upon this principle also are based the words of Elijah (peace be unto him!) who, when speaking of the unbelievers of his time, said of them, "Thou hast turned their hearts back," which means that, as they have sinned of their own accord, their punishment from Thee is that Thou hast turned their hearts away from repentance, by not permitting them to exercise free will, and thus have a desire to forsake that sin, in consequence of which they persevere in their unbelief. (*Eight Chapters* viii; p. 97)

Maimonides here broke with the philosophic tradition of Socrates, Plato, Aristotle, and their medieval continuators that made ignorance responsible for wrongdoing. Citing the Bible, Maimonides argued that the true relationship is the converse. Ignorance makes harmful action possible, but harm is not evil unless will is involved. Willful, knowing choice of sin produces ignorance through the psychological process of denial, a voluntary refusal to believe what one knows. Denial, an emotional disconnection or dissociation of knowledge and its affirmation, is integral to wrongdoing. Once denial has been instituted, it may become habitual and automatic. Denial, originally instituted willfully, may develop into an automatic and involuntary inhibition (Hartmann, 1958). The habit is then so complete that it may not be possible to recover the knowledge that was denied.

Because Maimonides' psychology started with a serious taking account of the normalcy of voluntary control over conduct, he could also conceptualize illnesses that involve losses of normal volition. Maimonides formulated his understanding of the topic in commentary on the biblical verse, "Then the

Lord said to Moses, 'Go to Pharaoh; for I have hardened his heart and the heart of his officials, in order that I may show these signs of mine among them'" (Ex 10:1; see also Ex 10:20, 11:10). Maimonides explained:

> God at times punishes man by withholding repentance from him, thus not allowing him free will as regards repentance, for God (blessed be He) knows the sinners, and His wisdom and equity mete out their punishment.... Just as some of man's undertakings, which ordinarily are subject to his own free will, are frustrated by way of punishment, as for instance a man's hand being prevented from working so that he can do nothing with it, as was the case of Jereboam, the son of Nebat, or a man's eyes from seeing, as happened to the Sodomites who had assembled about Lot, likewise does God withhold man's ability to use his free will in regard to repentance, so that it never at all occurs to him to repent, and he thus finally perishes in his wickedness. (*Eight Chapters*, viii; pp. 95–96).

Commenting on the biblical text, Maimonides came to the point of discussing what we are accustomed after Freud to call neurosis. Jereboam suffered what we describe as "hysterical paralysis" and the Sodomites were afflicted with "hysterical blindness." The concepts of neurosis and fixation presuppose the concept of freedom of will and are logically dependent on it. Ignorance can explain inability, but neurosis involves a loss of voluntary function.

In all, Maimonides resolved the inconsistency in Platonic and Aristotelian philosophy between ignorance and moral responsibility for evil by developing a sophisticated argument about voluntary ignorance. He briefly mentioned the logical alternative, that genuine ignorance is morally innocent, but, from his standpoint as a moralist, it was nevertheless problematic. Scientific psychiatry had its basis, however, in the separation of moral and medical concerns, beginning in the sixteenth century when witches ceased to be regarded as evil servants of Satan and instead came to be regarded as sufferers of mental disorders (Zilboorg & Henry, 1941). When Renaissance concepts of nature led to the widespread rejection of the demonic theory of disease, the way was opened for the understanding of mental illness as a morally neutral, medical concern. Much of Freud's thinking consisted precisely of pursuing the paradigm of morally innocent suffering as far as he could take it. We may nevertheless value Maimonides' contribution on the moral aspects of therapy as an important, early, and still partly unsurpassed observation of a discrete clinical syndrome: willful denial that leads to neurotic symptoms.

REPENTANCE

Because Maimonides interpolated the Jewish doctrine of free will within Aristotelian psychology, citing biblical and rabbinical sources in support of his teaching, he was able to conceptualize *teshuvah*, "repentance," as a kind of therapeutic change. Once sin had been punished with ignorance, paralysis, or blindness, it no longer sufficed to cultivate good habits. For *teshuvah* to occur, involuntary processes—in modern terms, resistances—had to be brought to an end, and only then could will resume its freedom to pursue virtue.

Maimonides was willing to allow acts of repentance and the performance of fasts not as ends in themselves, but "with respect to inculcating opinions that are correct and that are useful for belief in the Law" (*Guide* III:35; p. 535). The ritual acts had no magical efficacy. Their virtues were educational.

> An individual cannot but sin and err, either through ignorance—by professing an opinion or a moral quality that is not preferable in truth—or else because he is overcome by desire or anger. If then the individual believed that this fracture can never be remedied, he would persist in his error and sometimes perhaps disobey even more because of the fact that no stratagem remains at his disposal. If, however, he believes in repentance, he can correct himself and return to a better and more perfect state than the one he was in before he sinned. For this reason there are many actions that are meant to establish this correct and very useful opinion, I mean the *confessions*, the *sacrifices* in expiation of negligence and also of certain sins committed intentionally, and the *fasts*. The general characteristic of repentance from any sin consists in one's being divested of it. And this is the purpose of this opinion (*Guide* III:36; p. 540).

In keeping with his view of divine justice, Maimonides changed the meaning of *teshuvah*, literally "returning, reversion," from its conventional meaning in Scripture as penitent behavior that involves making restitution. At the beginning of the section of the *Mishneh Torah* that is entitled *Laws of Repentance*, Maimonides noted that only one precept in Scripture deals with *teshuvah*. This text states: "When a man or woman commits any of the sins that people commit by breaking faith with the Lord, and that person is guilty, he shall confess his sin which he has committed; and he shall make full restitution for his wrong, adding a fifth to it, and giving it to him to whom he did the wrong" (Num 5:6–7). However, when Maimonides quoted this biblical text, he ended the citation with the words: "he shall confess his sin which he has committed" (*BK, Laws of Repentance* I:1; p. 81b). The way in which he truncated the biblical text permitted him to develop an original emphasis on the act of confession. In his commentary on the verse, he specifically made the point that if one has injured someone or caused him financial damage and made what restitution he could, he must still confess and openly resolve never to commit the offense again (*Laws of Repentance* I:1; p. 81b). Maimonides advised that in all cases confessions must be made in words.

Maimonides transformed the precept, a precept that appears to have a strong meaning of restitution to some injured party, into something that was considerably more psychological. The essence of *teshuvah* for Maimonides was the enhancement of awareness about sin and virtue. *Teshuvah* was not penance. *Teshuvah* was not restitution. *Teshuvah* required confession, but only as a means to a further end that was psychological. True *teshuvah* was becoming increasingly aware, for only by the increase in awareness could evil be truly overcome. Consider his definition of repentance.

> What is Repentance? It consists in this, that the sinner abandon his sin, remove it from his thoughts, and resolve in his heart never to repeat it, as it is said, "Let the wicked forsake his way, and the man of iniquity his thoughts" (Is 55:7); that he regret the past, as it is said, "Surely, after that I turned I repented, after that I was instructed, I smote upon my thigh" (Jer 31:19); that he calls him who knows all secrets to witness that he will never again return to this sin again, as it is said, "Neither will we call any more the work of our hands our God, for in Thee the fatherless findeth mercy." (Hos 14:4) (*BK, Laws of Repentance* II:2; p. 82b)

Only at the end of this passage did Maimonides add: "It is also necessary that he make oral confession" (ibid.).

Maimonides' example of optimal repentance similarly emphasized the psychological dimension of repentance.

> What is perfect repentance? It is so when an opportunity presents itself for repeating an offence once committed, and the offender, while able to commit the offence, nevertheless refrains from doing so, because he is penitent and not out of fear or failure of vigour. For instance, if a man had sinful intercourse with a woman, and after a time was alone with her, his passion for her persisting, his physical powers unabated while he continued to live in the same district where he had sinned, and yet he refrains and does not transgress, he is a sincere penitent. (*BK, Laws of Repentance* II:1; p. 82b)

Because "the improvement of the moral qualities is brought about by the healing of the soul and its activities" (*Eight Chapters* i; p. 38), what was most important to Maimonides was the change in the mental state. Behavioral consequences then followed. *Teshuvah* for Maimonides was essentially an achievement of understanding that was fundamental to the soul's health. In this feature of his cure of souls, Maimonides anticipated by eight centuries the psychoanalyst Melanie Klein's (1935) emphasis of reparation and D. W. Winnicott's (1963) discussion of the capacity for concern.

CONCLUSIONS

Socrates had attributed evil or wrongdoing to ignorance, and both the Platonic and Aristotelian traditions sought to relieve ignorance partly through study and partly through contemplative experiences. In the Aristotelian formulation that reached Maimonides, the soul achieves perfection through its conjunction with the Active Intellect, an angelic process of mind that produces coherence or reason both in the human soul and in the perceptible world. The Active Intellect relieves ignorance when it actualizes the rational faculty's potential, causing it to know concepts that were previously unknown to it. Aristotle's psychology was pedagogical; it had no means to correct wrongdoing that had become habitual. The Muslim philosopher al-Farabi proposed the correction of bad habits through the political and juridical enforcement of good habits. Maimonides' cure of souls began with the contributions of Aristotle and al-Farabi, but added a behavioral program of countering bad habits with equal and opposing habits, in order to arrive finally at the mean. Maimonides also insisted on the biblical doctrine of free will. For Maimonides, evil or wrongdoing was a moral defect that people freely chose. Choosing evil had the effect of inducing ignorance that evil is evil; it rationalizes evil as good. The confusion of evil with good produces disorder in the emotions, and inappropriate emotions are the primary causes of the diseases of the soul. Once ignorance is induced through choice, ignorance becomes self-perpetuating and the scope for freedom of will is reduced. The losses of freedom to which wrongdoing led included physical symptoms, such as blindness and paralysis, in addition to the behavioral symptoms of wrongdoing. Maimonides' cure of souls required repentance before ignorance would cease to be self-perpetuating and its symptoms could be relieved.

TWO

Worship of the Heart

MAIMONIDES' CURE OF SOULS remained within the Aristotelian tradition in attributing transformative power to contemplative experience, but his own approach to contemplation was equally indebted to classical Jewish precedents. Aristotle's passing references to intuition throughout his writings suggest that his theory of actualizing the intellect through contemplation was a way of talking about creative inspirations on scientific topics (Lesher, 1973). Whenever scientific thinking was accurate, the ideas that the rational faculty attained were the same ideas that the Active Intellect produced objectively in nature and constituted an actualization of the rational faculty. In cases when scientific ideas were intuited or inspired, they were, by definition, contemplations.

In *The Book of Direction to the Duties of the Heart*, written two generations prior to Maimonides, Bahya ibn Paquda (c. 1050–c.1156) appropriated the Aristotelian program of contemplation as a medieval Jewish practice. The text, which is generally categorized as a work of Jewish ethics, was heavily influenced by Muslim Sufism of the early type that was ascetic and devotional, but not additionally concerned with unitive mystical experiences. For Bahya, meditations on scientific topics were to be employed in order to cultivate devotion to God.

> The meditation upon creation consists of the study of the world's foundations and the phenomena dependent on them, the study of the construction and use of every compound thing and the traces of wisdom manifested in its creation—its form and shape, its usage, and final purpose for which it has been created. It is also the observation of the spiritual and material elements of this world, its causes and effects, its speaking creatures and those not endowed with speech, its components moving, resting, and immovable, its plants and regions above and below....

> The clever and intelligent man should extract from this world the knowledge of its spiritual and subtle elements, making them into a ladder of demonstration of the Creator of the whole. He should take it upon himself to obey Him and worship Him in accordance with His greatness and glory as established in his heart. (Bahya, 1973, pp. 155–156)

Possibly referring to *Sefer Yetsirah*, Bahya suggested that the easiest and most obligatory topic of meditation was "the species of man, who is the microcosmos and the major reason for the existence of the macrocosmos" (p. 160). He alluded to Socrates when he wrote: "One of the philosophers has already said that philosophy is man's knowledge of himself" (p. 160). Bahya affirmed Aristotle's prioritizing of the rational faculty when he maintained, "The greatest favor God has done us is to give us a mind and the power of discrimination, by which He distinguished us from the rest of living creatures" (p. 166).

THE COMMANDMENTS OF MONOTHEISTIC BELIEFS AND AFFECTS

Maimonides endorsed Bahya's program of meditation, among other manners, in his commentary to the very first of the 613 commandments that he found in the Pentateuch. In his *Book of the Commandments*, he listed the first four commandments as:

> 1. To know that there is a God, as it is said, "I am the Lord, thy God" (Ex 20:2; Deut 5:6). 2. To acknowledge his unity, as it is said, "The Lord our God, the Lord is One" (Deut 6:4). 3. To love Him, as it is said, "And thou shalt love the Lord thy God" (Deut 6:5). 4. To fear Him, as it is said, "The Lord, thy God, shalt thou fear" (Deut 6:13; 10:20). (*BK* 5a)

Maimonides treated the four biblical items as commandments, even though it might be argued that they do not really qualify as commandments. A commandment ordinarily refers to conduct that is within the realm of volition, yet the first two of the four commandments are associated with cognition, while the third and fourth are associated with affect. The two cognitive items on the existence and unity of God concern what is true and false. They do not address right and wrong conduct. For Maimonides, the conceptualization of God as existing and the recognition of God's unity were nevertheless religious obligations. It is conventional to think of beliefs as something that one has, rather than as something one does, but Maimonides' listing of these beliefs as commandments indicates that he regarded them as actions. Consistent with his point of view, in the *Mishneh Torah* where he listed the *halakhot*, or rabbinic laws, that were predicated on the *mitzvot*, commandments, of the Pentateuch, he added a fifth law to the biblical four: "Not to permit the thought to enter the mind that there is any god but the Eternal" (*BK, Laws*

Concerning the Basic Principles of the Torah I; p. 34a). In addition to thinking of God as existing and as one, a person was forbidden to think of any other god as a god.

As for the two commandments of affect, because emotions are contingent on cognitions, they presuppose and imply beliefs. Maimonides explained:

> One loves God only in accordance with the knowledge that one may have of Him. One's love is according to one's knowledge. If it is little, then it is little. If it is much, then it is much. Therefore a person should devote himself singularly to understand and to comprehend the sciences and the studies which will inform him concerning his Possessor, according to the power that the person has to understand and to obtain. (*BK, Laws of Repentance* X:6; p. 93a)

Summarizing his position in the *Guide*, Maimonides stated, "Love [of God] is proportionate to apprehension" (*Guide* III:51; p. 620).

The commandments of affect remained problematic, however, because affects cannot themselves be willed. Affects imply beliefs that may be actions, but affects are not themselves voluntary. Maimonides asked how loving and fearing God can be performed as commandments. He answered, as Bahya had done, that devotion to God could be cultivated through meditation on God's work of creation. Commenting on the biblical text, "Thou shalt love the Lord, thy God" (Deut 6:5), Maimonides asserted that the study of nature "may serve the intelligent individual as a door to the love of God, even as our sages have remarked . . . 'Observe the Universe and hence, you will realize Him who spake and the world was'" (*BK, Laws Concerning the Basic Principles of the Torah* II:2; p. 35b).

> And what is the way that will lead to the love of Him and the fear of Him? When a person contemplates His great and wondrous works and his creatures and from them obtains a glimpse of His wisdom which is incomparable and infinite, he will straightway love Him. . . . And when he ponders these matters, he will recoil affrighted, and realize that he is a small creature, lowly and obscure, endowed with slight and slender intelligence, standing in the presence of Him who is perfect in knowledge. (*BK, Laws Concerning the Basic Principles of the Torah*, II;2; p. 35b)

Because study of the universe leads to the love and fear of God, the commandments to love and fear God can be performed through the study of nature, which is understood as the work of God.

MAIMONIDES' CURRICULUM

The systematic philosophical character of Maimonides' meditations on nature was reflected in the curriculum that he recommended for Jewish education. Consider the following passage from the *Mishneh Torah*.

> The time allotted to study should be divided into three parts. A third should be devoted to the Written Law; a third to the Oral Law; and the last third should be spent in reflection, deducing conclusions from premises, developing implications of statements, comparing dicta, studying the hermeneutical principles by which the Law is interpreted, till one knows the essence of these principles, and how to deduce what is permitted and what is forbidden from what one has learnt traditionally. This is termed Talmud. (*BK, Laws Concerning the Study of Torah* I:11; p. 58a)

Maimonides' curriculum was based on a saying in the Talmud: "One should always divide his years into three: [devoting] a third to Scripture, a third to Mishnah, and a third to Talmud" (*BT*, Kiddushin, 30a). By substituting "Oral Law" for Mishnah, Maimonides introduced a far-reaching alteration of the rabbinical ruling. In customary Jewish parlance, the Written Law was the text of the Pentateuch, to which Maimonides devoted his *Book of the Commandments*. The Oral Law designated the rabbinical teachings of the Mishnah and the Gemara, which Maimonides had discussed in both his *Commentary on the Mishnah* and his *Mishneh Torah*. The Mishnah and Gemara, taken together, are conventionally designated as *Talmud*, "study." Maimonides instead based himself on a Talmudic saying that reflected an older linguistic usage, in which the term *talmud* differed from the Mishnah and was synonymous with the text of the Gemara (Twersky, 1967, p. 107). The archaism provided Maimonides with an opportunity to depart from convention in an original direction. By paraphrasing the text of *Kiddushin* 30a in a manner that equated the Mishnah with the Oral Law, Maimonides diminished the status of the Gemara. Twersky (1967) explained:

> The basic text of the Oral Law *in toto* is the work redacted by Rabbi Judah ha-Nasi: the Mishnah. *Every other work* . . . stands in interpretive-commentatorial, but not actually innovating, relation to the Mishnah. . . . This interpretive relation characterizes also the Talmud, the Palestinian as well as the Babylonian; both continue the task of explanation. (pp. 107–108)

Maimonides' emphasis on the original meaning of *talmud* provided him with the opportunity to challenge the conventional treatment of the Gemara as its synonym. For Maimonides, *talmud* signified commentary on the Mishnah, whether consisting of Gemara or other works of the sages, as the rabbis of the Talmudic era are collectively known. Discussing the curriculum further, Maimonides stated:

> For example, if one is an artisan who works at his trade three hours daily and devotes nine hours to the study of the Law, he should spend three of these nine hours in the study of the Written Law, three in the study of the Oral Law, and the remaining three in reflecting on how to deduce one rule from another. The words of the Prophets are comprised in the Written Law, while

their exposition falls within the category of the Oral Law. The subjects styled *Pardes* (Esoteric Studies), are included in Talmud. (*BK, Laws Concerning the Study of Torah* I:12; p. 58a)

By suggesting that *talmud* consists of "reflecting on how to deduce one rule from another," Maimonides inserted philosophy within the curriculum. He might be taken to have referred to the thirteen hermeneutic principles of Rabbi Ishmael, by which the sages derived rabbinic law from the text of Scripture. Rabbinic hermeneutics rest, however, on a series of philosophical assumptions regarding the nature of the universe, law, the theological concerns of Scripture, and a variety of further topics. When Maimonides redefined *talmud* as rabbinic methodology, he opened the philosophical assumptions of Judaism to self-conscious reflection.

His ambition was not modest. The beginning of the *Mishneh Torah* identified the subject matter of its first four chapters as *Pardes* (*Laws Concerning the Basic Principles of the Torah* IV:13; p. 39b), explaining that "all the principles in the first two chapters are called Maaseh Merkabah" (II:11; p. 36b), while "the exposition of all the topics in chapter three and in [chapter] four are called Maaseh Bereshith" (IV:10; p. 39b). Maimonides claimed that the esoteric studies of Judaism were traditionally two: *Maaseh Bereshith*, the Account of the Beginning (Gen 1–3), and *Maaseh Merkabah*, the Account of the Chariot (Ezek 1). Throughout his writings, Maimonides asserted that "the Account of the Beginning is identical with natural science, and the Account of the Chariot with divine science" (*Guide* I:Introduction; p. 6; compare *Commentary on the Mishnah*, Hagigah 2:1; *BK, Laws of the Basic Principles of the Torah* 2:11; 4:10–11). For Maimonides, *Maaseh Bereshith* and *Maaseh Merkabah*, the natural and divine sciences, were the topics, respectively, of the *Physics* and *Metaphysics* of Aristotle—as interpreted from a Jewish point of view. Maimonides' *Guide* represented a later and expanded reexamination of the same topics and may consequently be regarded as a source book on the third part of the curriculum, the part that Maimonides called *talmud* in his idiosyncratic, archaizing sense of the term.

The continuation of the same passage in the *Book of Knowledge* further explains Maimonides' point of view. The curriculum was to be divided into thirds only for beginners. Advanced students were to allocate their time differently.

> This plan applies to the period when one begins learning. But after one has become proficient and no longer needs to learn the Written Law, or continually be occupied with the Oral Law, he should, at fixed times, read the Written law and the traditional dicta, so as not to forget any of the rules of the Law, and should devote all his days exclusively to the study of Talmud, according to his breadth of mind and maturity of intellect. (*BK, Laws Concerning the Study of Torah* I:12; p. 58a)

Thirteenth century kabbalists such as Moses de Leon, the presumed author of *Sefer Ha-Zohar*, and Abraham Abulafia, who founded the ecstatic kabbalah, read Maimonides and interpreted his statements as authority to devote themselves to the study of kabbalah. However, what Maimonides meant by *Talmud* was a more comprehensive group of studies. In the Epistle Dedicatory of the *Guide*, he stated:

> When thereupon you read under my guidance texts dealing with the science of astronomy and prior to that texts dealing with mathematics, which is necessary as an introduction to astronomy, my joy in you increased because of the excellence of your mind and the quickness of your grasp. I saw that your longing for mathematics was great, and hence I let you train yourself in that science, knowing where you would end. When thereupon you read under my guidance texts dealing with the art of logic, my hopes fastened upon you, and I saw that you are one worthy to have the secrets of the prophetic books revealed to you so that you would consider in them that which perfect men ought to consider. (*Guide* Epistle Dedicatory; p. 3)

Maimonides began his study of Talmud with astronomy because its findings established the unity of the creation, from which the unity of God could be inferred. "When a man reflects on these things, studies all these created beings, from the angels and spheres down to human beings and so on, and realizes the Divine Wisdom manifested in them all, his love for God will increase" (*BK, Laws Concerning the Basic Principles of the Torah* IV:12; p. 39b).

Maimonides included mathematics in the curriculum both because it was necessary to the understanding of astronomy and because the rigor of mathematical demonstrations formed a preparation for the practice of logic. Maimonides wrote:

> Sometimes, if you wish it, you can rid yourself of an unfounded predeliction, free yourself of what is habitual, rely solely on speculation, and prefer the opinion that you ought to prefer. However, to do this you must fulfill several conditions. The first of them is that you should know how good your mind is and that your inborn disposition is sound. This becomes clear to you through training in all the mathematical sciences and through grasp of the rule of logic. (*Guide* II:23; p. 321)

Maimonides was aware of the account given in Plato's *Meno* where Socrates manages to bring a slave boy to a demonstration of the Pythagorean theorem not by telling him anything, but only by asking such questions that the slave boy comes to understand of his own knowledge. Mathematics were included in the medieval curriculum for the specific purpose of teaching independence of thought. In mathematics, a person never has to depend on authority. One does proofs oneself. In the sciences, a person has to depend on others. One needs their data, their results, and so forth. Mathematics and logic differ. In the Middle Ages, some of the writings on pedagogy stated explicitly that a person learned mathematics to learn independence of thought. In anything else, whether the sciences or history, in the last analysis, one had to depend on a teacher to learn whether a thing was true or not. In mathematics, a person was independent, and learning mathematics was a means of learning self-reliance.

The intellectual path that Maimonides identified—astronomy, mathematics, logic, and the prophetic books—was a single coherent trajectory. The physical and divine sciences were a single continuous philosophic enterprise. Knowledge was one. Religion was intrinsically scientific. Differing terminologies created the impression that different disciplines existed, but the terminologies were interchangeable. Consider, for example, Maimonides' phrasing: "All natural things are called *the work of the Lord*" (*Guide* I:66; p. 160); "If you consider the divine actions—I mean to say the natural actions" (*Guide* III:32; p. 525). Religion and science were identical because both pertained to objectively existing realities. Like the astronomical concept of celestial spheres, the mathematical concepts of arithmeticals and geometricals were instances of forms or intelligibles that the rational faculty abstracted from sense perceptions through the process of the Active Intellect. The intelligibles were elements of the design of the creation, and their intellectual attainment was achieved through a conjunction of study and inspiration.

Philosophy and science were not something that differed from religion but could be made integral with it. Divine science was predicated on the physical sciences.

> God, may his mention be exalted, wished us to be perfected and the state of our societies to be improved by His laws regarding actions. Now this can come about only after the adoption of intellectual beliefs, the first of which being His apprehension, may He be exalted, according to our capacity. This, in its turn, cannot come about except through divine science, and this divine science cannot become actual except after a study of natural science. (*Guide* I:Introduction; pp. 8–9)

Nor was Maimonides presenting a theologically skewed system of thought that paid lip service to physical science while rationalizing untenable beliefs. Maimonides was sincere in his claim that Judaism, properly understood, has its foundation in natural science, builds its theology on its knowledge of nature, and develops its laws on the basis of its theology. Correct opinions regarding both the world and God were to be built from the bottom up.

> There is no possible inference proving [the existence of God] except [from premises] deriving from this existent [world] taken as a whole and from its details. Accordingly it necessarily behooves one to consider this existent [world] as it is and to derive premises from what is perceived of its nature . . .

it follows that you should know its perceptible form and nature, and then it will be possible to make an inference from it with regard to what is other than it [i.e., God]. (*Guide* I:71; p. 183)

Divine science was consequently to be reached at the end of the course of scientific study and reasoning. Theological propositions were not to be asserted dogmatically as unearned axiomatic premises. Even correct theological ideas were not to be accepted on a basis of speculation or trust in the opinions of others. Divine science was to be demonstrated methodically, working modestly with evidence and logical inferences, in order that theology be a science—and not simply a matter of opinion.

> Man should not hasten too much to accede to this great and sublime matter at the first try, without having made his soul undergo training in the sciences and different kinds of knowledge, having truly improved his character, and having extinguished the desires and cravings engendered in him by his imagination. When, however, he has achieved and acquired knowledge of true and certain premises and has achieved knowledge of the rules of logic and inference and of the various ways of preserving himself from errors of the mind, he then should engage in the investigation of this subject. When doing this he should not make categoric affirmations in favor of the first opinion that occurs to him and should not, from the outset, strain and impel his thoughts toward the apprehension of the deity; he rather should feel awe and refrain and hold back until he gradually elevates himself. (*Guide* I:5; p. 29)

Maimonides' reference to awe was not casual. In wedding monotheistic devotion to Aristotelian contemplation, Maimonides referred to something more than thinking about the universe in the pursuit of scientific understanding and inspiration. The attitude that Maimonides recommended was analogous to viewing a work of art in an emotionally open and responsive manner that makes one available to be moved by the art. Meditations on natural science were not to be performed in a dispassionate frame of mind that was analogous to looking at a work of art with indifference. Only if a person contemplates God's works and creatures with an openness to respond emotionally would one come both to love God and to be frightened of Him. The commandments of affects could be fulfilled as consequences of willed acts, although not as willed acts themselves.

What Maimonides described as the fear of God was an instance of the type of religious experience that Otto (1950) termed a feeling of creatureliness. Maimonides wrote:

> When a man reflects on these things, studies all these created beings, from the angels and spheres down to human beings and so on, and realises the Divine Wisdom manifested in them all, his love for God will increase, his soul will thirst, his very flesh will yearn, to love God. He will be filled with

fear and trembling, as he becomes conscious of his own lowly condition, poverty and insignificance, and compares himself with any of the great and holy bodies; still more when he compares himself with any one of the pure forms that are incorporeal and have never had association with corporeal substance. He will then realise that he is a vessel full of shame, dishonour and reproach, empty and deficient. (*BK, Laws Concerning the Basic Principles of the Torah*, IV;12; p. 39b)

Because God, in His omnipotence, could not be affected by human acts, neither belief in God's existence and unity, nor a realistic love and fear of God, had any impact on God. Observance of the four commandments did impact psychologically, however, on worshipers. The commandments of monotheism and contemplation were components of Maimonides' cure of souls.

MAIMONIDES' INTELLECTUALIST MYSTICISM

Maimonides understood the mental representation of the intelligibles, the actualization of the rational faculty by the Active Intellect, as a means to provoke the love and fear of God. Indeed, Maimonides was content to treat meditation as the only cultic—as distinct from ethical and social—behavior that was ultimately necessary for a human being.

To come near to this true deity and to obtain His good will, nothing is required that is fraught with any hardship whatever, the only things needed being *love of Him and fear of Him* and nothing else. For these two are, as we shall explain, the end of divine worship. (*Guide* III:29; p. 518)

Blumenthal (1977; 1980; 1988; 1999; 2006) identified Maimonides' program of the Active Intellect's actualization of the rational faculty as a Jewish instance of "intellectualist mysticism," in which "the experience of the divine is a function of philosophic, intellectualist preparation and such experience yields philosophic, intellectualist knowledge" (1977; pp. 27–28). Idel (1986, p. 86) agreed that Maimonides was concerned with "the philosophical *ascensio mentis ad Deum*." Merlan (1969) demonstrated that the Neoplatonists of late antiquity had distinguished two varieties of mystical experience. Differing from regression to the One, the "flight of the alone to the alone," was a distinct mystical experience of the second Neoplatonic hypostasis, the *nous*, "Intellect," a term and concept that Neoplatonism borrowed from Aristotle. The Neoplatonic distinction between union with the One and union with the *nous* was preserved in the medieval Islamic tradition, where Sufis favored the term *'ittihad*, "union, unification," which referred technically to the experience of the One, while Muslim philosophers generally wrote of *'ittisal*, "conjunction, contact," which designated mystical experience of the intellect, which was technically termed *'aql* in Arabic (Fakhry, 1971; Merkur, 2001a).

Blumenthal contended that medieval Jewish philosophers engaged in closely related practices, using the very same Arabic terms. Blumenthal noted the frequency of Maimonides' use of cognates of *'ittisal*. Where, for example, Pines translated, "For everyone with whom something of this overflow is united, will be reached by providence to the extent to which he is reached by the intellect" (*Guide* III:17, p. 474), Blumenthal (1977, pp. 30–31) carefully rendered, "For anyone who has had anything of this emanation contact him (*ittasala bihi shai*) will be reached (*yasiluhu*) by providence to the extent to which the intellect reaches him (*yasiluhu*)."

Blumenthal drew attention to the philosophic context in which Maimonides placed his mysticism. Maimonides wrote:

> There are those who set their thought to work after having attained perfection in the divine science, renounce what is other than He, and direct all the acts of their intellect toward an examination of the beings with a view to drawing from them proof with regard to Him, so as to know His governance of them in whatever way it is possible. . . . This is the rank of the prophets. (*Guide* III:51; p. 620)

> This kind of worship ought only to be engaged in after intellectual conception has been achieved. If, however, you have apprehended God and His acts in accordance with what is required by the intellect, you should afterwards engage in totally devoting yourself to Him, endeavor to come closer to Him, and strengthen the bond between you and Him—that is, the intellect. . . . The *Torah* has made it clear that this last worship to which we have drawn attention . . . can only be engaged in after apprehension has been achieved. . . . Now . . . love is proportionate to apprehension. After *love* comes this worship to which attention has also been drawn by [the sages], *may their memory be blessed*, who said: *This is the worship in the heart* [*BT* Taanit, 2a; BT, Berakhot IV]. In my opinion it consists in setting thought to work on the first intelligible and in devoting oneself exclusively to this as far as this is within one's capacity. (*Guide* III:51; pp. 620–621)

In commenting on these passages, Blumenthal (1977, p. 34; 1988, p. 4; 2006, pp. 132–141) emphasized three discrete phases in the procedure that Maimonides described. The first phase was an intellectual exercise in philosophizing that aimed at "an examination of the beings with a view to drawing from them proof with regard to Him." Topics of study were to be pursued not as ends in themselves but as evidence of the "governance" of the creation. Having attained an idea of God by inference from the evidence of nature—a theological "argument from design" (Paley, 1802)—a philosopher was said to possess "intellectual apprehensions." These were to be followed by the second phase, the "love of God." Because God remained ineffable, the cognitive content of this phase was "the first intelligible," which is to say, "the bond between you and Him—that is, the intellect." The Active Intellect served as a direction or pointer for the devotion of love toward the Creator who transcends intellect itself. The "love of God" (*al-mahabba*) was a yearning through intellect for more than intellect. It differed from and was followed by the third phase, the climactic "worship of the heart" (*al-'ibada*) that Maimonides characterized as "intellectual worship consisting in nearness to God and being in his presence in that true reality that I have made known to you and not by way of affections of the imagination" (*Guide* III:51; p. 623). Blumenthal (1988, p. 5) noted that Maimonides, who wrote the *Guide* in Arabic using the Hebrew alphabet, systematically distinguished between Arabic *mahabba*, "love," cognate with Hebrew *'ahavah*, and between Arabic *'ishq*, "passionate love," cognate with Hebrew *hesheq*, the latter being "a quantitative increment" of the former. "You know the difference between the terms *one who loves* [*oheb*] and *one who loves passionately* [*hosheq*]; an excess of love [*mahabbah*], so that no thought remains that is directed toward a thing other than the Beloved, is passionate love [*'ishq*]" (*Guide* III:51; p. 627). Passionate love was aroused as the desire for God gave way to the sense of "nearness to God and being in his presence" at which Maimonides' meditations aimed. Also aroused by the sense of God's immediate presence was Arabic *ghibta*, "bliss," corresponding to Hebrew *simhah* and *no'am* (Blumenthal, 1988, pp. 5–6), and approximating Aristotle's *eudaimonia*.

THE RATIONAL CHARACTER OF MAIMONIDES' INTELLECTUALIST MYSTICISM

The Aristotelian tradition of intellectualist mysticism may be regarded as a medieval expression of the type of religious experience that David Bakan discussed in modern contexts as "rational mysticism."

> For many people ... the term "intuition" implies the totally mysterious and irrational. I prefer the phrase "rational mysticism"; it suggests the noetic power of the process and also the fact that it is understandable and to some extent even predictable. Intuition is not an ultimately mysterious thing, as most people suppose. (Bakan, in Havens, 1968, p. 35)

As examples of rational mystics, Bakan (1966b) identified "Newton, Kepler, Pascal—and Fechner in psychology—who were profoundly mystical in their orientation. And in modern times there are people like Einstein, Schrödinger, Planck, Whitehead, Eddington, Jeans, Wittgenstein, and others in whom there are identifiable mystical streaks by any reasonable definition of the term" (p. 140). Bakan suggested that rational mysticism may be found not only among scientists, but also among some mystics, and as a general practice within psychoanalysis. In each instance, rational mysticism involves three beliefs.

1. The notion of the "one" entails a belief in a fundamental unity in spite of apparent disunity.
2. "Beyond" entails a belief in the distinction between what is manifest and what is not manifest, and the conviction that what is not manifest influences what is manifest.
3. The emphasis on meditation entails the conviction that through some kind of intrapsychic activity one can come into contact with what is not manifest. (Bakan, 1966b, p. 141)

Bakan attributed specific meditative practices to rational mysticism. We quote at length:

> It is possible and desirable to make portions of the unmanifest manifest by meditation. More generally, this is the belief that through engaging in certain specified intrapsychic processes it is possible to reach beyond the veil which covers the unmanifest; and that through the apprehension of what was unmanifest a radical overhaul of the human condition is possible.
>
> In this respect we can consider mathematics . . . as perhaps one of the highest forms of meditation. . . . In mathematics we seek to get at a kind of truth which is not manifest. We do it by means of a psychotechnical exercise. The reality to which we come is felt to be sounder than the ephemeral and unstable world of the informative sense organs. In mathematics there is that peculiar synthesis of discovery and invention which reaches out and comes to grips with the world in a way which would otherwise be completely impossible.
>
> The possibility of radical reform of the condition of human existence through meditation is one of the central features of the mystical position. The mystic starts with the sense of alienation and ends with a sense of union with what was unmanifest. The mathematician ends up with the deep experience of relationship which he did not have before. In those forms of meditation which we call introspection, free association, dream interpretation, etc., we have the experience of insight, an experience based on the apprehension of what was not manifest before and with it the possibility of radical reform of the condition.
>
> It is clear that the meditative exercise to the mystic, the discipline of logic, mathematics, and the scientific method, and of free association and dream interpretation can all be regarded as systematic forms of meditation, psychotechnical devices which are presumed to bring the individual into contact with regions of existence which would otherwise remain unmanifest. The objection that they differ from each other with respect to how much emotional or personal entailment there is in them does not really stand. For there are many mathematicians who "live for" their mathematics.
>
> In each of the three modes of thought the ultimate appeal is to the experience of the individual. This is certainly the case in science, where, for exam-

ple, so much stress has been made on such things as replicability, the fundamental idea being that a scientific truth is a truth which can be repeated for any individual if he but engages in the same procedures and "meditations." It is certainly the case in connection with mysticism which has always been related to a profound individualism as contrasted with authority and community. And it is certainly the case in psychoanalysis where the fundamental truths must be individual experience in order to be understood and accepted. And somehow, at least in psychoanalysis and mysticism, this individual experience is the way to a radical modification in the life of the individual, especially in the modification of desire. (Bakan, 1966b, pp. 147–149)

Neither medieval intellectualist mysticism nor the rational mysticism that is its modern analog involves the dissociated states, otherworldliness, logical paradoxes, and other departures from realism for which most of the world's mysticisms are deservedly notorious. It is, however, an error in thinking to confine the term "mysticism" to the irrational practices that are based on ecstatic trances, and so arrive at a categorical opposition of "science" and "mysticism." Such an opposition involves a caricature of both science and mysticism, and creates a disjunction that is completely fictional, unnecessary, and intellectually irresponsible.

When Maimonides wrote of rationality *in actu*, the actualization of the rational faculty through its conjunction with the Active Intellect, he had in mind what has been called the "aha!" experience of creative inspiration. It is the experience that Aquinas, who depended on Maimonides, called "understanding" and attributed to "helping grace." It occurs when someone "gets" an idea, when "the penny drops." It is the moment when a body of data is organized in thought in a fashion that crystallizes into a coherent concept.

Maimonides claimed that the experience of understanding a concept involved more than the rational faculty alone. It involved a function that was both intellectual and rational but was not limited in its reach to computation or calculation. It was not a question of simply doing sums, which the rational faculty can do on its own. The intellectual process to which the rational faculty gained access was also capable of exceeding the sum of previous knowledge and making discoveries. It was capable of organizing thoughts in a synthetic or integrative manner that results in the emergence of novel ideas, in synergies that produce paradigm shifts large and small. For example, when a child is taught multiplication, the child begins by learning the multiplication tables by rote, beginning with 1 times 1, and proceeding to 10 times 10. Eventually, through the repetition of the examples, the child grasps the concept of "multiplication" in principle. When the child first attains the concept of multiplication, it is a moment of intellectual discovery. For the child, the concept does not as yet possess a name. It is experienced in thought without images, as a concept about a procedure that can be applied to numbers. The concept does not involve more data than were known previously. It comprehends the same data at a higher level of organization that constitutes a paradigm shift in thought about numbers. With the concept of multiplication, the child is able to multiply any two numbers, without further need for rote memorization.

For Maimonides, the Active Intellect designated the intellectual process that imparted discoveries to the rational faculty. The Active Intellect was at work, in our example, at the moment that the child grasped the procedural concept of multiplication. Maimonides understood the Active Intellect in an Aristotelian fashion as a development out of empirical data. He did not approach it, as Ibn Sina did, through the heritage of Platonic interpretations of the Active Intellect, as a process of sudden access to preexisting Platonic ideas. MacDonald (2003) summarized the Platonizing concept as follows:

> [The agent intellect is] the function of abstraction, the 'power' which produces universals ... the agent intellect [is] an intelligent or spiritual being distinct and superior to the soul, acting upon the soul in order to actualize its potency for thought ... there is only one agent intellect for all human beings; each individual possessed its own receptive power which the action of the agent intellect 'changes' from potency to actuality. In other words, all human concepts flow into our individual souls from a purely spiritual being, one and the same for all humans. (pp. 161–162)

For Maimonides, the Active Intellect was the process within the rational faculty that *produced* or *constructed* abstractions. The abstractions did not preexist the process of their derivation from sensory data. The Active Intellect worked with the data that it had available. It was what Aristotelians called an intelligence and the Bible called an angel. But by these terms Maimonides meant what we today mean by speaking of a natural "function" or "process" and postulating that a physical "structure" produces it. Maimonides was not talking about angels composed of spiritual substances. He was talking about psychology.

Maimonides used a variety of tropes in reference to the Active Intellect, but always in keeping with Aristotle's original concept of the intellect as a natural process. At times, however, he drew on the illuminist language of medieval Platonism. Because selections from the *Enneads* of Plotinus, the third century founder of Neoplatonism, circulated in the Islamicate under the title *The Theology of Aristotle*, medieval Aristotelian philosophy routinely included a Neoplatonic component. The distinction between Platonists and Aristotelians can be less informative than the contrast between constructivists such as al-Farabi, Ibn Rushd, and Maimonides and Aristotelian illuminists such as Ibn Sina. Maimonides drew readily on illuminist language, which he understood, as he explicitly stated, "figuratively."

> The books of the prophets ... apply figuratively the notion of overflow to the action of the deity ... through the overflow of the intellect that has overflowed from Thee, we intellectually cognize ... receive guidance ... draw inferences, and apprehend the intellect (*Guide* II:11; p. 280).

Much as Maimonides conformed linguistically with Platonizing formulations of intellectualist mysticism, he placed a significantly different spin on the common wording. Maimonides explicitly stated that his use of the image of overflow was to be understood as a metaphor. Consider the two parts of the following sentence: "The overflow of the Active Intellect goes in its true reality only to [the rational faculty], causing it to pass from potentiality to actuality" (*Guide* II:38; p. 377). In the first part of this sentence, Maimonides conceived of the Active Intellect as overflow. The image makes one think of something, like information being downloaded from the divine to the human being. In the second part of the sentence, reference was made to the actualization of a potential, implying that all of the potentially generative components, such as information, exist in the human being. The Active Intellect then functions as a kind of triggering agent, empowering the rational faculty's assembly of the information out of unorganized components, and so causing potential knowledge to become actuality. Brentano's (1977) book on the Active Intellect explained that views on the Active Intellect after Aristotle were very distinctly bifurcated between these illuminist and constructivist views of prophecy. Maimonides mentioned both positions and allowed himself the advantage of both. His phrasing formed a kind of bridge between the two positions and is correctly understood, as he explained, by treating the illuminist language as an imaginative metaphor that referred to a process that was natural.

The differences between the constructivist and illuminist positions within medieval philosophy had important consequences. Illuminists allowed themselves no possibility of being in error. Because they were convinced that their mystical experiences provided them with access to externally existing spiritual beings and other phenomena, they feared demons and attributed magical consequences—supernatural rewards and punishments—to their every deed. Maimonides agreed that human beings have access to objective truths, but he was not claiming that the psychological process of abstraction is infallible. He was claiming the revelation or inspiration of objective truths, but he was also leaving ample opportunity for the process of abstraction to result in error. Maimonides' epistemology freed him from the necessity of believing in demons and magic, making possible the turn to psychology that allowed him to conceptualize the sickness and cure of souls.

MAIMONIDES' PRACTICE OF THE PRESENCE OF GOD

Maimonides repeatedly associated "worship of the heart," the most advanced phase of his practice of intellectualist mysticism, with "nearness to God and being in his presence" (*Guide* III:51; p. 623) or "standing in the presence of Him who is perfect in knowledge" (*BK, Laws Concerning the Basic Principles of the Torah*, II;2; p. 35b). Maimonides' emphasis of the divine presence rested firmly on traditional Jewish precedents. Psalm 16:8 stated: "I have set the Lord always before me always; because he is at my right hand, I shall not be moved." Because the Hebrew verb *shivah*, which is understood in Psalm 16:8 to mean "to place, set," ordinarily means "to compare, liken; to level, even; to equalize," the sages interpreted the verse as a biblical precedent for their own meditations during synagogue prayers: "One who prays should perceive the divine presence before him" (*BT*, Sanhendrin 22a), thereby placing God on an even, level, or equal footing with himself (Verman, 1996, p. 5). The Talmudic practice of meditation included the cultivation of an anthropomorphic mental image, standing within four cubits of the meditator (Wolfson, 1996). The mental image was conceptualized variously as God, the archangel Metatron, the prophet Elijah, and, in the late Middle Ages, the meditator himself.

Maimonides insisted on an abstract concept of God, but otherwise endorsed the Talmudic practice. Using the term *kawwanah*, literally "turning" or "facing a particular direction" (Wolfson, 1996, p. 140), but idiomatically, "intention" or "intentionality" when engaged in prayer, Maimonides stated: "*Kawwanah* means emptying the heart of all thoughts, and to think of oneself as if standing before the Presence" (*BK, Laws or Prayer* IV:16). In part through Maimonides, *kawwanah* became the conventional term for "meditation" in the kabbalah (Scholem, 1934). In the *Guide*, Maimonides additionally recommended meditation on an abstractly conceptualized Presence as a private practice: "When . . . you are alone with yourself and no one else is there and while you lie awake upon your bed, you should take great care during these precious times not to set your thought to work on anything other than that intellectual worship consisting in nearness to God and being in His presence in that true reality that I have made known to you and not by way of affections of the imagination" (*Guide* III:51; p. 623).

Blumenthal (1977) expressed uncertainty in translating his findings about the stages of Maimonides' meditations into experiential categories: "What was the exact nature of the experience of cognition or providence? What was it really like to be the recipient of the divine emanation, to attain to true knowledge? We do not know exactly" (p. 31). Blumenthal recognized that it involved "the transition from thinking-about-God to being-in-the-presence of God" (Blumenthal, 2006, p. 133). Maimonides described it as a cognitively rich and varied process of inspiration that he identified with biblical prophecy. Consider the following passage from the *Mishneh Torah*.

> When one . . . enters the "Paradise" and continuously dwells upon those great and abstruse themes—having the right mind capable of comprehending and grasping them; sanctifying himself, withdrawing from the ways of

the ordinary run of men . . . [and] keeping his mind disengaged, concentrated on higher things as though bound beneath the Celestial Throne, so as to comprehend the pure and holy forms and contemplating the wisdom of God as displayed in His creatures, from the first form to the very centre of the Earth, learning thence to realize His greatness—on such a man the Holy Spirit will promptly descend. (*BK, Laws on the Basic Principles of the Torah*, 7:1; pp. 42a–b)

Writing the *Mishneh Torah* for a popular audience, Maimonides asserted that meditation on an argument from design would result in a mingling of the person's soul with the angels. Because Maimonides equated angels with Aristotelian forms, he was claiming that successful meditation precipitated revelation from the Active Intellect—the Holy Spirit—that consisted of rational knowledge of the angelic forms. In the *Guide*, where Maimonides addressed the philosophically inclined, he wrote of the same experience more straightforwardly.

These people are those who are present in the ruler's council. This is the rank of the prophets. Among them there is he [or they] who because of the greatness of his apprehension and his renouncing everything that is other than God, may he be exalted, has attained such a degree that it is said of him, *And he was there with the Lord* [Exod 54:28], putting questions and receiving answers, speaking and being spoken to, in that holy place. (*Guide* III:51; p. 620)

Both formulations, mingling with the angels and engaging God in a prophetic dialogue, indicate that a cognitively limited or seemingly empty experience was emphatically not the content of Maimonides' contemplative experiences.

How did Maimonides' meditations accomplish the transition from contemplation of nature in the Aristotelian tradition to a classically Jewish communion and prophetic dialogue in the presence of God? The matter is considerably obscure. Neither Maimonides' son Abraham Maimonides (1927, 1938) nor grandson Obadyah Maimonides (1981), in their treatises on Jewish mysticism, provided instructions; Abraham Abulafia, the great kabbalistic expositor of the *Guide*, was sufficiently puzzled that he considered Maimonides' account incomplete. Abulafia wrote:

Indeed, I did inform you that the true knowledge of the Name cannot be known, from *Sefer Yezirah* alone, even if you know all the above-mentioned commentaries on it, nor from the *Guide of the Perplexed* alone, even if you know all commentaries on it; but only when the two types of knowledge of those two books will be linked together. (Cited in Idel, 1990, p. 67)

Abulafia used meditative techniques belonging to the *Hasidei Ashkenaz* that pertained to letter combinations that were based on *Sefer Yetsirah*, in order to attain alternate states of consciousness, but he depended on the *Guide* to direct the states toward the desired contemplative experiences (Idel, 1990, pp. 66–69; 2004, p. 209).

Aryeh Kaplan (1985) suggested that Maimonides' meditations progress from the topic of God's work of creation to the topic of oneself as a part of the creation. "One asks the questions, 'If God created this vast universe, then who am I? How do I fit into all of this?'" (p. 50). The reflexive character of the meditations is reflected by the traditional designation of Maimonides' procedure as *hitbonenut*, "observation, consideration, reflection," deriving from the reflexive (*hitpa'el*) form of the verb *biyen*, "to understand, know, perceive, or discern oneself." Trying to understand oneself, not from one's own perspective, but from God's perspective, in order to understand God's purposes for oneself, on a moment-to-moment and day-by-day basis, is an effort to empathize with God's perspective, to know God's will for oneself. It is a performance during meditation of the practice that Martin Buber (1965) described as the life of dialogue (see also Merkur, 2008). Meditations on the topic of one's personal teleology may lead to inspirations regarding the services that one may render—not only in a calling or vocation that is a life's work, but also on the simpler scale of highly variable daily tasks. In keeping with Maimonides' epistemology, when inspired self-knowledge outlines a realistic and appropriate course of action, the inspirations may be regarded as objective and truthful in precisely the same sense that inspired discoveries in the natural sciences are counted as valid. Belief in the genuinely revelatory character of the inspirations may easily surround their intellectual experience with an affective sense of presence.

A passage in the *Guide* indicates that Maimonides found synagogue liturgy to be helpful in achieving the sense of presence.

> While reciting the *Shema'* prayer, you should empty your mind of everything and pray thus. You should not content yourself with being intent while reciting the first verse of *Shema'* and saying the first benediction. When this has been carried out correctly and has been practiced consistently for years, cause your soul, whenever you read or listen to the Torah, to be constantly directed—the whole of you and your thought—toward reflection on what you are listening to or reading. (*Guide* III:51; pp. 622–623)

In the *Mishneh Torah*, Maimonides had required *kawwanah* during the first verse of the *Shema'* as a routine synagogue devotion. A Jew fulfilled his obligation at prayer if he remained conceptually alert as he spoke the one verse, "Hear O Israel, the Lord our God, the Lord is One," and otherwise recited the balance of the liturgy by rote, in a conceptually inattentive manner (*Book of Adoration, Laws concerning the Reading of the Shema'* II:1). In the *Guide*, however, Maimonides was concerned to cultivate a meditative state that was elective rather than requisite; he advised that practitioners be "constantly directed—the whole of you and your thought—toward reflection on what you are listening to or reading" throughout the whole of the synagogue service.

With these words, Maimonides simultaneously discouraged the monotonous repetition of the first verse of the *Shema'* that Jews have used to achieve the type of mystical experience that kabbalists prioritized. He insisted that once the liturgy had been committed to memory, neither prayers nor Scriptural passages were to be recited unthinkingly or repetitively. For the purposes of meditation, each and every word was instead to be pondered, both intellectually and emotionally, during the whole of each prayer service. The *Shema'* was not to be used as Hindus use mantras, Greek Orthodox use the Jesus prayer, and Muslims employ the *la illaha*. The meditative use of prayer was to remain discursive, rational, intellectually complex, and varied. It was to be intentional (*kawwanah*) and heartfelt.

Maimonides' recommendation of meditation on the contents of prayer may explain how he accomplished the transition between meditation on angelic forms and an immediate sense of the presence of God. In one of his discussions of worship of the heart, Maimonides contrasted thinking about God with thinking of God.

> This chapter . . . is to confirm men in the intention to set their thought to work on God alone after they have achieved knowledge of Him. . . . This is the worship peculiar to those who have apprehended the true realities; the more they think of Him and of being with Him, the more their worship increases. (*Guide* III:51; p. 620)

When meditating on philosophic topics, a person may think of God in the third person, as a logical cause responsible for the intelligence implicit in the topics being pondered. During prayer, however, the texts of both the biblical Psalms and many prayers of later composition often shift from discussing God in the third person to addressing God in the second person, as "Thou." Every blessing, for example, begins with this intellectual movement from the third to the second person, with the verbal formula, "Blessed art Thou O Lord our God, who. . . ." The word "blessed" conceptualizes God in the third person; the word "Thou" requires the speaker to reorient toward God in the second person. A person deeply practiced in achieving a state of creative inspiration by philosophizing could bring the developed capacity for achieving the alternate state to bear during liturgical prayer. The person would then be guided by the prayers to achieve further creative inspirations in which God was conceptualized in the second person. The contents of the experiences would consist of a sense of presence, in which God was felt emotionally to be in close physical proximity. Maimonides understood the experience of a sense of presence philosophically as an experience not of God, but of the first intelligible, the Active Intellect, which the sages had called the *Shekhinah*, the "immanence" or "presence" of God. (For psychological discussions of the sense of presence, see James, 1902; Merkur, 1999).

The sense of presence was compatible with an active and busy life, precisely as it was compatible with studies of astronomy, mathematics, logic, and other topics of Maimonides' curriculum. According to Maimonides, rare individuals were able to maintain worship of the heart continuously as they went about their daily lives.

> And there may be a human individual who, through his apprehension of the true realities and his joy in what he has apprehended, achieves a state in which he talks with people and is occupied with his bodily necessities while his intellect is wholly turned toward Him, may He be exalted, so that in his heart he is always in His presence, may He be exalted, while outwardly he is with people, in the sort of way described by the poetical parables that have been invented for these notions: *I sleep, but my heart waketh; it is the voice of my beloved that knocketh, and so on* [Song 5:2]. (*Guide* III:51; p. 623)

Maimonides attributed a continuous sense of God's presence to Moses and the patriarchs. He termed their condition "a permanent state of extreme perfection" (*Guide* III:51; p. 624). Maimonides denied that he himself aspired so high. "This rank is not a rank that with a view to the attainment of which someone like myself may aspire for guidance. But one may aspire to attain that rank which was mentioned before this one through the training that we described" (ibid.). The ambiguity of the syntax makes it unclear whether Maimonides was disavowing the ability to teach permanent perfection or was instead claiming that a continuous sense of presence could not be achieved through human efforts, but rather depended on the providence of God (Pines, in *Guide*, p. 624, n. 32). In either event, Maimonides was apparently remarking on the phenomenon that Abraham Maslow termed "plateau experiences" that are milder but more protracted experiences of the same cognitive and emotional contents that occur briefly and intensely as transient "peak experiences" (Cleary & Shapiro, 1995; Krippner, 1972; Maslow, 1964).

THE THERAPEUTIC EFFECTS OF MEDITATION

Because Aristotle attributed vice to ignorance of the good, he regarded contemplation of the good as a sufficient corrective. Maimonides' emphasis on the will to illness fundamentally altered the Aristotelian paradigm by reversing the relation between wrongdoing and ignorance. Ignorance had to be overcome, but general education regarding virtue—the program of Platonists and Aristotelians alike—was not sufficient to correct the particular ignorance that prevented *teshuvah*. Neither was Maimonides' behavioral therapy particularly effective. Without having a term for the phenomenon, moralists had always been aware that moral education fails whenever people are unable to learn lessons—that is, to know knowledge—that moral educators make available to them. Freud called the psychological obstacle to knowledge "resistance" and designed psychoanalysis to address its biographical sources. Maimonides thought in terms of a willfully chosen ignorance that persisted despite education by precept and habituation. Although he followed Aristotle in prescribing contemplation as a therapeutic practice, his cure of souls did not consist of contemplation alone.

Maimonides expressed himself in the medieval idioms of Aristotelian intellectualist mysticism, but within that discourse he positioned himself as a rational mystic, in Bakan's sense of the term. In keeping with the medieval convention of argumentation from design, Maimonides emphasized that a rational, scientific understanding of the world of nature is a logical proof of universal intelligibility that leads to a rational understanding of God, but he turned to the Bible and rabbinical teaching for guidance in his critique of Aristotelianism. In Maimonides' view, the Bible commanded both the ideas of the existence and unity of God and the attendant emotions of love and fear. The philosophic privileging of the rational faculty did not validate unemotional intellectualism. Maimonides' emphasis of the rational faculty took for granted the natural fact that no greater pleasures exist than the joys of rationality. The pleasure that may be taken in a rational understanding of the world of nature and its many phenomena leads naturally to the pleasure from a rational relationship with God. In moments whose cognitive aspects consist of inspiration and communion, the attendant pleasures of rationality may intensify to become ecstasy or bliss. These emotions never cease to be rational. In rational mysticism, the bliss is never postrational or nonrational. The bliss is intrinsic, proportional, and responsive to the experiences of rationality. It is because intense rationality is joyous and blissful, and bliss capable of being rational, that reason was Maimonides' way to the love and fear of God.

Maimonides' cure of souls proceeded from the premise that both vice and ignorance may be freely chosen. Intellectual truths may be unknown, but they may also be known and disbelieved. Maimonides consequently valued meditative practices both for the intellectual truths that they disclosed and, more important, for their promotion of belief in those truths. Sinners know what the good is, but they are unable to connect emotionally with their knowledge, as is necessary in order to make use of it, because they have no belief or faith in their knowledge of the good. Belief consists of knowledge that is affirmed. Its mere knowledge or cognition does not make it a belief. "There is no belief except after a representation; belief is the affirmation that what has been represented is outside the mind just as it has been represented in the mind" (*Guide* I:50, p. 111). In Maimonides' view, education addresses knowledge; the cure of souls turns on the knowledge's affirmation. Unlike pedagogical instruction, meditation cultivates affirmations through rational love and rational fear.

Maimonides theorized that contemplative experiences of the love and fear of God were curative because they addressed disorders of the particular faculties of the soul that are involved in virtue and sin. "Know that transgressions and observances of the Law have their origin only in two of the faculties of the soul, namely, the *sensitive* and the *appetitive*, and that to these two faculties alone are to be ascribed all transgressions and observances" (*Eight Chapters* ii; p. 47). After dividing virtues into "two kinds, *moral* and *intellectual*" (pp. 49–50), he assigned the intellectual virtues of wisdom, reason, sagacity and cleverness to the rational faculty, but moral virtues to the appetitive faculty.

> Moral virtues belong only to the appetitive faculty.... The virtues of this faculty are very numerous, being moderation, [i.e., fear of sin], liberality, honesty, meekness, humility, contentedness [which the rabbis call "wealth," when they say, "Who is truly wealthy? He who is contented with his lot"], courage, [faithfulness], and other virtues akin to these. The vices of this faculty consist of a deficiency or of an exaggeration of these qualities (*Eight Chapters* ii; p. 50).

Moral vices consisted, in Maimonides' view, of misplaced desires. "The wicked man ... continually longs for excesses which are really pernicious, but which, on account of the illness of his soul, he considers to be good" (*Eight Chapters* iii; p. 51). Maimonides' pursuit of the behavioral mean sought to correct individual desires by force of habit. His program of meditation addressed the generic motivation for pursuit of the mean by producing correctly placed desires directly. The love and fear of God that could be achieved through meditation on nature implicitly functioned, in Alexander and French's (1946) felicitous phrase, as "corrective emotional experiences" that placed the relationship to God on a realistic and emotionally valid footing. A person who achieved love and fear through meditation on God's creation acquired intelligibles that might subsequently serve as an emotional compass. In medieval idiom, the memories of moments of actualization were termed the Acquired Intellect; we would today speak of the mental structures of a self-representation. However it may be formulated, the solace of blissful love for God can become both an emotional goal at which to aim and a motive for doing so. In its turn, the fear of God is an existential fear—an instance of "real anxiety"—whose contrast with experiences of neurotic anxiety can be sobering, humbling, and corrective of histrionic melodramatics.

Maimonides' prescription of contemplative experiences was consistent with modern findings about the therapeutic value of mystical union (Fauteux, 1994). Mystical experiences manifest religious ideals in connection with intense emotions (or emotionlessness) that favor the ideals' integration within the personality as personal standards for self-esteem, identity, and the sense of authenticity. Mystical experiences can be effective forms of supportive psychotherapy. They can ameliorate the degree of health whose achievement is possible without altering or dismantling the resistance. Like all other supportive psychotherapies, mystical experiences can enhance the conscious portion of the personality, greatly reducing the secondary complications of neurosis, but without undoing the neurosis itself. Between them, the contemplative love and fear of God can consolidate the healthy portion of the personality, limiting the spread of neurosis beyond the areas of primary repression, and transforming at least some irrational defenses into wholesome sublimations.

CONCLUSIONS

Maimonides listed belief in the existence and unity of God, and the obligation to love and to fear God, as the first four of the 613 commandments in the Law of Moses. For Maimonides, belief in the existence and unity of God was a logical necessity that could be demonstrated to anyone who was willing to reason through the topic. Agreeing with Bahya ibn Paquda's *Duties of the Heart*, Maimonides recommended rational meditations on the natural sciences, especially mathematics and astronomy, to persuade individuals that the universe possesses a design and so attests to its creation by God. Gratitude, wonderment, and humility would then arouse the love and fear of God, fulfilling the commandments. Maimonides augmented the philosophical tradition of meditation on nature with the rabbinical tradition of communing with God. Arguing that divine science was properly conducted as a rational procedure that was continuous with the physical sciences, Maimonides proposed that Jews follow their meditations on physical science with additional meditations on being in the immediate presence of God. These meditations sought not merely to know about God, but directly to know God. Subsequent tradition called Maimonides' meditations *hitbonenut*, "self-reflection," in reference to their focus on God's purposes for the meditator, that is, on the self in perspective of God. Maimonides described three phases of his meditative practice of the presence of God, of which the third, "worship of the heart" was a religious ecstasy. Maimonides conceptualized worship of the heart in biblical language as prophecy, and in philosophical language as a conjunction of the soul with the Active Intellect. Worship of the heart was an instance of what medievalists call "intellectualist mysticism," in reference to the soul's union with the Active Intellect. It is also an instance of the type of meditation that Bakan termed "rational mysticism." In Maimonides' view, contemplative love for God was therapeutic because it corrected disordered affects and motivated repentance.

THREE

Imagination and the Interpretation of Prophecy

MAIMONIDES ADDRESSED his philosophical tour de force, the *Guide of the Perplexed*, to individuals who were already familiar with his psychological views. He wrote: "This Treatise has been composed only for the benefit of those who have philosophized and have acquired knowledge of what has become clear with reference to the soul and all its faculties" (*Guide* I:68; p. 166). Modern scholars commonly treat the *Guide* as a work of philosophy—indeed, as the single greatest achievement of medieval Jewish philosophy—but the text is correctly understood, Maimonides asserted, as a psychological document. Perplexity is not to be understood as a reference to intellectual puzzlement. By "perplexity," Maimonides denoted a state of spiritual crisis. Perplexity was a medical condition that Maimonides considered symptomatic of the illness of the soul.

When Maimonides treated ignorance as consequent rather than causal of wrongdoing, he recognized that Aristotelian psychology lacked a cogent explanation of wrongdoing. To complete his own model, he needed to devise a theory to explain how the affective faculty can err and desires can come to be misdirected. To develop the needed theory, Maimonides massively expanded the significance of Aristotle's predication of intellect on imagination. Aristotle had made various points in the course of arguing that reason is a faculty that is part of a unified and embodied soul, and is not a discrete soul on its own. Among other observations, he remarked: "Without an image thinking is impossible. For there is in such activity an affection identical with one in geometrical demonstrations" (*On Memory* 450^a 1–2). With this argument, Aristotle claimed that the Platonic project of pure reason was humanly impossible because reasoning is predicated on imaginative combinations of memories of sense. Maimonides recognized the extraordinary clinical importance of what for Aristotle had been a passing observation. In keeping with Aristotle's theory of mental imagery, Maimonides implicated imagination in wrongdoing. Moral failures arise, Maimonides wrote, when "men err as regards . . . qualities, imagining that one of the extremes is good, and is a virtue" (*Eight Chapters* iv; p. 57). "Those whose souls are ill, that is the wicked and the morally perverted, imagine that the bad is good, and that the good is bad" (*Eight Chapters* iii; p. 51). These formulations replaced ignorance with imagination as the condition of wrongdoing.

Maimonides' formulation inverted the relationship between vice and imagination that al-Farabi had noted. In al-Farabi's (1961) view, disorders of imagination were symptoms of vice.

> Wicked and vicious men, being sick in their souls, are led to imagine that wicked deeds are good and good deeds wicked. The man virtuous with the ethical virtues desires and longs always for the ends that are good in reality and makes them his aim and purpose. The wicked man desires always the ends that are wicked in reality, but imagines them good, on account of the sickness of his soul. (p. 45).

When Maimonides regarded disordered imagination as the cause and not merely the consequence of vice, he introduced an innovation that has had abiding importance for the historical development of psychotherapy. According to Maimonides, mental illness was a product not of ignorance but of imagination. The will to do wrong—the will to illness—is made possible by the imagination "that the bad is good, and that the good is bad." Maimonides' theory explained why the general philosophic program of correcting ignorance through education was unable to effect the cure of souls. Psychotherapy had additionally to address the vicissitudes of imagination.

Meditation was curative only insofar as the love and fear that it cultivated for God were rational and moral emotions. The same emotions, and the meditations that might incur them, could instead be pathogenic whenever they were devoted to irrational imaginations. The difference between therapeutic and crazy-making uses of meditation turned on the vicissitudes of imagination.

Maimonides' formulation was epoch-making. In developing a theory that replaced ignorance with imagination as the cause of mental illness, Maimonides inaugurated the paradigm shift that led—through the medieval kabbalah, Renaissance esotericism, and German Romanticism—to Freud's ideas about unconscious fantasies that underlie neurotic symptoms. Maimonides wrote the *Guide*, as Freud (1900) later wrote *The Interpretation of Dreams*, because the theory that mental images undergird mental illness led him to attribute curative power to rational interpretations of the imagery.

IMAGINATION AND ANTHROPOMORPHISM

As previously with his understanding of ignorance, when Maimonides uncovered a logical flaw in Aristotelianism, he turned to Judaism as an intellectual resource for the development of his cure of souls. Judaism was intrinsically critical of imagination. The Second Commandment asserts: "You shall not make for yourself a graven image, or any likeness of anything that is in heaven above, or that is in the earth beneath, or that is in the water under the earth" (Ex 20:4); and the commandment had already been understood psychologically in the biblical period. The second Isaiah wrote:

> He plants a cedar and the rain nourishes it.... Then it can be used as fuel.... The rest of it he makes into a god, his idol, bows down to it and worships it; he prays to it and says, "Save me, for you are my god!"
>
> They do not know, nor do they comprehend; for their eyes are shut, and their minds as well, so that they cannot understand. No one considers, nor is there knowledge or discernment ... a deluded mind has led him astray. (Is 44:14b–15a, 17–19a, 20a)

Maimonides considered these teachings to be the very foundation of Judaism. He wrote: "The first intention of the Law as a whole is to put an end to idolatry" (*Guide* III:29; p. 517).

The sages agreed for their own reasons with Aristotle's theory that mental images underlie thinking. They held that anthropomorphism, which wrongly attributes human characteristics to God, was an inevitable concomitant of human thought and speech. The Talmud repeatedly stated: "The Law speaks in the language of human beings" (*BT*, Yevamot, 71a; Baba Metsia, 31b; Berakhot, 39b). Maimonides expressed the same teaching in close detail, for example, in the course of the following discussion about popular misconceptions concerning angels.

> When it was established as true among some belonging to the multitude that the deity is not a body or that He does not draw near to that which He does, they imagined that He gives commands to the angels and that they accomplish the actions in question through immediate contact and the drawing near of one body to another, as we do with regard to what we act upon. They also imagined that the angels were bodies.... All this follows imagination. (*Guide* II:12; pp. 279–280)

In rabbinical teaching, the best that one could do would be to become aware of, and to discount, one's inevitable anthropomorphisms. In medieval terms, one was to engage in negative theology, knowing and owning one's imaginations.

Maimonides' project in the *Guide*, to refute anthropomorphism by teaching the interpretation of biblical dreams, visions of prophecy, and other scriptural imagery, may be seen in its entirety as a component within his cure of souls. The *Guide* is a compendium of psychological insights into mental imagery.

INTELLECTUALIST MYSTICISM AND PROPHECY

Maimonides composed the *Guide* as a commentary on Scripture rather than as a more overtly psychological genre of text because he was convinced that biblical prophecy was the *locus classicus* of rational mysticism. Maimonides' orientation to Scripture was a commonplace of medieval mysticism. Medieval Jews routinely discussed prophecy as precedents for their own contemplative experiences (Heschel, 1996). Maimonides both recommended "worship of the heart" to his contemporaries and identified the soul's perfection with biblical prophecy. "Those who have apprehended the true realities.... This is the rank of the prophets" (*Guide* III:51; p. 620). In passing references, Maimonides sometimes employed mixed expressions, treating scriptural prophets and contemporary worshipers as equivalents (Blumenthal, 1977). Maimonides wrote: "all prophets or excellent and perfect men" (*Guide* III:51; p. 624) and "the other prophets and the excellent men" (*Guide* III:51; p. 628).

Within Judaism, Maimonides' affirmation of the possibility of prophecy was not considered outlandish. What was original was his expression of the common view in philosophical terms. Maimonides offered a learned Aristotelian explanation of phenomena that many Jews experienced. He was challenged by his contemporaries for denying the objective reality of supernal realms, but he was not criticized for maintaining the possibility of prophecy in his own time. Jews routinely applied biblical language to mystical experiences in antiquity and the Middle Ages. Many medieval Jews claimed experiences of prophecy. Heschel (1996, pp. 6–22, 32–37) catalogued Jewish claimants to the status of prophet in the Talmudic era, in the eleventh and twelfth centuries, among the leaders of the Issaite movement among Iranian Jews in the eighth century, among the Tosafists, and among the founders of the kabbalah. Rashi personally claimed inspiration (p. 38), and Saadia Gaon considered poetic inspiration to be prophetic (p. 40). Maimonides mentioned a Rabbi Moses Al-Dar'i, who claimed prophecy in Andalusia in 1122 (p. 29). Joseph Ibn Aknin, the student to whom Maimonides addressed the *Guide*, claimed to be a prophet and intimated in his correspondence with Maimonides that Maimonides secretly regarded himself as a prophet too (pp. 80–91). Maimonides used several expressions that tended to the same effect. He claimed to be among those "over whom lightning flashes time and time again . . . the level of the majority of the prophets" (*Guide* I:Introduction; p. 7). He boasted that his discussion of Satan was "akin (*ki-demut*) to prophecy" (*Guide* III:22; p. 488). Heschel (1996) concluded:

A soul as refined and noble as Maimonides' would not point to himself and say, "Behold, I am now fit and ready for the highest perfection." A man does not declare himself a prophet. Nevertheless, this secret, which was so well hidden in the folds of his personality, does peep forth in hints scattered throughout his writings, slight in some places and fuller in others. (p. 79)

Beginning with al-Farabi, Muslim Aristotelian philosophers had accounted for prophecy with reference to intellectualist mysticism. Although their individual formulations differed in points of detail, they commonly maintained that the Active Intellect's production of ideas in the rational faculty of the soul was responsible not only for every person's attainment of abstract concepts, but also for every other order of inspiration, including prophetic revelation (Davidson, 1992; Rahman, 1958). Al-Farabi worked with an Aristotelian epistemology that had intelligibles abstracted from sense impressions. He maintained that the rational faculty was sometimes equal to the intelligence that the Active Intellect revealed. At the same time, he also held that prophecy revealed theoretical truths that were consistent with scientific procedures (Davidson, 1992, p. 121). Inspired by the Neoplatonic hierarchy of hypostases, al-Farabi constructed an intricate scheme of the emanation of ten cosmological regions, each with its own intellect and its own soul, ending with the original *nous* of Aristotle in the sublunar zone of the four elements (Netton, 1992). Other philosophers were more sympathetic to the Neoplatonic trends within medieval Aristotelianism. Ibn Sina maintained that the rational faculty acquires all of its knowledge of abstract forms through emanation directly from the Active Intellect (Rahman, 1958, p. 1). For Ibn Sina, all ideas were attained exclusively through revelation; no ideas were generated within the soul on a prior basis of sense perception. All knowledge depended directly on revelation, none on scientific procedures (Davidson, 1992, p. 117). Ibn Bajjah (the Latin Avempace) attributed knowledge of the future to the rational faculty's conjunction with the Active Intellect, but he attributed knowledge of theoretical truths to scientific procedures and ratiocination. His extant writings make no mention of the figurative representation of scientific truths. Ibn Rushd (the Latin Averroes), an elder contemporary of Maimonides, similarly attributed prophecy to the rational faculty's conjunction with the Active Intellect, yet he asserted that theoretic truths are known exclusively through scientific procedures (Davidson, 1992, pp. 127–139, 340–344, 350).

The general contours of medieval Muslim Aristotelianism informed Maimonides' thought as early as his *Commentary on the Mishnah*; he opened his *Mishneh Torah* with a systematic presentation of the medieval Aristotelian concepts of God, the universe, and humanity. Neither legal work contains a deeper acquaintance with Aristotelianism than was available through Arabic handbooks on philosophy (Davidson, 2005, pp. 91, 305). The *Guide* shows evidence of further research. It names Aristotle's *Physics, On the Heavens, Nicomachean Ethics, Rhetoric,* and *Metaphysics* (p. 99). It also displays familiarity with two of Aristotle's biological works, but Maimonides seems not to have known Aristotle's *On the Soul* or *On Generation and Destruction* (p. 105). The doctrines that Maimonides attributed to the *Metaphysics* of Aristotle were instead derived from the *Metaphysics* of Ibn Sina, a text that blended Aristotelianism with Neoplatonism and was never mentioned by Maimonides (pp. 102–103, 111). Maimonides was presumably unconscious of his debt to Ibn Sina (p. 115). In a letter to the *Guide*'s Hebrew translator, Ibn Tibbon, Maimonides discussed al-Farabi, Ibn Sina, Ibn Bajjah, and Ibn Rushd. He preferred al-Farabi and recommended his *Political Government*. He considered Ibn Sina inferior, though still valuable. He called Ibn Bajjah "a great philosopher" whose writings were "correct," and he recommended Ibn Rushd's commentaries on Aristotle (p. 113). In correspondence, Maimonides stated that he had studied astronomy with a student of Ibn Bajjah and conversed with others (pp. 79–80). He owed his doctrine of the four perfections to Ibn Bajjah (Altmann, 1972); and obtained Ibn Rushd's commentaries on Aristotle when the *Guide* was in an advanced state of composition or already completed (Davidson, p. 109). He may also have known works by Ghazali and Ibn Tufail (p. 115).

Although Maimonides' practice of meditation and his phrase "worship of the heart" were presumably indebted to Bahya ibn Paquda's *Duties of the Heart*, Maimonides otherwise had little interest in Jewish philosophers (Davidson, 2005, p. 121). In his basic positions on intellectualist mysticism and prophecy, Maimonides agreed with the formulations of Abraham ibn Daud (c. 1110–c. 1180), the first Jewish Aristotelian philosopher and, like both Ibn Rushd and Maimonides, a native of Cordoba in Spain (Husik, 1916, pp. 197–198, 221–226). However, Maimonides nowhere referred to Ibn Daud, and debts to him have not been demonstrated persuasively (Davidson, 2005, p. 117). Maimonides may have arrived independently at the same preferences among the formulations of Muslim Aristotelians.

Without naming the different Muslim philosophers, Maimonides positioned his own version of intellectualist mysticism within their debate. For Maimonides, the idea of the Active Intellect's role in prophecy provided a theoretic solution to the following problem: Is prophecy a process whereby information is generated naturally in the mind or is the mind some kind of receiver of information from a divine source? The common understanding of prophecy is as a communication that has its origin with the divine and is directed toward the person who is called the prophet. Prophecy's direction was assumed to be from God to man. However, Maimonides rejected the common view of prophecy that "God ... chooses whom He wishes from among men, turns him into a prophet, and sends him with a mission," providing only that the person has "a certain goodness and sound morality." This wrong opinion of prophecy was shared both by pagans and by "some of the common people professing our Law" (*Guide* II:32; p. 360). For Maimonides, prophecy occurred as a natural disposition of the healthy, imaginative, and philosophically developed human mind. "For it is a natural thing that everyone who according to his natural disposition is fit for prophecy and who has been trained in his education and study should become a prophet" (*Guide* II:32; p. 361). The divine will that is necessary for prophecy is neither miraculous nor a special dispensation to a chosen few, but rather is consistent with the divine creation of nature as a whole. Prophecy is part of nature. It is a psychological process that the Active Intellect produces in the human soul. It is "a certain perfection in the nature of man . . . achieved . . . after a training that makes that which exists in the potentiality of the species pass into actuality, provided an obstacle due to temperament or to some external cause does not hinder this" (*Guide* II:32; p. 361).

With the exception of the prophecy of Moses, Maimonides characteristically considered prophecy to be a form of apprehension. The ultimate act of prophecy for Maimonides was the apprehension of the divine. In Maimonides' view, the direction of prophecy, in all cases other than Moses, was from the prophet to God. Consider, for example, how Maimonides described his own experience of the actualization of his rational faculty: "No divine revelation has come to teach me that the intention of the matter in question was such and such . . . but rightly guided reflection and divine aid" (*Guide* III:Introduction; pp. 415–416). This formulation rejected the popular misunderstanding of prophecy when Maimonides asserted that he did not depend passively on an infusion of revelation. He instead affirmed a constructivist theory when he stated that he reached out with his intellect to seek the divine aid of the Active Intellect.

Although medieval Aristotelians agreed on the rational faculty's actualization by the Active Intellect, they were of divided opinion regarding the role of imagination in prophecy. Al-Farabi and Ibn Sina both attributed dreams and prophetic visions to the action of the Active Intellect on the imaginative faculty. In their theories, the Active Intellect acted on the rational faculty, which transmitted the actualized ideas to the imaginative faculty for it to transform into imagery. Because only the final imagery were experienced as the contents of dreams and visions, both the conjunction of the Active Intellect with the rational faculty, and the conversion of actualized ideas into imaginations, implicitly proceeded unconsciously (Davidson, 1992, p. 121). In maintaining that prophetic images were always figurative presentations of intelligibles, al-Farabi was simultaneously offering a theory of the soul's production of metaphors as ways to express ideas for which non-metaphoric language is unavailable. Ibn Sina also allowed that a second and higher category of prophetic visions directly perceived externally existing spiritual beings, creatures, sceneries, constructions, and the like. In this respect, Ibn Sina pushed the Muslim Aristotelian theory in a Neoplatonic direction, making it account for mystical visions of *malakut*, the supernal world of angels and disembodied forms.

Citing the rabbinic saying, "The Law speaks in the language of human beings" (*BT*, Yevamot, 71a; Baba Metsia, 31b; Berakhot, 39b), Maimonides taught that prophets—with the exception of Moses, who was in a class by himself—experienced the actualization of both their rational and their imaginative faculties.

> The very overflow that affects the imaginative faculty... is also the overflow that renders perfect the act of the rational faculty, so that its act brings about its knowing things that are real in their existence, and it achieves this apprehension as if it had apprehended it by starting from speculative premises. (*Guide* II:38; p. 377)

Maimonides explained that the imaginative faculty retains "things which are perceived by the senses, combining things, and imitating them" (*Guide* II:36; p. 370). The imaginative faculty can be active when the senses are not being stimulated. Because the imaginative faculty can produce combinations that are representative of things that have never been directly experienced, it can be misleading, but it can also be revelatory. Maimonides wrote that "the greatest and noblest action [on the part of the imaginative faculty] takes place only when the senses rest.... It is then that a certain overflow overflows to this faculty... and it is the cause of veridical dreams. This same overflow is the cause of the prophecy" (*Guide* II:36; p. 370).

The prophecy of the prophets other than Moses depended on the combined actions of both the rational and the imaginative faculties. In the case of dreams, there was an overflow "toward the rational faculty in the first place and thereafter toward the imaginative faculty" (*Guide* II:36; p. 369). Similarly, in a vision of prophecy "the overflow in question comes to the rational faculty and overflows from it to the imaginative faculty" (*Guide* II:41; p. 385). The essential feature for both dreams and visions of prophecy was that the Active Intellect actualized both faculties. "If... this overflow reaches both... the rational and the imaginative... and if the imaginative faculty is in a state of ultimate perfection... this is characteristic of the class of prophets" (*Guide* II:37; p. 374).

Maimonides regarded prophecy as "the highest degree of man and the ultimate term of perfection that can exist for his species; and this state is the ultimate term of perfection for the imaginative faculty" (*Guide* II:36; p. 369). He consequently drew a distinction between the intellectualist mysticism of the philosophers and the phenomenon of prophecy. The Active Intellect's actualization of the rational faculty produced philosophy, but the additional actualization of the imaginative faculty was a further condition of prophecy.

> The case in which the intellectual overflow overflows only toward the rational faculty and does not overflow at all toward the imaginative faculty—

either because of the scantiness of what overflows or because of some deficiency existing in the imaginative faculty in its natural disposition, a deficiency that makes it impossible for it to receive the overflow of the intellect—is characteristic of the class of men of science engaged in speculation. (*Guide* II:37; p. 374)

The rational faculties of "men of science," that is, philosophers, were actualized by the Active Intellect, leading them to knowledge of the universals and other intelligible truths. Theirs was an intellectualist mysticism that meditated on nature in Aristotle's fashion, but not one that culminated in love and fear for God. "By means of his speculation alone, man is unable to grasp the causes from which what a prophet has come to know necessarily follows" (*Guide* II:38; p. 377).

Maimonides distinguished two discrete functions of imagination: the retention of images by the senses, and the generation of completely imaginative constructions. "I do not consider that you might confuse intellectual representation with imagination and with the reception of an image of a sense object by the imaginative faculty" (*Guide* I:68, p. 166). In agreement with al-Farabi, Maimonides maintained that the imaginative constructions in visions of prophecy may consist either of parables or of apprehensions of the intelligibles.

In a *vision of prophecy* only parables or intellectual unifications are apprehended that give actual cognition of scientific matters similar to those, knowledge of which is obtained through speculation.... This is the meaning of its dictum: *I do make Myself known unto him in a vision.* (*Guide* II:45; p. 403)

In allowing that visions of prophecy may include "parables" as well as intelligibles, Maimonides agreed with al-Farabi and Ibn Sina that the actualization of imagination proceeds through the intermediacy of the actualization of the rational faculty, resulting in figurative images that are rational but whose meaning is not part of their experience. The intermediacy of the rational faculty was unconscious. Only the figurative images manifested consciously. Maimonides insisted, however, that the manifest images provided figurative expressions for rational meanings. Like al-Farabi, Maimonides restricted prophecy to intelligibles and figurative images that symbolized intelligibles. He rejected the assumption shared by illuminists such as Ibn Sina, Muslim Sufis, and Jewish kabbalists that visions also provide access to a "supernal region" that exists outside the human soul.

The psychological concepts that al-Farabi and Maimonides expressed in their formulations of prophecy remain current. We would today describe the process of abstracting concepts from sense perceptions as experiences of creative inspiration and agree with al-Farabi and Maimonides that in addition to rationality an element of imagination is operative. Piaget (1951, p. 210), for example, maintained that generalization and abstraction are developmentally advanced forms of the processes that Freud (1900) called condensation and displacement, respectively, and defined as different ways of combining separate mental images into single symbolic images. Bion (1962, 1963, 1967) proposed that a single "alpha function" performs both conceptual thinking and the dreamwork. Creativity in a general sense can proceed through rational calculation or deduction, but inspired creativity, involving an "aha!" experience of sudden discovery, invariably involves a metaphor or another mental image (Merkur, 2001b).

DREAMS AND VISIONS OF PROPHECY

Maimonides distinguished between the prophecy of Moses and the visions and dreams of prophets other than Moses on the basis of a story in Scripture about Moses, his brother Aaron, and their sister Miriam (*Guide* II:36; p. 370). The Bible tells how Aaron and Miriam grumble about the way in which Moses has arrogated authority to himself. They are appalled that he was assigning himself special privilege by allowing himself to marry a Cushite woman. They say, "Has the Lord spoken only with Moses? Has he not also spoken with us?" In response to their grumbling, God calls a meeting of the three of them. God descends in a pillar of cloud, defends Moses, and rebukes Aaron and Miriam. The point of the narrative is what he says at this juncture. God says, "If there is a prophet among you, I, the Lord, do make myself known to him in a vision, I do speak with him in a dream. With respect to my servant Moses it is not so.... With him I do speak ... openly and not in dark speeches" (Num 12:6–7).

These verses, which Maimonides cited repeatedly and alluded to variously, are critical. There is a major difference between God's relationship to Moses and His relationship to prophets other than Moses. These relationships sharply distinguish the prophecy of Moses, the commandments and their explanation, the Jewish law, from the prophecy of all the prophets other than Moses. All the prophecies of the prophets other than Moses come either as a vision or dream. Regarding the prophecy of prophets other than Moses, Maimonides stated:

> [God] has informed us of the true reality and quiddity of prophecy and has let us know that it is a perfection that comes in a dream or in a vision [*mar'eh*]. The word *mar'eh* [vision] derives from the verb *ra'oh* [to see]. This signifies that the imaginative faculty achieves so great a perfection of action that it sees the thing as if it were outside.... In these two groups, I mean vision and dream, all the degrees of prophecy are included. (*Guide* II:36; p. 370)

In explaining the difference between visions and dreams, Maimonides said of dreams, "I do not need to explain what a dream is" (*Guide* II:41; p. 385). A vision, on the other hand, "is a fearful terrifying state which comes to a prophet when he is awake.... In such a state as this the senses ... cease to function. ... Thereupon the terror and the strong affection ... become intensified and then prophetic revelation comes" (*Guide* II:41; p. 385). A dream differed from a vision in that speech was heard in dreams in accordance with the biblical phrasing, "I do speak to him in dream." As for prophetic visions in which speech was heard, Maimonides said that "every vision in which you find the prophet hearing speech was [only] in its beginning a vision, but ended in a state of submersion and became a dream" (*Guide* II:45; p. 402). The prophetic experience of speech was similarly limited to the content of a dream or a vision of prophecy. "In the case of everyone about whom exists a scriptural text that an *angel* talked to him or that speech came to him from God, this did not occur in any other way than *in a dream* or *in a vision of prophecy*" (*Guide* II:41; p. 386).

Maimonides was adamant that the visions and dreams of the prophets were not real events such as one could observe with the senses. He stated:

> In the case of prophetic parables seen or enacted in a vision of prophecy, when the parable requires a certain action, when things are done by the prophet, when intervals of time are mentioned within the parable between the various actions and the transportation from one place to another, this takes place only in a vision of prophecy, they are not real actions, actions that exist for the external senses. Some of them are set forth in the books of prophecy without qualification. For since it is known that all these things occur in a vision of prophecy, Scripture ... may dispense with reiterating that that happened in a vision of prophecy. Similarly a prophet may say, And the Lord said unto me, without having the need to state explicitly that this happened in a dream. Therefore the multitude think that these actions, transportations, questions and answers, occurred all of them in a state in which they could have been perceived by the senses, not in a vision of prophecy. (*Guide* II:46; p. 404)

Maimonides continued this passage with a kind of composite ideal narrative that was made up of elements variously drawn from Scripture, and he explained that its events all occur in a vision of prophecy.

> After this introduction you should know that just as a man sees while sleeping that he has made a journey to a certain country, has married there, has stayed for a certain time, that a son was born to him there, that he called him by a certain name, and that his son's circumstances and state were such and such; so in the case of prophetic parables seen or enacted *in a vision of prophecy*, when a parable requires a certain action, when things are done by the prophet, when intervals of time are mentioned within the parable between the various actions and the transportation from one place to another, this takes place only *in a vision of prophecy*, they are not real actions, actions that exist for the external senses. (Ibid.)

Maimonides claimed that the authors of Scripture were so familiar with visions of prophecy that they often did not trouble to say that the events described were not real but imaginary: "For some [accounts] are set forth in the books of prophecy without [saying] that they happened *in a vision of prophecy*. Similarly a prophet may say, *And the Lord said unto me*, without having ... to state explicitly that this happened in a dream" (ibid.). In other cases, the awareness that a prophecy was not a real event may not have extended to the prophet. A prophet might apprehend a prophecy with "this secret [about prophecy being in the form of visions and dreams] not having as yet been revealed to him" (*Guide* II:45; p. 395). Maimonides made this point in commentary on the verse about Samuel's first prophetic apprehension when he was a child. The biblical text states that "Samuel did not yet know the Lord, neither was the word of the Lord yet revealed to him" (I Sam 3:7). Maimonides stated that this "means that he did not know and that it had not yet been revealed to him that the word of the Lord comes in this way" (*Guide* II:45; p. 395).

THE PSYCHOLOGY OF IMAGINATION

Maimonides repeatedly asserted that prophecy comes to the prophets other than Moses through an angel. "The fundamental principle ... which I have never ceased explaining [is] that to every prophet except Moses ... prophetic revelation come through an angel" (*Guide* II:35, 367). After the Active Intellect had actualized the rational faculty, a second process—a second angel—transformed the actualized ideas into the imagery of a vision. The angel that mediated visions of prophecy was the process within the soul that Maimonides called the imaginative faculty. Maimonides maintained, "Our principle states that all prophets [other than Moses] hear speech only through the intermediary of an angel ... the intermediary is the imaginative faculty" (*Guide* II:46; p. 403). On at least some occasions, Moses was no exception to this general rule. "Moses too depended on an angel. Even in the case of *Moses our Master*, his prophetic mission is inaugurated *through an angel: And there appeared unto him an angel of the Lord in the heart of fire*" (*Guide* III:45; p. 576).

Maimonides asserted that the imagination is limited in its capacity to the representation of bodies. "According to the imagination, there are no existents except bodies or things in bodies" (*Guide* I:73; p. 211). For example, although angels are processes, acts, or forces that are intelligible and incorporeal, they may appear to have visible shapes when human imagination portrays them in dreams and visions of prophecy. "Every form in which an *angel* is seen, exists *in the vision of prophecy*" (*Guide* II:6; p. 265; see also II:42; p. 388). These forms were imaginary, however, and not real.

> The Sages say in *Bereshith Rabbah*: *The flaming sword which turns every way*, is called thus with reference to the verse: *His ministers a flaming fire*. [The

expression], which turns every way, alludes to the fact that sometimes they turn into men, sometimes into women, sometimes into spirits, and sometimes into angels. Through this dictum they have made it clear that the angels are not endowed with matter and that outside the mind they have no fixed corporeal shape, but that all such shapes are only to be perceived in *the vision of prophecy* in consequence of the action of the imaginative capacity. (*Guide* I:49; pp. 108–109)

Because imagination portrays the corporeal, it can lead a person to bad judgment and bad belief, even when reading the law. Maimonides mentioned specifically the combination of literal reading and imaginative supplementation. "The external sense of these texts leads ... to a grave corruption of the imagination and [thereby] to giving vent to evil opinions with regard to the deity" (*Guide* II:29; p. 347). Drawing on the rabbinic teaching that will is free because it is positioned between two contrary motivations, *yetser ha-tov*, "will for the good," and *yetser ha-ra'*, "will for the bad," Maimonides maintained that what the sages had called *yetser ha-ra* was no other than the imagination. "Imagination ... is ... in true reality the *evil impulse* (*Guide* II:12; pp. 279–280).

Updating a psychological insight of the sages, Maimonides treated Satan as a personification of imagination. "It is their dictum in the *Talmud: Rabbi Simon ben Laqish said: Satan, the evil inclination, and the angel of death are one and the same*" [*BT*, Baba Batra, 16a] (*Guide* III:22; p. 489). Imagination functioned as an evil inclination when its capacity for fiction led the appetitive faculty to desire what it should not. The evil inclination "indubitably turns people away from the ways of truth and makes them perish in the ways of error" (*Guide* III:22; p. 489).

Maimonides similarly identified *yetser ha-tov*, "the good inclination," with an angel.

> Now, as they have explained to us that *the evil inclination* is *Satan*, who indubitably is an *angel*—I mean that he too is called an *angel* inasmuch as he is found in the crowd of *the sons of God*—*good inclination* must consequently also be an *angel*. Consequently that well-known opinion figuring in the sayings of the *Sages* [*BT*, Hagigah, 16a], *may their memory be blessed*, according to which every man is accompanied by *two angels*, one to his right and the other to his left, identifies these two with *good inclination* and *evil inclination*. (*Guide* III:22; p. 490)

Maimonides' statement, "*Good inclination* is only found in man when his intellect is perfected" (*Guide* III:22; pp. 489–490), indicates that the good inclination, or good angel, was the Active Intellect.

Maimonides' identification of imagination with the evil inclination was consistent with his assertion in *Eight Chapters* that the imaginative faculty is not a seat of morality. He took for granted the sages' view that the good and evil inclinations are not themselves good and evil, respectively. Because the opposition of the two inclinations provides alternatives that together guarantee the freedom of human will, even the inclination to do evil serves the good purposes of God. Imagination, the evil inclination, may inspire but does not participate in immorality.

> The faculties of *nutrition* and *imagination* do not give rise to observance or transgression, for in connection with neither is there any conscious or voluntary act.... The proof of this is that the functions of both these faculties, the nutritive and the imaginative, continue to be operative when one is asleep, which is not true of any other of the soul's faculties. (*Eight Chapters* ii; p. 47)

For Maimonides, moral responsibility was borne exclusively by the will, which is shaped by the desires of the appetitive faculty. Imagination had a potential to corrupt desire and will, but it also had a potential to exceed reason's reach in the accomplishment of good. Accordingly, neither does God do evil, nor is the evil inclination itself evil. Evil is a misuse that human beings can make of imagination, when imagination is not coordinated with rationality.

THE PLACE OF IMAGINATION IN THE INTERPRETATION OF SCRIPTURE

Incorrect interpretations of Scripture were one of the most common causes of perplexity. Because the prophets who wrote Scripture had all been philosophers, they had all intended their writings to be be understood in fashions consistent with philosophy. Readings of Scripture that were inconsistent with philosophy were necessarily mistaken. The failure to understand biblical language correctly resulted in the reader's adoption of fallacious or "imaginary beliefs to which he owes his fear and difficulty ... heartache and great perplexity" (*Guide* I:Introduction; p. 6). "All this is due to people being habituated to, and brought up on, texts that it is an established usage to think highly of and to regard as true and whose external meaning is indicative of the corporeality of God and of other imaginings with no truth in them, for these have been set forth as parables and riddles" (*Guide* I:31; p. 67).

Maimonides warned against interpretations of Scripture that employ "the imagination" as was done by "homilists [*darshanin*] and the sorry commentators." Their readings encouraged the corporeality that is intrinsic to imagination. To be read properly, Scripture had to be comprehended "with the true nature of the intellect, and after [attaining] perfection in the demonstrative sciences and knowledge of the secrets of prophecy" (*Guide* II:29; p. 347). As an example of Maimonides' exegetical method, consider his rejection of the idea that God is subject to emotions. "God, may He be honored and magnified, is not a body or subject to affections. For affection is a change, and He, may He be exalted, is not touched by change" (*Guide* I:35; p. 81).

One of the major misgivings that Maimonides had of Judaism as it had been handed down to him was that it promoted a view of God as angry. Anger, for Maimonides, is "a pernicious characteristic, arising ... from an evil psychic condition" (*Eight Chapters* iv; p. 67). For Maimonides, in spite of the numerous indications of God as angry in Scripture, the ascription of anger to God was wrong. He made this point specifically in the very first chapter of the *Mishneh Torah*, where he cited: "Is it I whom you provoke to anger?" (*BK, Laws Concerning the Basic Principles of the Torah*, I:12;p. 35a; citing Jer 7:19). Maimonides explicitly denied the plain meaning of the biblical text in connection with the attribution of anger to God. God's anger was variously displayed in Scripture. Most notably it was exhibited in connection with the golden calf episode, where the text stated that God said to Moses, "And now let me alone, that my anger may wax against them, and I will consume them" (Ex 32:10). Maimonides brought the principle of negation to bear in connection with all attributions of human characteristics to God, including anger specifically. In the *Mishneh Torah*, after enumerating various characteristics that have been attributed to God historically and denying that they are appropriate, he stated, "This being so, the expressions in the Pentateuch and books of the Prophets ... are all of them metaphorical and rhetorical." Among his examples he specifically mentioned anger, citing Deut 32:21, where the words "They have angered me with their vanities" are attributed to God. Maimonides indicated that all of these anthropomorphisms were to be dismissed because "the Law speaks in the language of men" (*BK, Laws Concerning the Basic Principles of the Torah*, I:12; p. 35a; citing *BT*, Yevamot, 71a; Baba Metsia, 31b; Berakhot, 39b).

At the same time that Maimonides denied that God was ever angry, he maintained the value of the metaphor. Scripture's account of God's anger was useful in its promotion of human welfare.

> The Law ... makes a call to adopt certain beliefs, belief in which is necessary for the sake of political welfare. Such, for instance, is our belief that He, may He be exalted, is violently angry with those who disobey Him and that it is therefore necessary to fear Him and to dread Him and to take care not to disobey. (*Guide* III:28; p. 512; see also *Guide* I:25, p. 54; *Guide* III:28; p. 514)

Our responsibility is to explain the text, allowing that the text may be difficult and that some readers may understand it better than others. Anthropomorphisms are not to be reified, but are instead to be understood as metaphors that arise out of human tendencies to speak of God in anthropocentric manners.

Not only certain motifs, such as God's anger, but entire biblical narratives, such as the tales of Noah's flood and of Sodom and Gomorrah, were to be understood in terms of their value for inculcating correct opinions. "The story of the *Flood* and the story of *Sodom and Gomorrah* were recounted in order to bring proof for the following correct opinion: *Verily there is a reward for the righteous; verily there is a God that judgeth on the earth* [Ps 58:12]" (*Guide* III:50; p. 614).

THE PROPHECIES OF ABRAHAM

Prophets' need for competence in philosophy arose from the role that imagination played in prophecy. Maimonides urged the reader to distinguish carefully among four things, three of which have an imaginative contribution to them: "What has been said by way of a parable, what has been said figuratively, what has been said by way of a hyperbole, and what has been said exactly according to the first conventional meaning" (*Guide* II:46; p. 409). If one held the four distinctions in mind: "Then all the prophecies will become clear and manifest to you. And then only intelligible beliefs will remain with you, beliefs that are well ordered and that are pleasing to God" (ibid.). And then Maimonides made a statement that may be taken as his ultimate theological credo. "For only truth pleases Him . . . and only that which is false angers Him" (ibid.).

One of the critical contributions of a philosophical background is to be able to distinguish the real from the imagined. Decisions regarding correct interpretations of prophecies were always to be made with reference to natural science. The intelligible beliefs that were expressed imaginatively as prophetic parables, figures, and hyperboles belonged to natural science. "In whatever chapter you find me discoursing with a view to explaining a matter already demonstrated in natural science . . . know that that particular matter necessarily must be a key to the understanding of something to be found in the books of prophecy, I mean to say of some of their parables and secrets . . . regarding the belief in a true opinion belonging to the beliefs of Law" (*Guide* II:2; p. 254).

These general principles informed Maimonides' understanding of the historical achievement of Abraham. He considered Abraham to have been both the first philosopher and the first prophet. It was because he was a philosopher that he was able to be a prophet. Prior to Abraham, there had been false prophets, as there continued also to be after him. According to Maimonides, there are "some people [who] have . . . extraordinary imaginings, dreams and amazed states, which are like the vision of prophecy so that they think about themselves as prophets." These people, he says, "bring great confusion into matters of great import, true notions being strangely mixed up in their minds with imaginary ones" (*Guide* II:37; p. 374). False prophets, such as the prophets of Baal and the prophets of Asherah (*Guide* II:32; p. 363), invariably depended on developed imaginative faculties, but their rational faculties were weak. Abraham's perfection of his rational faculty through his engagement in philosophy permitted him not only to prophesy, but to prophesy truly.

Maimonides maintained that Abraham was not only the first of the prophets, but also—with the exception of Moses—the greatest of them. Maimonides differentiated twelve types of prophetic experience. He ranked them hierarchically. He generally termed them "degree" but at one point used the term "station" (*Guide* I:46; p. 100) that was favored by Muslim Sufi mystics. The twelfth and highest degree was unique to Moses, but Abraham exemplified the eighth through the eleventh degrees.

Maimonides wrote that "the eighth degree" of prophecy "consists in the fact that a prophetic revelation comes to the prophet *in a vision of prophecy* and that he sees parables, as *Abraham in the vision between the pieces*, for these parables came *in a vision* during the day, as has been set forth" (*Guide* II:45; p. 401). Expanding on a narrative that he classified as an instance of the eighth degree of prophecy, Maimonides spoke of

> a fearful terrifying state, which comes to the prophet when he is awake.... The speech of the *angel* to him and his setting him upright, all this happened *in a vision of prophecy*. In a state such as this the senses too cease to function, and the overflow in question comes ... the terror and the strong affection consequent upon the perfection of the action of the imaginative faculty become intensified and then prophetic revelation comes, as is recounted of *Abraham*. (*Guide* II:41; p. 385)

Maimonides stated that "the ninth degree" of prophecy "consists in the prophet's hearing speech *in a vision*, as is said with regard to *Abraham: And, behold, the word of the Lord came unto him, saying, This shall not be thine heir*" (*Guide* II:45; pp. 401–402). The ninth degree of prophecy similarly involved a vision of prophecy.

> It is said of *Abraham: The word of the Lord came unto Abram in a sight, saying*. And it is said in the same *vision of prophecy: And He brought him forth abroad, and said: Look now toward heaven, and count the stars*. It is therefore clear that it was in a *vision of prophecy* that he saw that he was brought out from the place he was in so that he should see the heavens. (*Guide* II:45; p. 405; see also *Guide* II:46; p. 404)

Maimonides emphasized that Abraham did not physically walk out of doors to behold the stars through sight perception, but instead envisioned himself doing so as the content of a vision of prophecy.

"The tenth degree" of prophecy "consists in the prophet's seeing *a man* who addresses him *in a vision of prophecy*, as *Abraham* again by the *terebinths of Mamre* and as *Joshua* in *Jericho*" (*Guide* II:45; pp. 401–402). Regarding the tenth degree of prophecy, Maimonides cited Rabbi Hiyya, a rabbinic sage, as his authority for treating the biblical story of Abraham's entertainment of God and two angels as the content of a further vision of prophecy.

> He ... says of *Abraham's* dictum—*And he said: My lord, if I now have found favor in thy sight, pass not away, I pray thee, from thy servant*—that it too is a description of what he said in a *vision of prophecy* to one of them; he says in fact: *He said it to the greatest among them* (Genesis Rabbah, XLVIII) ... this story ... concerning *Abraham* ... at first informs us in a general way, *And the Lord appeared unto him, and so on*, and then begins to explain in what way this happened. (*Guide* II:42; p. 389)

"The eleventh degree" of prophecy "consists in the prophet's seeing an *angel* who addresses him *in a vision*, as *Abraham at the time of the binding*. In my opinion, this is the highest of the degrees of the prophets whose states are attested by the prophetic books, after the perfection of the rational faculties of the individual, considered as necessary by speculation, has been established, and provided one exempts *Moses our Master*" (*Guide* II:45; pp. 401–402). The story of the "binding" of Isaac, which is traditionally called the *Akedah*, is one of the most gripping stories to be found in Scripture. It is not ordinarily interpreted as the content of a vision of prophecy, but Maimonides indicated that it should be. The biblical text says that in Abraham's old age, after much grief over not having a son with his wife, the Lord remembered Sarah, as he had promised, and she bore a son, whom Abraham named Isaac. After some years, it says, the Lord sought to prove, to test, to try, Abraham. God appeared to Abraham and told him to take his son to the land of Moriah, and offer him up as a burnt offering. Dutifully, Abraham rose early in the morning, saddled his ass, took Isaac and two of his young men with him, cleaved wood for the burnt offering, and proceeded to the place that he had been ordered to go. After a three day journey, they arrived where they could see the place. Abraham left the young men, had Isaac carry the wood, took what he needed to ignite a fire and a knife, and proceeded. Just as Abraham was about to slay Isaac, he was stopped by an angel who called out to him, "Abraham, Abraham," and told him "Do not lay your hand on the boy and cause him no injury." Abraham lifted his eyes and behold there was a ram caught with his horns in the bush. Abraham took the ram and offered it as a burnt offering instead (Gen 22:1ff.).

Maimonides regarded the story of the *Akedah* as a problem, because it was a story of a trial by God and God did not make trials. Maimonides called the concept of God making trials for people, which he says occurs six times in Scripture, "very difficult" (*Guide* III:24; p. 497). "It should not be believed that God ... wants to test and try out a thing in order to know that which He did not know before" (*Guide* III:24; p. 502). Another concept of divine trials was equally untenable. It was generally held that God caused calamities to occur to people without their having sinned in order that the reward might be increased, but Maimonides insisted that there was no such principle in the law (*Guide* III:24; p. 497).

Maimonides' solution to this problem, and to many of the problems associated with narratives in Scripture, was to comprehend them as visions of prophecy. In his view, the account of the *Akedah* concerns an event that took place as the content of a vision or dream. The events did not occur physically in the world of the senses. The account of the *Akedah* is not commonly regarded as a vision or a dream in any of the three Western monotheisms that narrate the story. Quite the contrary. The story is taken as the paradigm of, not the parable of, faith. The common interpretation of the *Akedah* is that God tested Abraham by indicating to him that he should sacrifice his son; and that Abraham proceeded to do so in the literal sense. The moral of this account is that Abraham's faith in God was so great, that even when God ordered him to sacrifice his own son, he willingly obeyed. It can be argued that it is critical to the meaning of the *Akedah* that the story be real, that the very force of the story would be undercut if the story does not represent a real occurrence in the external world of the senses, but only a vision and dream. This was not so for Maimonides.

Maimonides indicated the imaginative character of the *Akedah* by citing rabbinic teachings on Satan's role in the proceedings.

> You will find that they say in a number of passages that *Satan* wanted to tempt *Abraham our Father* not to agree to offer *Isaac* as a sacrifice, and that he also wanted to tempt *Isaac* not to obey his father. And with reference to that story, I mean to say the *binding* [of Isaac], they say likewise: *Sammael came to our Father Abraham and told him: What, old man! have you lost your senses, and so on* [Genesis Rabbah, LVI]. Thus it has become clear to you that *Sammael* is *Satan*. (*Guide* II:30; p. 356)

Because Satan personified the imagination, Satan's address of Abraham in the course of the *Akedah* narrative indicated the activity of his imagination, implicitly during a vision of prophecy; because imagination must be credited with part of Abraham's experience, Maimonides left his reader to infer that imagination was also active in other, less negative ways.

Maimonides' view of the *Akedah* as the content of a vision of prophecy agreed with his comment elsewhere that child sacrifice was a polytheistic rite, not a Jewish one.

> This Law of God, which was prescribed to *Moses our Master*, to whom in consequence it is ascribed, came to facilitate the actions of worship and to lighten the burden.... It behooves you to compare a rite in which for reasons of divine worship a man burns his child with one in which he burns a

> young pigeon. The *Law* states literally: *For even their sons and their daughters do they burn in the fire to their gods*. This was the worship they rendered to their gods. What corresponds to this in our worship is the burning of a young pigeon or even of a handful of flour. (*Guide* III:47; p. 592)

Maimonides implied that God cannot have commanded Abraham to sacrifice Isaac because the law opposed child sacrifice as an idolatrous practice. For the *Akedah* to be understood as a real event, both God and Abraham had to be credited with patent irrationality and immorality. God cannot have commanded Abraham to do something idolatrous, immoral, and ignorant. If Abraham felt himself commanded to perform a polytheistic rite, it can only have occurred in a vision or a dream.

Abraham's response to the command similarly indicated that the *Akedah* was not a physical event in the perceptible world, but only the content of a vision. Maimonides explained: "If a dream of prophecy had been obscure for the prophets, or if they had doubts or incertitude concerning what they apprehended *in a vision of prophecy*, they would not have hastened to do that which is repugnant to nature, and [Abraham's] soul would not have consented to accomplish an act of so great an importance if there had been *a doubt* about it" (*Guide* III:24; pp. 501–502). Abraham's soul consented to the proposed sacrifice not as an act of his will, but as an imaginary event during a vision of prophecy.

Maimonides emphasized that the prophecy was experienced by Abraham as a real event, much as a dream is believed to be real while it is being dreamt. Maimonides wrote: "[Scripture] wished to make it known to us that all that is seen by a prophet in a vision of prophecy is, in the opinion of the prophet, a certain truth, that the prophet has no doubts in any way concerning anything in it, and that in his opinion its status is the same as that of all existing things that are apprehended through the senses or the intellect" (*Guide* III:24; p. 501). The story was meaningful because Abraham regarded it as a physical event during the occurrence of his vision, but the story was not to be interpreted in the same manner by the reader. It is critical to our understanding that we do not recognize it as a true story because we should then be obliged to believe that both God and Abraham were guilty of incomprehensible behavior.

Neither should we assume that Abraham remained credulous of his vision for the remainder of his life. Maimonides remarked that "the story of the *binding* . . . was" originally "known only to God and the two individuals involved" (*Guide* III:24; p. 498), indicating that the story of the *Akedah* was transmitted by Abraham to his children and household. Maimonides implied that the interpretation that he placed on the story originated with Abraham, as his understanding of his vision of prophecy, after the vision had ended.

> It was fitting that this story, I mean the *binding*, should come to pass through the hand of *Abraham*. . . . For *Abraham our Father* was the first to make

known the belief in Unity, to establish prophecy, and to perpetuate this opinion and draw people to it ... just as they followed his correct and useful opinions, namely, those that were heard from him, so ought one to follow the opinions deriving from his actions. (*Guide* III:24; p. 502)

Maimonides' position on the *Akedah* was not destructive of the message of the story. To the contrary, it added strength to the story's fundamental notion of faith. The power of the presumed historical account was vulnerable to questions about its literal credibility, but its treatment as a prophetic parable was not. The message of faith in the story of the *Akedah* is weakened when readers expect the story to be true and are then disillusioned because they cannot find it credible. But there is no reason to become disillusioned with Maimonides' reading of the story. Because the *Akedah* was the content of a vision and not an occurrence in any other sense, there was no deficiency or culpability for either God or Abraham. The lesson of the *Akedah* for the reader is about loving and fearing God (*Guide* III:24; p. 500). It was a story with a point, but the truth of the point did not depend on the truth of the external aspects of the story. Accepting the *Akedah* as a parable allows it never to surrender its meaning. (On the psychological significance of the *Akedah*, see Bakan 1966a, 1971, 1979, 1991; Rubenstein 1975.)

CONFIRMATION FROM EZEKIEL

Immediately following his discussion of the *Akedah* in Chapter II:46 of the *Guide*, Maimonides provided a series of remarks about the prophecies of Ezekiel that served simultaneously as oblique comments on his discussion of the *Akedah*. He explicitly stated that what was being exemplified and discussed directly might be applied by the reader to something that was not being discussed immediately.

> As to this I shall cite you an example about which no one can have fanciful notions, and I shall add to it some other examples belonging to the same species. And from these examples you will be able to draw an inference regarding those that I shall not mention. (*Guide* II:46; p. 404)

His first example was from Ezekiel: "I sat in my house and the elders of Judah sat before me, and so on. And a spirit lifted me up between the earth and the heaven and brought me in the visions of God to Jerusalem" (Ezek 8:1,3). This transportation was, as he indicated, patently something that was not to be understood literally. Maimonides then moved to another example that he placed in the same category, even though it was less obvious that it should not be read literally. "Similarly when he says, *Then I arose, and went forth into the plain* [Ezek 3:23], this also only happened *in the visions of God*" (*Guide* II:46; p. 404). An examination of the biblical passage that contains Maimonides' citation makes his reading self-evident: "And the hand of the Lord came upon me; and He said unto me: 'Arise, go forth into the plain, and I will there speak with thee.' Then I arose, and went forth into the plain; and, behold, the glory of the Lord stood there, as the glory which I saw by the river Kebar; and I fell on my face" (Ezek 3:22–23). Maimonides intimated that the reader was to appreciate the story of Abraham in parallel by referring immediately to the similarity of expression in the story of Abraham: "*And he brought him forth abroad* [Gen 15:5], this occurred *in a sight* [Gen 15:1]" (*Guide* II:46; p. 404).

By way of conclusion to his discussions of Abraham and Ezekiel, Maimonides criticized those who read visions of prophecy literally.

> God is too exalted than that He should turn His prophets into a laughing stock and a mockery for fools by ordering them to carry out crazy actions ... in addition to ordering them to commit acts of disobedience. ... All those happenings are parables *in a vision of prophecy*. ... [T]here remains no room for obscurity as to any of these things having a real existence. ... [E]ven if such actions should have had a long duration and should have been attached to certain times ... individuals ... and places, you should—as soon as it has become clear to you that the action in question is a parable—have certain knowledge that it occurred *in a vision of prophecy*. (*Guide* II:46; pp. 405–407)

At the same time, Maimonides presented his remarks about the *Akedah* in an oblique fashion. He permitted the reader who did not understand him fully to at least get the point about the importance of loving and fearing God. The lesson about loving and fearing God was apparent from the story of the *Akedah*, whether it was understood as a historical narrative concerning events apparent to the senses or as the content of a vision of prophecy.

CONCLUSIONS

Because wrongdoing involves the imagination that evil is good, Maimonides addressed the topic of imagination as an integral component of his cure of souls. He followed rabbinical teachings that corporeal, anthropomorphic conceptions of God and the angels are inevitable because imagination cannot produce images of the incorporeal. Imagery could not be avoided. If it was not to lead to wrongdoing, it had to be both experienced and interpreted. Differing from the views of Muslim Aristotelians who attributed prophecy to the Active Intellect's actualization of the rational faculty, Maimonides argued that prophecy involves the actualization of both the rational and the imaginative faculties. He maintained that all the prophecies of prophets other than Moses, and some of the prophecies of Moses, occurred either in visions of prophecy or else in dreams. In both cases, prophecies routinely portrayed imaginative events. Prophets similarly heard voices and engaged in prophetic dialogues in visions of prophecy. The imaginative process or faculty of the soul was an angel that the Talmud had variously called Satan, the angel of death, and the evil inclination. Because its existence made freedom of will possible, it was itself good. Visions of prophecy were not to be treated at face value, but were instead to be interpreted, in order to discover the rational meanings that the imaginative faculty had represented in images. The practice of interpretation was consequently integral to Maimonides' cure of souls. Maimonides used biblical materials concerning Abraham and Ezekiel to illustrate both his theory of imagination and his technique for interpreting visions of prophecy therapeutically.

FOUR

Perplexity and the World to Come

THE *GUIDE* ADDRESSED the circumstance of "a man ... perfect in his religion and character" who had "studied the sciences of the philosophers" and become perplexed as a result. His perplexity concerned "whether he should follow his intellect ... and consequently consider that he has renounced the foundations of the Law. Or he should hold fast ... not let himself be drawn on together with his intellect, rather turning his back on it and moving away from it, while at the same time perceiving that he had brought loss to himself and harm to his religion" (*Guide* I:Introduction; pp. 5–6).

The relation of revelation and reason was a major intellectual concern in the Middle Ages, and the polarization of the debate has left a legacy of confusion that divides modern scholars in their views regarding Maimonides' handling of the topic. The assumption that Maimonides intended to reconcile reason and revelation presupposes contemporary ideas about science, religion, and their relationship. It takes for granted that science is valid, religion is not, and efforts to reconcile the two are essentially misguided and self-deceiving. The *Guide* is then seen as a historical curiosity, a quaint but mistaken medieval philosophy, from which we moderns have nothing to learn. We could not disagree more.

Maimonides would not have agreed to the assumptions that modern scholars have brought to his corpus. He never granted that revelation and reason are opposed. He insisted that religion is rational and scientific in principle and should always be maintained so in practice. Perplexity was to be resolved by means of interpretation.

> The most beloved of things for the multitude [of adherents] of the Law and the most pleasant thing according to their foolishness is to represent the Law and intellect as extremes of contradiction and to separate everything from what is intelligible and claim that it is a miracle. And they avoid [saying] that

a thing follows the course of nature [when speaking] either about what is related about what has already come to pass or about what is observed in the present state or about what is said will occur in the future. But we ourselves yearn to harmonize the Law with what is intelligible and to regard [lit., cause to follow a course] all things as following a possible natural order, other than that concerning which there has come down an open declaration that it is a miracle and concerning which one is altogether unable to interpret, for then we are compelled to say that this is a miracle.

We have already made clear in the "Guide" clear texts of *Scripture* and also texts of the *sages (may their memory be a blessing)* that state that many *parables* occur in *prophetic statements*. (*Resurrection*, p. 167)

Maimonides maintained that the "state of perplexity and confusion" that found reason and revelation in conflict was a product of the misunderstanding of Scripture. The debate about reason and revelation was nonsensical because a correct understanding of Scripture found no conflict. Reason, the intellectual faculty, was actualized by the Active Intellect, thereby creating revelations within the soul. Reason could not then conflict with revelation, nor revelation with reason. They were the content and process of a single phenomenon. Due to the "overflow" of revelations to the imaginative faculty prior to the manifestation of a vision of prophecy, some prophecies were figurative and could be misinterpreted. Ignorance of the intelligible meaning of figurative revelations was possible, but dreams and prophecies were never intrinsically irrational. False prophecy was an oxymoron, a contradiction in terms. What was popularly called false prophecy was more appropriately described as fallacious interpretations of prophetic visions that would prove rational and truthful when rightly understood. False prophets existed not because their prophecies were false, but because the interpretations that they promoted were in error. Like prophecies, scriptural texts might be interpreted in either ignorant or learned manners. Perplexity was to be avoided by interpreting Scripture "as following a possible natural order." Passages that might seem inconsistent with the order of nature were to be understood as parables that were completely consistent with nature.

At the same time, when Maimonides treated the physical and divine sciences as a single continuum, he assumed that divine science, just like any other science, involves a single self-consistent body of universally valid truths. As a result, he would not have equated science with religions in general. Historical religious traditions were mostly not scientific because they were devoted mostly to errors. They were inconsistent with science to the extent that they were in error regarding the true nature of religion. True religion was scientific. Only false religion was not. And Judaism, alone among the world's religious traditions, happened to concur with the true nature of religion—but only when Judaism was understood and practiced correctly.

Maimonides' concept of perplexity was a diagnostic category with a considerable range of severity. In its mildest forms, perplexity consisted of intellectual puzzlement that could be resolved through the traditional pedagogical techniques of philosophy. Perplexity could also be more profound. It then required a cure of souls. Guidance in the management of meditative experiences was appropriate, however, for a person who had attained the love and fear of God but did not know how to reconcile the experiences with his or her worldview and/or community. In its more severe forms, however, perplexity was a pathological response to spirituality that included everything from confusion and uncertainty to the psychiatric syndromes that Grof and Grof (1989, 1990) termed a "spiritual emergency" and the fourth (1994) edition of the American Psychiatric Association's *Diagnostic and Statistical Manual of Mental Disorders* classified as category V62.89, "Religious or Spiritual Problem."

MAIMONIDES' ESOTERICISM

Perplexity has always been pandemic among Jewish mystics. From the apocalyptic literature of the Second Temple era, through the *hekhalot* literature of the Talmudic era, and the medieval and modern kabbalah, Jewish meditation and mysticism have largely been surrounded with esotericism (Halbertal, 2007). Often the writings were written, copied, and sold in secret. Manuals on meditation were extremely few. Many highly prized texts circulated only in rarely copied manuscripts for centuries after the introduction of print. Most of the writings were comprehensible only to advanced students. Texts routinely omit all sorts of introductory materials that were transmitted, if at all, only orally. Many published commentaries include rather bad guesses at the original meanings of the texts. And a substantial number of texts were composed in a secretive literary style that requires decoding before its intended message can be understood. Under the circumstances, Jewish esotericism has historically been shielded from public discussion and clarification. Errors have gone uncorrected and multiplied over the centuries, creating an ever-worsening culture of perplexity. The problem had already been remarked in the Talmud, and significant aspects of Maimonides' cure of souls were addressed specifically to esotericians' needs.

Maimonides' *Guide* is the classic example of a text that employed an esoteric literary style. Precisely because it was his purpose to address the perplexity of Jewish esotericians, he wrote it in a style that would earn esotericians' respect. At the same time, he provided non-esotericians with enough education in reading his text that they would be able to decode the coded portions of the *Guide*. In the Introduction to the *Guide*, Maimonides openly stated that he encoded his remarks on topics whose open discussion the sages had forbidden. Maimonides composed coded passages in his writings as early as his

Commentary on the Mishnah, but he did not publicly declare that he was doing so until the *Guide*. In telling us that he was concealing secret teachings within the *Guide*, Maimonides was not suddenly becoming secretive after a lifetime of open statement. To the contrary, he was becoming more openly spoken than he had ever previously been and ever was to be again. By 1191, when he composed the *Treatise on the Resurrection*, which refers to the *Guide* as a completed work that was in public circulation, Maimonides had returned to his former standard of secrecy. In the *Treatise*, he urged readers to consult the *Guide* if they wished more candor from him.

In the coded sections of his writings, Maimonides relied on a combination of esoteric literary techniques. Some were rabbinic. Others were widely used in the Islamicate and termed *ta'wil* in Arabic. The term covered a variety of literary procedures. Allegorizing exegesis was practiced by Muslim esotericians for the purpose of concealing secrets (Hodgson, 1960; Nanji, 1985; Ryding, 1989), but by Muslim philosophers as a means for asserting the coherence of incomprehensible or objectionable passages in the Qur'an (Galston, 1990, pp. 22–54; Heath, 1992). Maimonides' exegesis of the *Akedah* was an instance of rational *ta'wil*. Esoteric *ta'wil* was sectarian, concealing different subtexts among different esoteric circles, but rational *ta'wil* was multiconfessional (Wasserstrom, 1995, pp. 133–146). Wasserstrom (1995) remarked:

> There was a moment in the ninth and tenth centuries in which Rabbanite and Karaite Jews, Coptic Christians, and Zaydi and Twelver Shi'ites, along with Sunni theologians, all used Mu'tazilite ta'wil. All these establishment leaders utilized this technique to defend the rationality of their own scriptures and to attack the irrationality of their opponent's scriptures. (pp. 142–143)

The Arabic alchemical writings attributed to Balinas and Jabir ibn Hayyan expanded the techniques of *ta'wil* to include what, for want of a better term, may be called a cipher. Alchemical cipher consisted extensively of allegory, but it also interrupted the one-to-one correspondence through any or all of several types of misdirection. Ciphers were typically self-contradictory or incoherent on their manifest level. Only their subtexts were coherent. "The upper, narrative level is frequently destroyed, reduced to incoherence or impossibility on its own terms in the interest of the lower, physical level" (Vickers, 1990, p. 28). Haq (1994) described one of Jabir's innovations as follows:

> Quite unlike the ancient practice of using cover names and allegories, Jabir's "esotericism" consists in what he calls *tabdid al-'ilm*, the Principle of Dispersion of Knowledge: truth was never to be revealed completely at one place. Rather, it was the aim of the author to cut it up and, like so many pieces of a jigsaw puzzle, spread it all over the maze of a vast corpus. . . .

The application of the Principle of Dispersion of Knowledge may also explain the fact that in the same treatise, without contextual justification, the author often deals with vastly disparate subject matters. Thus, all individual writings of the Jabirian corpus are full of digressions, shifts of perspectives, discontinuities and half truths: these features present difficulties of a serious order.

Finally, one is confronted with the problem of an irritating lack of consistency. (pp. 6–7)

The practice of *ta'wil* entered Judaism no later than the tenth century, when Saadia Gaon adopted Muslim philosophers' practice of an allegorical *ta'wil* (Altmann, 1969, p. 145). Maimonides composed the *Guide* in the more complicated literary style of alchemical cipher. In his Introduction to the *Guide*, Maimonides referred explicitly to both the rabbinic technique of "chapter headings" and the Jabirian technique of dispersion: "You should not ask of me here anything beyond *the chapter headings*. And even those are not set down in order or arranged in coherent fashion in this Treatise, but rather are scattered and entangled with other subjects that are to be clarified" (*Guide* I:Introduction; p. 6).

Egyptians who were familiar with pseudonymous Ismaili additions to the Jabirian corpus of alchemy (Kraus, 1943) may have brought the alchemical techniques of *ta'wil* to Maimonides' attention in connection with the pharmaceutical aspects of his medical practice. Maimonides arrived in Egypt in 1160, where esoteric *ta'wil*, called *batini*, "inner" or "esoteric," had been adopted by an entire Muslim sect, the Ismailis, whose Fatimid dynasty had ruled Egypt since the tenth century. Maimonides was familiar with their writings. He criticized interpreting "the miracles figuratively also, as was done by the Islamic internalists [*ahl al-batin*]" and resulted "in some sort of crazy imaginations" (*Guide* II:23; p. 328). Maimonides presumably had personal acquaintance with Ismaili writings. Saladin, who replaced the Fatimids in 1171, gave his vizier al-Fadil the deceased Fatimid caliph's book collection; Maimonides was al-Fadil's personal physician (Heschel, 1982, p. 182). We know from his letter to the Jews of Marseilles, in which Maimonides discussed "thousands of ... false astrological works, whose notions are essentially pagan," that he was widely read in non-Jewish religious literature. "I ... read extensively about all pagan practices. There was not a single book translated into Arabic on the subject that I have not studied and investigated in depth" (Maimonides, *Letters*, pp. 119–120). In his correspondence, Maimonides sometimes complained of having to wait around all day at al-Fadil's home in order to be available to treat the vizier's family (Friedländer, 1904, p. xxiv). He presumably explored the library while he waited.

To alchemical *ta'wil*, Maimonides added the literary device of employing "contradictory or contrary statements" (*Guide* I:Introduction; pp. 17–20). He explained in detail seven different reasons why a text may be self-contradictory, but he left his readers to decide which, where, and how the motives were to be applied to apparent problems in understanding the *Guide*.

Before turning to the *Guide*, let us examine an earlier passage that secretly pertained to the problem of perplexity.

THE WORLD TO COME

In the portion of his *Commentary on the Mishnah* that is traditionally known as *Perek Helek*, the "Chapter on the Portion," Maimonides commented on a passage in the Mishnah that begins, "All Jews have a portion in the world to come." In his commentary, Maimonides took the occasion to present his views on the messianic era and other topics that were popularly associated with it. In the *Eight Chapters*, Maimonides asserted that divine punishment is sometimes accomplished in the world to come. "Sometimes, He punishes only in this world, sometimes only in the world to come, sometimes in both" (*Eight Chapters* viii; p. 95). What Maimonides meant by the phrase *olam ha-ba*, "the world to come," differed profoundly from Muslim expectations of a corporeal Paradise postmortem, as he explained in *Perek Helek*. He stated that "it is almost impossible to find anyone whose opinion is uncontaminated by error" with respect to the matter of the world to come.

> Concerning this strange world to come, you will rarely find anyone to whom it occurs to think about it seriously.... What everybody wants to know, both the masses and the learned, is how the dead will arise. They want to know whether they will be naked or clothed, whether they will rise in the same shrouds with which they were buried, with the same embroidery, style, and beauty of sewing, or in a plain garment which just covers their bodies. Or they ask whether, when the Messiah comes, there will still be rich men and poor men, weak men and strong men, and other similar questions. (*Helek*, p. 97)

Maimonides then explained that it was customary to provide children with rewards in order to encourage them to study.

> Imagine a small child who has been brought to his teacher so that he may be taught the Law.... Of necessity ... his teacher ... must bribe him to study.... Thus, the teacher may say, "Read and I will give you some nuts or figs ... a bit of honey." ... [Later] the teacher will stimulate his desire for whatever he wants then ... beautiful shoes or nice clothes ... money. ... [Later] he will desire something more honorable. His teacher may say to him then, "Study so that you may become the president of a court, a judge, so that people will honor you...."
>
> Now all this is deplorable. However, it is unavoidable because of man's limited insight, as a result of which he makes the goal of wisdom something other than wisdom itself. (*Helek*, pp. 97–98)

Because good was always its own reward, Maimonides was of the opinion that learning was the true reward of study. He accepted, however, that for pedagogical purposes it was practical to offer students further rewards as incentive to studying the law. In its context within *Perek Helek*, this illustration of pedagogical method may be understood as a parabolic comment on popular ideas regarding the world to come. Popular ideas of the world to come compare with nuts, figs, honey, shoes, clothes, money, or social honors. The true nature of the world to come was something else.

In the *Mishneh Torah*, Maimonides discussed the world to come in a manner that hinted clearly at his secret teaching.

> That form of soul which is identical with the intelligence ... apprehends the Creator, as far as it is able, and apprehends other abstract concepts and things.... That life, as it is immortal—death being only incidental to the body, which does not exist in the hereafter—is called 'the bond of life,' as it is said, "but the soul of my lord shall be bound in the bond of life; and the souls of thine enemies, them he shall sling out ..." (I Sam. 25:29). And this is a recompense than which there is none higher; a bliss beyond which there is nothing more blissful. And for this, all the prophets yearned.... Its general name is 'the world to come.' (*BK, Laws of Repentance* VIII:3–4; p. 90b)

The bliss that prophets' intellects know in their apprehension of God and other abstract concepts was not reserved to a future era or condition.

> The reason why the sages styled it 'The world to come' is not because it is not now in existence and will only come into being when this world shall have passed away. That is not so. The world to come now exists, as it is said, "which Thou hast treasured up (for them that fear Thee), which Thou hast wrought (for them that trust in Thee before the children of men)" (Ps. 31:19–20). It is called the world to come, only because human beings will enter into it at a time subsequent to the life of the present world in which we now exist with body and soul—and this existence comes first. (*BK, Laws of Repentance* VIII:8; p. 91a)

Maimonides' phrasing in the *Mishneh Torah* was equivocal. His assertion that "the world to come" existed at present could be interpreted in either of two ways. Maimonides clearly referred to a state of bliss when consciousness of "body and soul" gives way to an intellectual experience of the intelligibles. He explicitly contrasted this state of bliss with "the days of King Messiah" that will involve "material things" in a future era "when sovereignty will be restored to Israel" (*BK, Laws of Repentance* VIII:7; p. 91a). What Maimonides did not specify was whether prophets attained "the bond of life" during the course of their mortal human existence. Maimonides could be taken to have referred to a condition that disembodied intellects attain following the mortal demise of the body and the faculties of the soul that depend on the body.

Writing more boldly in the *Guide* some years later, Maimonides again explicitly rejected the idea of an eschatological age and realm. Implicitly in *Perek Helek*, but unequivocally in both the *Mishneh Torah* and the *Guide*, there was for Maimonides no *olam ha-ba* in a literal sense.

> The passing-away of this world, a change of the state in which it is, or a thing's changing its nature and with that the permanence of this change, are not affirmed in any prophetic text or in any statement of the *Sages* either... you constantly find as the opinion of all *Sages* and as a foundation on which every one among *the Sages of the Mishnah and the Sages of the Talmud* bases his proofs, his saying: *There is nothing new under the sun*, and the view that nothing new will be produced in any respect or from any cause whatever. (*Guide* II:29; p. 344)

Maimonides affirmed belief in the world to come but in a sense that differed from popular notions. In Maimonides' view, the world to come was the true reward of a human being—not an eschatological fantasy, but an achievable reality. What was the world to come? What did the term mean? In *Perek Helek* Maimonides stated explicitly that it meant to actualize oneself as a human being.

> The world to come is the ultimate end toward which all our effort ought to be devoted. Therefore the sage who firmly grasped the knowledge of the truth and who envisioned the final end, forsaking everything else, taught: "All Jews have a share in the world to come" (*BT*, Sanhedrin, 10:1).... As a decent man, one must cultivate the virtues and avoid the sins. In so doing, he will perfect the specifically human which resides in him and will be genuinely different from the animals. When one becomes fully human, he acquires the nature of the perfect human being; there is no external power to deny his soul eternal life. His soul thus attains the eternal life it has come to know which is the world to come. (*Helek*, p. 215)

What was the eternal life of the world to come? In the *Guide*, Maimonides suggested that people who contemplated the intelligibles might be said to be "permanently with God."

> He should take as his end that which is the end of man qua man: namely, solely the mental representation of the intelligibles, the most certain and the noblest of which being the apprehension, in as far as this is possible, of the deity, of the angels, and of His other works. These individuals are those who are permanently with God. They are those to whom it has been said: *Ye are gods, and all of you children of the Most High*. This is what is required of man; I mean to say that this is his end. (*Guide* III:8; p. 432)

For Maimonides, the world to come was a term that signified the worship of the heart, the final phase of his meditative practice.

To be sure, Maimonides affirmed the afterlife of the form of the soul, but it was a very limited and specific concept. It did not include the nutritive, appetitive, and sensitive faculties of the soul, which depend on the physical body, and it is unclear whether it partook of imagination. All that Maimonides attributed to it was a capacity for intellectual perception.

> This form of the Soul is not compounded of elements into which it would again dissolve. Nor does it exist by the energy of the vital [or, nutritive] principle so that the latter would be necessary to its existence, in the way that the vital principle requires a physical body for its existence. But it comes directly from God in Heaven. Hence, when the material portion of our being dissolves into its component elements, and physical life perishes—since that only exists in association with the body and needs the body for its functions, this form of the Soul, is not destroyed, as it does not require physical life for its activities. It knows and apprehends the Intelligences that exist without material substance; it knows the Creator of All things; and it endures for ever. Solomon, in his wisdom said, "And the dust returneth to the earth as it was, and the spirit returneth to God who gave it" (Eccl 12:7). (*BK, Laws Concerning the Basic Principles of the Torah*, IV:9; p. 39b)

The form of the soul existed eternally with God in a manner that may be analogous to the eternal existence of the form of the circle. Because "what thinks and what is thought are identical" (Aristotle, *On the Soul* 430^a 4), God's knowledge of the soul was of a soul that was eternally engaged in knowing intelligibles and knowing God. Maimonides nowhere states, however, whether there was one form for all human souls or individual forms for each human soul. Ibn Rushd maintained that each person had a separate acquired intellect during life, but, for lack of a body, its individuality was lost at death, when it was absorbed into the Active Intellect. Maimonides possibly held to a similar view (Husik, 1916, p. xlvii), but it is also possible that he believed in precisely the sort of afterlife that he achieved. The form of his soul, "which is identical with the intelligence," is present with us as the ideas that we actualize in reading his writings.

The ever-lasting existence of the form of the soul should not be confused with the concept of eternal life. Strictly speaking, the form of the soul neither lives nor dies. Life and death pertain to the body. Generation and decay are processes that occur within the sublunar world of the four elements; they are not processes to which intelligibles are subject. In connection with the idea of eternal life, Maimonides remarks that biblical references to "living" often pertain to the acquisition of knowledge.

> The term [living] is often used . . . in the sense of acquisition of knowledge. Thus: *So shall they be life unto thy soul; For whoso findeth me findeth life; For they are life unto those that find them.* This use is frequent. In accordance with

it, correct opinions are called *life* and false opinions *death*. God, may He be exalted, says accordingly: *See, I have set before thee this day life and good, and so on*.... Because of this figurative sense being generally known in the Hebrew language, the Sages have said: *the righteous even in death are called living, [whereas] the wicked even in life are called dead* [*BT*, Berakhot, 18a–b]. (*Guide* I:44; pp. 92–93)

Maimonides here credited rabbinical tradition with an alternative way of referring to the world to come. As a figurative trope, eternal life was a concept that may also be found in the *Nicomachean Ethics*, where Aristotle applied it to the experience of rational mysticism. Aristotle wrote:

And we ought not to listen to those who counsel us *O man, think as man should* and *O mortal, remember your mortality*. Rather ought we, so far as in us lies, to put on immortality and to leave nothing unattempted in the effort to live in conformity with the highest thing within us. Small in bulk it may be, yet in power and preciousness it transcends all the rest. We may in fact believe that this is the true self of the individual, being the sovran and better part of him. It would be strange, then, if a man should choose to live not his own life but another's ... the intellect more than anything else *is* the man. (*Nicomachean Ethics* 1177^b 32–1178^a 8).

In asserting that divine punishment sometimes occurs in this world, and sometimes in the world to come, Maimonides was speaking of sober and contemplative states of consciousness during mortal life. He was not speaking of mortal life and an afterlife.

THE THIRTEEN FOUNDATIONAL PRINCIPLES OF THE LAW

Perek Helek, in which Maimonides most fully discussed the figurative trope of the world to come, commented on a paragraph in the Mishnah. The context of this mishnaic paragraph is significant. It occurs at the end of Sanhedrin, which discussed laws concerning the more serious criminal cases, especially capital cases. After addressing the topics of the courts, its judges and rules of procedure, and the methods of executing criminals, the Mishnah raised the question of participation in the world to come. The literary context, following the rules for executing people convicted of capital crimes, implies that we are considering what crimes a Jew might commit that would lead to his exclusion from the world to come. The Mishnah then asserts: "All Jews have a share in the world to come [save] the one who says that the resurrection of the dead is not taught in the Law, one who says that the Law is not from heaven, and the Epicurean."

Maimonides' discussion of the world to come in *Perek Helek* occurred by way of preface to his presentation of thirteen principles that he regarded as the sine qua non of Judaism. Maimonides referred regularly to *yesodei ha-Torah*, "foundations" or "fundamental principles of the Law." From medieval times onward, the principles have been incorporated in the daily liturgy of Judaism. They occur in the poem *Yigdal*, and in the recital of the *Ani ma'amin be-emunah shlemah*, "I believe with complete faith." Reflecting the liturgical formulation, Maimonides' thirteen principles are sometimes termed "articles of faith" and interpreted as though Maimonides had intended to formulate a creed for Judaism. Maimonides had no ambition, however, to articulate a consensus statement of Jewish beliefs. He had no interest in dogmatic creeds, and he was well aware that some Jews took exception to some of his principles.

The literary context of the thirteen principles makes plain that Maimonides' purpose was to identify thirteen conditions that must be met for a person to qualify for the world to come. The thirteen principles pertained not to consensual, historical Judaism, but only to Maimonides' distinctive approach to rational mysticism. They were foundational for "worship of the heart." They were doctrinal implications of Maimonides' rational mysticism that he developed by building from the natural sciences to experiences of the actualization of his rational faculty. They were not axiomatic postulates of his philosophy, nor dogmatic statements of a creed. They were his considered conclusions regarding divine science, a succinct summary statement of the distinctive philosophical position that he regarded as scientifically correct theology.

The Mishnah on which Maimonides commented listed three conditions of exclusion from the world to come: denial of the resurrection of the dead, denial that the law is from God, and Epicureanism. Maimonides' thirteen foundational principles were commentaries that explicated the three conditions, but they proceeded in the reverse order.

From the *Guide*, we learn Maimonides' understanding of Epicurus: "Epicurus ... does not believe in the existence of a deity and all the more does not believe in prophecy" (*Guide* II:32; p. 360). Thus, when the Mishnah stated that the Epicurean did not have a share in the world to come, Maimonides took the saying as the occasion to advance the first seven foundational principles regarding God and prophecy. The first through fifth of Maimonides' foundational principles concerned God:

> To believe in the existence of the Creator. . . .
> We are told to believe that God is one. . . .
> We are to believe that God is incorporeal. . . .
> We are to believe that the One is absolutely eternal. . . .
> Only God, blessed be He, is rightfully worshiped, magnified and obeyed.
> (*Helek*, pp. 337–338)

The sixth foundational principle concerned prophecy in general. The seventh addressed the uniqueness of the prophecy of Moses.

> Among men are found certain people so gifted and perfected that they can receive pure intellectual form. Their human intellect clings to the Active Intellect, whither it is gloriously raised. These men are the prophets; this is what prophecy is....
>
> Moses ... was the chief of all other prophets before and after him ... superior in attaining knowledge of God to any other person who ever lived or ever will live.... All his powers of sense and fantasy were repressed, and pure reason alone remained. (*Helek*, pp. 338–339)

These seven foundational principles summarized major features of Maimonides' rational mysticism: their devotion exclusively to God, who was approached by means of a negative theology, together with a practice of prophecy that was commonly available through appropriate meditations, but differed from the distinctive prophecy of Moses. These postulates were descriptive of Maimonides' practice of meditation and the results to which it led. Maimonides was not offering speculative religious ideas that he wanted people to believe in the absence of evidence. He was reporting the empirical reality of the spiritual state that the sages had called "eternal life" in "the world to come."

The Mishnah's teaching that the world to come was unavailable to one who denies that the law came from heaven became the basis for Maimonides' eighth and ninth foundational principles.

> The Law came from God....
>
> The authenticity of the Law, *i.e.*, that this Law was precisely transcribed from God and no one else. (*Helek*, p. 340)

Talmudic tradition claimed that the Five Books of Moses were composed in their entirety by God through Moses, with the exception of the final verses describing Moses' death, which some rabbis attributed to Joshua. Maimonides alluded to the Talmudic claim, but carefully phrased himself in a fashion that opens the door to other possibilities. "We do not believe that this *Law* in its entirety is from *the mouth of Moses our Master*. All of it is only from the mouth of the Force [*ha-geburah*, i.e., God]" (*Resurrection*, p. 172). Maimonides acknowledged that Moses was not the sole author of the law. He insisted only that the whole of the law was inspired by God.

Maimonides' assertion that the law came from God, although not necessarily through Moses, again reported the empirical experience of rational mysticism. Scripture stated that wisdom served God as a master-builder in the creation of the universe (Proverbs 8:30). In equating wisdom with the five books of Moses, the sages had asserted that the law was the blueprint for natural law throughout the universe. Maimonides championed the sages' position. Every actualization of every person's rational faculty, in all matters of natural and divine science, is a revelation of law from God.

Maimonides' tenth through thirteenth foundational principles may be seen as commentaries on the Mishnah's affirmation that the law teaches the resurrection of the dead. The principles are:

> God knows all that men do and never turns His eyes away from them, as those who say, 'The Lord has abandoned this earth' [Ezekiel 8:12, 9:9] claim. . . .
> God rewards those who perform the commandments of the Law and punishes those who transgress its admonitions. . . .
> We are to believe as fact that the Messiah will come. . . .
> The Resurrection of the Dead. (*Helek*, p. 341)

In his discussion of the tenth foundation of the law, Maimonides took the occasion to respond to those who argue that because God had no further role to play in the world after the creation, there cannot be a resurrection. To the contrary, Maimonides maintained that God has an ongoing role in the world.

The eleventh principle affirmed the concept of rewards and punishments, but implicitly in the mishnaic sense that the reward of a commandment is the commandment, and the punishment of a misdeed is the misdeed.

Coming to the resurrection of the dead, Maimonides defined it as "the return of this soul to the body after separation" (*Resurrection*, p. 163). He insisted that some biblical references to the resurrection are not parables, even though others are (*Resurrection*, p. 165). He affirmed that resurrection is a miracle (*Resurrection*, p. 167), but he insisted "that with belief in the Creation of the world it follows necessarily that all the miracles are possible, and therefore *Resurrection of the Dead* is also possible" (*Resurrection*, p. 172). At the same time, he implicitly understood the resurrection of the dead in an esoteric sense. He wrote:

> The resurrection of the dead is one of the cardinal principles established by Moses our Teacher. A person who does not believe in this principle has no real religion, certainly not Judaism. However, resurrection is only for the righteous. This is the meaning of the statement in *Bereshith Rabbah* (ch. 13) which declares: "The creative power of rain is for both the righteous and the wicked, but the resurrection of the dead is only for the righteous." How, after all, could the wicked come back to life, since they are dead even in their lifetimes? Our sages taught: "The wicked are called dead even while they are still alive; the righteous are alive even when they are dead" (*BT*, Berakhot, 18b). All men must die and their bodies decompose. (*Helek*, p. 214)

By juxtaposing the sages' teaching that "the righteous are alive even when they are dead" with his own observation that "all men must die and their bodies decompose," Maimonides implied that the death of the righteous differs from the death that involves bodily decomposition. What had he in mind?

Although modern scholars often trace the biblical doctrine of the resurrection of the dead to the prophetic books, the Mishnah specified that it was taught in the Five Books of Moses. "All Jews have a share in the world to come [save] the one who says that the resurrection of the dead is not taught in the Law." Maimonides did not elaborate on the scriptural source of the concept in *Perek Helek*, but he explained his understanding in an ostensibly unrelated context within the *Guide*. Maimonides there asserted that it "is well known and universally admitted in our community" that everyone at the gathering at Sinai, in the time of Moses, experienced the voice of God in a vision of prophecy (*Guide* I:46; p. 100). They heard God speak the first two commandments, "I am the Lord your God who brought you out of the land of Egypt, out of the house of bondage. You shall have no other gods before Me" (Exodus 20:2–3).

> [The sages] have a dictum formulated in several passages of the Midrashim and also figuring in the *Talmud*. This is their dictum [*BT*, Makkot, 24a; Midrash on the Song of Songs, 1:2]: *They heard "I" and "Thou shalt have" from the mouth of the Force.* They mean that these words reached them just as they reached *Moses our Master* and that it was not *Moses our Master* who communicated them to them. (*Guide* II:33; p. 364)

Maimonides states that the first two commandments belong "to the class of the intellecta," by contrast with all other commandments, which "belong to the class of generally accepted opinions and those adopted in virtue of tradition" (*Guide* II:33; p. 364). They are true rather than false, and not good rather than bad. The intellectual commandments can be attained through philosophy and do not require a vision of prophecy to become known.

> For these two principles, I mean the existence of the deity and His being one, are knowable by human speculation alone. Now with regard to everything that can be known by demonstration, the status of the prophet and that of everyone else who knows it are equal; there is no superiority of one over the other. Thus these two principles are not known through prophecy alone. (*Guide* II:33; p. 364)

At Sinai, however, the two intellectual commandments were prophesied, causing all Israel to experience terror and the fear of death.

> All *Israel* only heard at that *Gathering* one *voice* one single time—the *voice* through which *Moses* and all *Israel* apprehended *I* and *Thou shalt not*, which commandments *Moses* made them hear again as spoken in his own speech.... It was after they had heard that first *voice* that they, as is mentioned, were terrified of the thing and felt a great fear, and that they, as is reported, said: *And ye said, Behold the Lord [our God] hath shown us, and so on. Now therefore why should we die, and so on. Go thou near and hear, and so on.* (*Guide* II:33; pp. 364–365)

To make sense of the biblical narrative, Maimonides alluded to a rabbinic narrative that stated that the assembly at Sinai lost their souls, only to have their souls restored to them immediately following their deaths (Chernus, 1982).

> As for *the voice of the Lord*, I mean the created voice from which the *speech* [of God] was understood, they heard it once only, according to what the text of the *Law* states and according to what the *Sages* make clear in the passage to which I drew your attention. This was *the voice on hearing which their soul went out of them*, and through which *the first two commandments* were apprehended. (*Guide* II:33; p. 365)

Like the world to come and eternal life, the resurrection is a figurative reference to an experience that occurs during the course of mortal life as a phenomenon of rational mysticism. Maimonides located the soul's return to the body as an event that occurs prior to the actualization of the rational faculty. "*Resurrection of the Dead* is one of the foundations of the Law of *Moses our Master* [although] it is not the ultimate end; rather, the final end is *life in the World to Come*" (*Resurrection*, p. 157). As Maimonides' explication of the Sinai event indicates, resurrection was a recovery from the eighth degree of prophecy: the deathly terror that sometimes occurs during spiritual experiences. Acknowledgment that resurrection is taught in the law is, accordingly, not a dogmatic article of faith, but a simple statement of fact. It is taught in the text of Exodus 20:18–20.

Maimonides intimated that experiences of mystical death were products of the imaginative faculty when he cited the Talmudic saying, "*Rabbi Simon ben Laqish said: Satan, the evil inclination, and the angel of death are one and the same*" [*BT*, Baba Batra, 16a] (*Guide* III:22; p. 489). Precisely because people recover from experiences of mystical death, finding themselves alive after they have died, their deaths become self-evident as imaginations; experiences of mystical death are invaluable object lessons in the imaginative nature of "visions of prophecy." Maimonides' emphasis of the rabbinic saying, "There is no death without sin and no sufferings without transgression" (*Guide* III:24; p. 497; citing *BT*, Shabbat, 55a), implies that he regarded mystical death as a punishment for allowing imagination to function as the evil urge. Mystical death is a punishment for guilt that occurs when knowledge of guilt is actualized during a rational mystical experience. At the same time, it functions as a corrective of imagination in a manner that was integral to Maimonides' cure of souls.

In presenting his account of the world to come immediately after discussing cases of capital crimes, Maimonides implicitly raised the question of the relationship between ethics and prophecy. In *Eight Chapters*, he asserted that "it is not ... an indispensable requirement that a prophet should possess all the moral virtues, and be entirely free from every defect," and he cited biblical instances of lust, cruelty, anger, and fear among the prophets.

At the same time, he allowed that "a few moral imperfections lessen the degree of prophetic inspiration; in fact, we find that some moral vices cause prophecy to be entirely withdrawn" (*Eight Chapters* vii; p. 81). In affirming the rabbinic saying, "All Jews have a portion in the world to come," Maimonides asserted that rational mysticism was within reach of people quite generally. The extent of the prophecies might be diminished, but their occurrence was normally possible.

Maimonides' teachings in *Perek Helek*, regarding the foundational principles of the law that make a person eligible for the world to come, provide a context for understanding Maimonides' legal rulings concerning capital punishment in the *Mishneh Torah*. Relying only partly on the Talmud, Maimonides stated that heretics, idolators, those who deny the law and the phenomenon of prophecy, and even rebels against the law, whose sins are limited to eating nonkosher meat or wearing clothes that mix wool and linen, used to be executed in former times. He advocated that law courts in his own time administer whippings and, if necessary, the death penalty (Davidson, 2005, p. 229). Implicit in the Mishnah that Maimonides expounded in *Perek Helek* was the notion that a mystical death, followed by a resurrection from the dead, was the nature of the capital punishment under rabbinical discussion. During rational mystical experience, a person may prophesy guilt over moral imperfections, precipitating a mystical death. Guilt can be aroused even over minor violations, for example, in matters of diet and clothing, just as with major sins.

All thirteen of Maimonides' foundational principles of the law are conclusions that may be reached through acquaintance with experiences of rational mysticism. The first five principles, concerning monotheism, arise from reflection on the natural world and the argument from its design that leads to the postulation of a Creator. The sixth principle, affirming prophecy, acknowledged the human experience of rational mysticism itself. The seventh principle, affirming that the prophecy of Moses belongs in a class to itself, confirms the place of the miraculous in an otherwise naturalistic worldview. Both the divine origin of the Law and its authenticity are conclusions that may be drawn from experiences of scientific discovery during rational mysticism. What is at stake from the perspective of rational mysticism are the law's *experiential* origin and authenticity. The tenth principle, affirming God's ongoing involvement in creation, is proved by the fact of rational mysticism. Were God uninvolved, mystical experiences would not exist. The eleventh principle, reward and punishment, is instantiated by the resurrection of the dead, which occurs as a punishment when actualization of the rational faculty leads a person to discover reasons for guilt.

The thirteenth principle also has implications for the therapy of the soul. Not only is the love of God achieved through conjunction with the Active Intellect—in the rabbinic trope, by attaining the world to come—by means of scientific study that culminates in a rational mystical experience, but the fear of God is achieved through a mystical death and resurrection. In this way, the thirteenth foundational principle of the law intimates that personal experiences of rational mysticism, which are means to fulfill the commandments to love and to fear God, have the capacity to set the appetitive faculty in rational order, and so provide a foundation for mental health.

The twelfth principle, concerning the messiah, was understood by Maimonides to refer to the restoration of a sovereign Jewish state in the world we know under the leadership of a descendant of King David. Because the messianic era would commence with the popularization of prophecy among the general public, the twelfth principle expressed Maimonides' expectation that rational mysticism, and its consequences for public mental health, would sooner or later become sufficiently widespread to have the sociopolitical repercussions that Scripture anticipates.

THE FOUR WHO ENTERED PARADISE

Where *Perek Helek* outlines the program of rational mysticism that Maimonides advocated, various passages in the *Guide* addressed Jewish esotericism that he considered perplexed. For Maimonides, the paradigmatic instance of perplexity was to be found in the following Talmudic narrative.

> Four entered into *pardes*. They were Ben Azzai, Ben Zoma, Aher and Rabbi Akiva. Rabbi Akiva said to them: When you come up to the pure marble stones do not say, Water, Water. For it is said: One who speaks lies cannot before my eyes [Ps 101:7]. Ben Azzai glanced and died. Concerning him, the verse says: Precious at the fountain of the Lord is the death of His saints [Ps 116:15]. Ben Zoma glanced and went mad. Concerning him, the verse says: Have you found honey? Eat just enough for you, lest you be filled and vomit it up. Aher chopped down the saplings. Rabbi Akiva emerged in peace. (*BT*, Hagigah, 14b)

Pardes was a loanword from Persian meaning "garden." It referred to the botanical gardens, full of exotic plants, that royal palaces housed between their outer walls and their residential buildings. In post-Talmudic literature, the term Paradise acquired its continuing meaning as a reference to a dwelling place for souls of the worthy in the afterlife. In the Talmud, however, the term regularly meant a fruit orchard with the one exception of the above narrative of the four who entered Paradise, where it signifies "the Orchard" as though only a single orchard merited consideration. The word had the same sense in Tractate Hagigah 14b that it had in St. Paul's account of his ascension to Paradise, where it similarly referred to the Garden of Eden as a botanical garden that implicitly surrounded the palace of God.

Scholem (1965) argued that the Talmudic narrative of the four who entered Paradise originated in the *hekhalot* literature of early Jewish mysticism and concerned the possible dangers of misadventure through mystical experience. Most scholars concur with his reading. Paradise and the world to come were equivalent tropes. The story of the four who entered Paradise belongs to the esoteric tradition within Judaism and was regarded by the Talmudic sages as an admission by esotericians of the dangers that surrounded their practices. Elsewhere in the Talmud, Ben Azzai and Ben Zoma were notable because their opinions were highly regarded even though they were not ordained as rabbis. The story of the four who entered Paradise conveyed the message that one was in jeopardy if one had not been sufficiently educated. Of the four who entered Paradise, only one was called a rabbi, and only he ascended and returned safely. We understand Maimonides to have believed that Akiva alone approached the secrets of the law correctly.

How did Maimonides' interpret the story of the four who entered Paradise? The Gemara appended two of Ben Zoma's rulings immediately following the story of the four who entered Paradise. These rulings concerned a prohibition regarding the means of neutering a dog, and the permissibility of a priest marrying a virgin who became pregnant (*BT*, Hagigah, 14b). Ben Zoma's preoccupation with bizarre sexual concerns may be inferred. The Gemara ended by observing, "Ben Zoma is still on the outside" (*BT*, Hagigah, 15a), a euphemism that meant that his opinion was incorrect. At the same time, the precise wording hinted that his madness on entering Paradise consisted of treating his vision "on the outside," that is, at its face value. He did not inquire regarding the inner meaning of his vision as a metaphor.

Ben Azzai was notable for the fact that his opinions concerning laws regulating sexual conduct were valued, even though he himself never married. This circumstance might be taken to indicate that his inexperience of sexuality contributed to his death in Paradise.

Elisha ben Avuyah, referred to as *Aher*, "Other," was notorious among the scholars mentioned in the Talmud for having become an apostate. Aher's scholarship was highly respected, but his approach to the biblical text was considered unduly literal. His apostasy was attributed to the literalism with which he approached his entrance into Paradise.

> Aher chopped down the saplings. Upon him the verse states: "Let not your mouth bring guilt upon your flesh" [Eccl 5:5]. What was it? He saw Metatron who was given permission to sit in order to record the merits of the Jewish people. Aher said, "We have a tradition that above there is neither sitting, nor competition, nor the back of a head, nor weariness. Perhaps there are two authorities [God and Metatron]." They took Metatron out and inflicted upon him sixty blows of fire. They said to him, "Why did you not stand before [Aher] when you saw him?" He was given permission to erase the merits of Aher. The echo of a voice emerged and said, "Return, O wayward sons [Jer 3:14]—except for Aher." He said, "Since that person has been

banished from that world [to Come], let him go out and indulge [himself] in this world. Aher strayed to bad society. He went out, found a harlot, and asked for her. She said to him, "But are you not Elisha ben Avuyah?" He uprooted a radish from a patch on the Sabbath, and gave to her. She said, "This must be someone else." (*BT*, Hagigah, 15a)

The tradition to which Aher referred was a teaching of the sages concerning Ezekiel's vision of the Glory of God enthroned on a chariot drawn by four living creatures. Regarding the creatures, Maimonides explained:

> [Ezekiel] states that their feet are straight; he means that they have no articulations. This is the meaning of his dictum *straight feet* [Ezek 1:7], according to its external sense. [The sages] have likewise said: *And their feet were straight feet—this teaches [us] that above, there is no sitting* [Genesis Rabbah, lxv]. Understand this also. (*Guide* III:2; p. 418)

Maimonides implied that because angels do not sit, Aher mistakenly regarded the angel that he beheld sitting on a heavenly throne as a second deity. Having embraced dualism, he apparently saw his way clear to sexual improprieties. If the Gemara is treated at face value, he consorted with a prostitute. If the rabbinic narrative is instead parabolic, it might be intimating that he attributed sexual activity to the two deities in whom he had come to believe. Maimonides indicated the presence of some sort of inner meaning when he appended "Understand this also" to the passage previously cited. The external sense concerned straight feet. What was *also* to be understood—the inner meaning—pertained to the word "sitting."

Rabbi Akiva was distinguished in the Talmud for two things: his attention to things outside of Jewish law, and his metaphoric readings of the biblical text. The Gemara remarked:

> Rabbi Akiva ascended in peace and descended in peace. Upon him, the verse states: "Draw me, we will run after you [Song 1:4]." And even Rabbi Akiva, the ministering angels wished to push. The Holy One, Blessed Is He, said to them, "Leave this elder be, for he is deserving to make use of my glory." (*BT*, Hagigah, 15b)

Rabbi Akiva implicitly understood that what he beheld when he entered Paradise was not God, but God's visible glory.

Maimonides' reference in the *Guide* to the four who entered Paradise indicated that his area of interest in the narrative included its contrast of literalism with a metaphoric sensibility. Maimonides wrote:

> With regard to the fact that that which is above the *firmament* is called water in name only and that it is not the specific water known to us, a statement setting this forth has also been made by the *Sages, may their memory be blessed*. They made it in the following passage: *Four entered the Paradise, and so on*.

> *Rabbi Akiba said to them: When you come to the stones of pure marble, do not say, Water, Water, for it is written: He that speaketh falsehood shall not be established before mine eyes.* (Guide II:30; p. 353)

Scholem (1954) asserted that "this famous passage . . . clearly enough refers to a *real* danger in the process of ascending to 'Paradise'" (p. 52), and illustrated his contention by quoting in full the relevant passage from the esoteric *hekhalot*, "Palaces," literature that was the Talmud's source.

> But if one was unworthy to see the King in his beauty, the angels at the gates disturbed his senses and confused him. And when they said to him: 'Come in,' he entered, and instantly they pressed him and threw him into the fiery lava stream. And at the gate of the sixth palace it seemed as though hundreds of thousands and millions of waves of water stormed against him, and yet there was not a drop of water, only the ethereal glitter of the marble plates with which the palace was tessellated. But he was standing in front of the angels and when he asked: 'What is the meaning of these waters,' they began to stone him and said: 'Wretch, do you not see it with your own eyes? Are you perhaps a descendant of those who kissed the Golden Calf, and are you unworthy to see the King in his beauty?' . . . And he does not go until they strike his head with iron bars and wound him. And this shall be a sign for all times that no one shall err at the gate of the sixth palace and see the ethereal glitter of the plates and ask about them and take them for water, that he may not endanger himself. (Scholem, 1954, pp. 53, 361 n. 47; citing Ms. Munich 22 f. 162b)

The esoteric teaching in the *hekhalot* literature was that mystics who failed to reify mental images, who failed to believe that an image of a marble floor was as solid as a floor of physical marble, were at risk of precipitating experiences of mystical death. Wolfson (1994) has shown that the reification of mental images, resulting in visions that Corbin (1972) termed "imaginal," has been the common practice of Jewish esotericians for two thousand years.

The talmudic phrasing of the *hekhalot* narrative reversed its significance. When "Rabbi Akiva said to them: When you come to the stones of pure marble, do not say, Water, Water," what was at stake was no longer a reifying, imaginal treatment of mental imagery. The Talmudic version revised the narrative in a manner that introduced a concern with truth. Akiva was made to explain: "for it is written: He that speaketh falsehood shall not be established before mine eyes." Falsehood incurred guilt, and guilt deservedly earned a mystical death.

Maimonides expanded on the Talmudic teaching when he separated Rabbi Akiva's final remarks from his main presentation of the story of the four who entered Paradise, and used the quotation to comment on the waters in Genesis 1:6–7. Not only was it incorrect to reify mental images, but it was obligatory to interpret them. For Maimonides, the *hekhalot* advice, to avoid experiences of mystical death and their correction of disordered imagination, violated a foundational principle of the law. It was an instance of perplexity, a grossly unscientific interpretation of mental imagery that led to aberrant behavior.

Of the four who entered Paradise, only Rabbi Akiva possessed the metaphoric sensibility that permitted him to emerge safely. The negative outcomes of his three companions owed to their treating literally what was correctly understood as metaphor. For Maimonides, the story of the four who entered Paradise illustrated the syndrome of the disease of the soul: perplexity, misadventure during mystical experience, and sexual misconduct.

At the very beginning of the *Guide*, Maimonides brought his historical narrative down to his own time. He asserted that: "It is not the purpose of this Treatise to make its totality understandable to the vulgar or to beginners in speculation, nor to teach those who have not engaged in any study other than the science of the Law—I mean the legalistic study of the Law" (*Guide* I:Introduction; p. 5). The three character types—the vulgar, philosophical tyro, and exclusive legalist—openly indicated how not to interpret the *Guide*. The typology also corresponded to the three who came to tragedy when they entered Paradise. Ben Azzai, the unmarried authority on sexual laws, exemplified the vulgar. His interest in Paradise was implicitly prurient, and he died. Ben Zoma, whom Maimonides described as a mathematician, exemplified "beginners in speculation" who lacked the thorough grounding in philosophy that was needed to make coherent sense of prophecy. His perplexity led him into madness. Lastly, Aher was a great legalist whose opinions were sought even after he committed apostasy. He exemplified "those who have not engaged in any study other than . . . the legalistic study of the Law." He beheld the enthroned glory; but he was no philosopher. Lacking the flexibility of mind to make parabolic sense of his vision, he ended in apostasy.

MONISTIC MYSTICAL UNION

Maimonides adopted a similarly critical approach to the type of unitive mystical experience that Neoplatonists had prized in late antiquity and both Muslim Sufis and Jewish kabbalists adopted in the Middle Ages. Consider, for example, the phrasing of Maimonides' elder contemporary, the Muslim Aristotelian philosopher Ibn Tufail.

> He continued to cultivate solitude in his cave, head bent, eyes closed, unaware of all sensual objects and bodily forces, struggling only to concentrate on the Being whose existence is necessary. . . .
>
> He continued to strive for sincerity in witnessing and for the annihilation of his self, and finally achieved it. The heavens and the earth and all that lies between them vanished from his thoughts and his memory. So also did

spiritual visions, bodily forces and all the non-material forces which are the essences conscious of that Being which is Truth; and his own essence vanished with them. All became scattered as dust, shrunk, vanished. Only the Truth, the One, the Being whose existence is permanent, remained. (Ibn Tufail, 1982, p. 45)

Ibn Tufail here described the achievement of a deep trance in which sense perception, imagination, bodily experiences, and even ideas vanished, leaving only the necessarily existent in consciousness.

Kabbalists pursued similar experiences. *Sefer HaBahir*, which was contemporary with Maimonides, termed them *makhshavah*, "thinking" or "consciousness." Scholem (1987) explained:

> This pure *mahshabah* is ... elevated to the highest rank in the *Bahir* ... this "thought," as conceived by the *Bahir*, connects human and divine thinking ... we may, perhaps, assume that here, too, the pure thought of man, detached from any concrete content and meditating upon no definite object but itself, is conducted along a path of pure meditation to the divine thought and enters into communion with it. (Scholem, 1987, p. 127)

Later kabbalists were to designate equivalent experiences of the first hypostasis as *'ayin*, "nothingness" (Matt, 1990).

Without referring by name to the mystics whose theologies he rejected, Maimonides offered the following interpretation of monistic mystical experiences.

> Perhaps they—I mean what these people apprehend—are merely opinions that they once had had and of which traces have remained impressed upon their imaginings together with everything else that subsists in their imaginative faculty. Accordingly when they void and annul many of their imaginings, the traces of these opinions remain alone and become apparent to them; whereupon they think that these are things that have unexpectedly occurred to them and have come from outside. To my mind they may be compared to a man who had with him in his house thousands of individual animals. Then all of them except one individual, which was one of those that were there, went out of that house. When the man remained alone with that individual, he thought that it had just now entered the house and joined him, whereas that was not the case, that individual being the one among the multitude that did not go out. This is one of the points that lead astray and cause perdition. How many among those who have aspired to obtain discernment have perished through this! (*Guide* II:38; p. 378)

Maimonides here explained claims of mystical monism as misunderstandings of opinions. Meditation on the necessarily existent was, in Maimonides' view, meditation on *the idea* of the necessarily existent. It was meditation on an intelligible. Its experience as God, rather than as a concept about God, was an imagination, and its misinterpretation was a category mistake that often had tragic consequences. Union with the Active Intellect was both possible and highly desirable. Union with God was a category mistake.

CONCLUSIONS

Perplexity arose through naive views that treated imagination at face value, leading to erroneous beliefs that prophecy and Scripture are in conflict with reason. Perplexity varied in severity from intellectual puzzlement, which could be addressed pedagogically, to acute and chronic spiritual crises that required therapeutic interventions. The paradigmatic example of spiritual crises was the Talmudic tale of the four who entered Paradise, a narrative that the Talmud had borrowed from the esoteric literature of Jewish *hekhalot* mysticism. In his discussion of the narrative, Maimonides preserved the secrecy of both the mystics and the Talmud. His techniques of encoding subtexts within his writing had rabbinical precedents but were also indebted to more recent Muslim and alchemical literary conventions. In *Perek Helek*, a section of his *Commentary on the Mishnah*, Maimonides esoterically explained that the Talmudic rabbis had referred to blissful religious experiences as "the world to come" and had treated terrifying religious experiences together with recovery from them under the images of "death" and "resurrection." Maimonides' thirteen foundational principles of the law, which he asserted were conditions of eligibility for the world to come, may be understood in the same esoteric context, as conditions for blissful "worship of the heart." Maimonides discussed the tale of the four who entered Paradise in a similarly secretive manner, explaining that the mystics who came to grief when they entered "Paradise"—a synonym for "the world to come"—erred by reifying imagination. They also engaged in aberrant sexuality—variously abstemious, perverse, and promiscuous—that was symptomatic of their perplexity. As a further instance of perplexity, Maimonides discussed the type of monistic mystical experience that kabbalists termed *makhshavah*, "consciousness," and *'ayin*, "nothingness."

FIVE

Secrets of the Law

IN JEWISH TRADITION, unconstrained exposition is a primary duty and primary activity. It is the one prescribed excess in the whole of the Jewish tradition. The law commands: "And these words that I command you this day shall be upon your heart; and you shall teach them diligently to your children, and shall talk of them when you sit in your house, and when you walk by the way, and when you lie down, and when you rise up" (Deut 6:4–7). Maimonides made the claim, however, that "the *sages* . . . specified in a number of places in the *Talmud* that *the words of the Law* have both a literal and a hidden meaning—the hidden meanings accordingly being called *secrets of Law*" (*Resurrection*, p. 160).

The secrets of the law were unfinished business for Maimonides when he set out to write the *Guide*. In his *Commentary on the Mishnah* and the *Mishneh Torah*, he had remarked that the sages forbade the public discussion of three topics. The Mishnah stated:

> One does not expound the *Arayot* to three, nor the *Maaseh Bereshith* to two, nor the *Maaseh Merkabah* even to one, save that he were wise, and one who is understanding of his own knowledge. As for anyone who should attempt to discern the meaning of [the following] four terms, pity him, for it were as though he had not come into the world. What is above, what is below, what is prior, and what is after. As for anyone who is not forebearing with respect to the glory of his maker, pity would have been shown to him had he not come into the world. (*BT*, Hagigah 11b)

The Gemara stated that one is not to expound on *arayot*, "nakednesses," to three people, nor the *Maaseh Bereshith*, "Account of the Beginning," to two people, nor the *Maaseh Merkabah*, "Account of the Chariot," to one, unless he is wise and capable of understanding on his own. The Gemara explains that three is too many for the *arayot* because while the teacher is discussing with one student, the other two might go off to speak to each other. Two is too many for the Account of the Beginning because it takes away from the one-to-one engagement of a teacher with a student. Finally, in connection with the Account of the Chariot, one should expound only enough to promote the self-understanding of the student. For the task of learning the Account of the Chariot involves coming to understand what one already knows.

Because Aher's vision of Metatron, which had led him to apostasy, had been an instance of *Maaseh Merkabah*, Maimonides' cure of souls was incomplete without explaining the correct interpretation of Aher's vision. But how was Maimonides to explain the interpretation of the vision, when he was forbidden to expound the vision itself? He had either to leave his cure of souls incomplete or publicly address the secrets of the law.

Maimonides took his position as a physician of the soul. His very title, *Guide of the Perplexed*, claimed permission to abrogate the Mishnah. Rabbinic law permits all obligations, save three, to be abrogated for medical reasons. The obligation of secrecy is not one of the three laws for which a Jew must accept death rather than transgress; Maimonides' purpose, to cure the diseases of the soul, justified his discussion of the secrets of the law.

Further to excuse his behavior, Maimonides claimed that he was not revealing anything that had been told to him on condition of secrecy. Maimonides pointed out that he had not been in receipt of secret communications.

> Knowledge of this matter has ceased to exist in the religious community, so that nothing great or small remains of it. And it had to happen like this, for this knowledge was only transmitted from one chief to another and has never been set down in writing. . . . On the other hand, if I omitted setting down something of that which has appeared to me as clear, so that knowledge would perish when I perish, as is inevitable, I should have considered that conduct as extremely cowardly with regard to everyone who is perplexed. It would have been, as it were, robbing one who deserves the truth of the truth, or begrudging an heir his inheritance. And both theses traits are blameworthy. (*Guide* III:Introduction; pp. 415–416)

Maimonides also remarked: "In that which has occurred to me with regard to these matters, I followed conjecture and supposition . . . [I did not] receive what I believe in these matters from a teacher" (*Guide* III:Introduction; p. 416). There was, however, a certain ingenuousness in Maimonides' claim. Anyone "wise, and . . . understanding of his own knowledge" who was told nothing more than "chapter headings" could claim with equal justice that he "followed conjecture and supposition." Maimonides was being more candid when he acknowledged: "Every man endowed with knowledge who has come to possess an understanding pertaining to these secrets . . . must indubitably say something" (*Guide* II:29; p. 347).

At the same time, Maimonides struggled to violate the obligation of secrecy as little as necessary. To minimize his violation, Maimonides opened the *Guide* with what Pines, the English translator, designated as an "epistle dedicatory." It is addressed to a certain Rabbi Joseph ibn Aknin, one of Maimonides' students. Rabbi Joseph moved away from Cairo in 1187, and Maimonides said that he was continuing his education by means of the pages that made up the *Guide*. "Your absence moved me to compose this Treatise, which I have composed for you and for those like you, however few they are. I have set it down in dispersed chapters. All of them that are written down will reach you where you are, one after the other" (*Guide*, Epistle Dedicatory; p. 4). These remarks imply that the *Guide* conformed with the Mishnah by being written essentially for a single addressee, Rabbi Joseph. The *Guide* was addressed to other readers only accidentally. Maimonides wrote the book in the second person singular as if to suggest that the book was consistent with the injunction to teach the Account of the Chariot only to one person at a time. His purpose was to signal his approach.

Maimonides was fully aware that when one writes a book, anyone can read it. He acknowledged, "Now if someone explained these matters in a book, he in effect would be teaching them to thousands of men" (*Guide* I:Introduction; p. 7). To achieve conformity with the Mishnah, Maimonides relied on the second part of the sages' injunction, not to expound on the secret of the Account of the Chariot even to one person unless that person understood it independently. Maimonides made the point obliquely, as was necessary to meet his obligation, when he wrote to Rabbi Joseph, saying that after he had studied astronomy, mathematics, and logic, "I saw that you are one worthy to have the secrets of the prophetic books revealed to you. . . . Thereupon I began to let you see certain flashes and to give you certain indications" (*Guide*, Epistle Dedicatory; p. 3). By alluding to the rabbinical technique of "chapter headings" (*BT*, Hagigah, 14b), Maimonides claimed the authority of the sages for his manner of communicating secrets. He permitted his readers to infer what he was prepared to intimate but was prohibited by rabbinic tradition from saying openly and fully. By discussing the secrets of the law in secretive ways, Maimonides was able to teach the secrets unapologetically without falling into violation of rabbinic law—but only to a reader "understanding of his own knowledge."

To restrict the secrets to readers who were able to understand of their own knowledge, Maimonides used a variety of literary devices, including misdirection. One such example occurs in the course of Maimonides' discussion of the Account of the Beginning, where he wrote:

> Reflect, if you are one of those who reflect, to what extent he has made clear and revealed the whole matter in this statement, provided that you consider

it well, understand all that has been demonstrated in the 'Meteorologica' and examine everything that people have said about every point mentioned in that work. (*Guide* II:30; p. 353)

Meteorologica is a work by Aristotle that concerned the weather. It also included a passage that discussed the derivation of the four elements from "a common and ultimate substrate" (*Meteorologica* 339^b 1–2; p. 556), a point of view to which Maimonides held. However, to read all that Aristotle and his commentators wrote on the *Meteorologica* would famously include Ibn Sina's *Kitab al-Shifa*, the "Book of the Remedy," which treats Aristotle's discussion of the four elements as a point of departure for the discussion of alchemy (Linden, 2003, pp. 94–98). Accordingly, the literature pertinent to Aristotle's *Meteorologica* would include the whole of the literature of alchemy; its consultation would occupy a lifetime, which was the intention of Maimonides' words. If a reader was incapable of interpreting the *Guide* in conformance with Maimonides' intention of rational mysticism, he would be fooled by Maimonides' suggestion, accept its misdirection, and pursue the study of alchemy rather than apply himself to understand Maimonides' subtext.

Most of Maimonides' enciphered passages are otherwise transparent. Although extensive sections of the *Guide* were written in cipher and have to be deciphered to be understood, most of what he discussed in these passages is also to be found openly stated in other locations in the *Guide*. Very little of what he wrote in cipher proves, after deciphering, to have been secret. In order to discover Maimonides' actual secrets, it is necessary, however, to decipher all of the enciphered passages and then arrive by a process of elimination at the small number of passages whose open explanation is not to be found elsewhere. The pedagogical function of Maimonides' technique was presumably deliberate and shaped by his desire not to limit his secrets to esotericians, but to reveal them to all interested and diligent inquirers. By presenting readers with ciphers whose correct solutions he provided elsewhere in the *Guide*, Maimonides offered opportunities for readers to learn and practice their skills at deciphering, much as a mathematics text might include both lessons and sample questions for students to solve, in order to gain experience at working with the ideas in the lessons. By presenting his readers with many more ciphers than contained secrets, Maimonides prepared his readers to be able to "understand of their own knowledge" the comparatively few passages that were both enciphered and unexplained elsewhere in the *Guide*.

ARAYOT

What are the restricted topics *arayot*, the Account of the Beginning, and the Account of the Chariot? They are texts whose public reading in synagogue is subject to restrictions: Leviticus 18, Genesis 1–3, and Ezekiel 1, 8–10.

Because it is not the reading of these biblical texts but only their explanation that the sages restricted, it is evident that the sages understood the texts to contain two levels of meaning. One was manifest in the reading, and the other was hidden in the exposition.

Leviticus 18, which prohibits various sexual relations, is termed *arayot*, "nakednesses." It begins with "No one shall go near anyone close to him in flesh to uncover the nakedness, I am the Lord" (Lev 18:6). The text then goes on to forbid the uncovering of the nakedness of father, mother, sister, grandchild, aunt and uncle, and so on. Despite the general thrust toward teaching and learning in the Jewish tradition, there is constraint in connection with instruction concerning sexuality. Instruction in connection with sexuality is done with reasonable privacy.

Interestingly, the third century Christian Church Father, Origen, reported in his commentary on the Song of Songs that Jews taught their children all of the Hebrew Bible but deferred four portions to the end of the education: "The beginning of Genesis, in which the creation of the world is described; the first chapters of Ezekiel, which tell about the cherubim; the end of that same, which contains the building of the Temple; and this book of the Song of Songs" (Origen, 1957, p. 23). Elior (2004, p. 162) associated this curriculum with the Mishnaic injunctions regarding the teaching of the Account of the Beginning, the Account of the Chariot, and *Arayot*, implying that the Jews of Origen's acquaintance in the Galilee in the third century included the text of Song of Songs among the restrictions concerning *Arayot*. Because the Song of Songs is openly erotic and celebrative of permissible sexuality, its restriction may indicate that it was sexuality, and not incestuous relations alone, that was the concern of the prohibition in the early Talmudic era.

Idel (1986) noted that Maimonides used the Gemara phrase *sitre 'arayot*, "secrets of nakedness," in his *Commentary on the Mishnah*, but followed Mishnaic usage and referred only to *'arayot* in the *Guide*. Citing statements by Maimonides in both the *Commentary* and the *Mishneh Torah* that thinking about the body and its desires interferes with contemplation of intelligibles, Idel suggested that for Maimonides the forbidden sexual relations of *'arayot* included any concern with sexuality whatsoever, when engaged in contemplation. In the *Guide*, however, Maimonides dropped the term *sitre*, "secrets of," in reference to *'arayot*, because it was the manifest content of *'arayot* that the sages had intended. The restrictions on the accounts of the beginning and the chariot differed in being addressed to the esoteric content of the two topics.

If the Mishnaic constraint against teaching about the nakednesses were freestanding, it would not be noteworthy in our present discussion of Maimonides' cure of souls. It is not freestanding, however, but is instead conjoined with greater constraint against explaining the Account of the Beginning, and still greater constraint with respect to the Account of the Chariot. An order of secrecy is clearly indicated by the order of constraint. The Account of the

Chariot is the most secret, while the least secret is the *Arayot*. The association of the three texts raises the possibility that concerns with sexuality and its representation may be involved in all three.

Certainly Maimonides intimated as much. The Talmud compared the chariot vision of Ezekiel 1:6 with the temple vision of Isaiah 6:2–3 (*BT*, Hagigah, 13a); and Maimonides concurred (*Guide* III:6; p. 426). At one point in his discussion of the temple vision, Maimonides cited a Talmudic teaching that explained why the rabbis surrounded sexuality with secrecy. After noting the discrepancy between the six wings of the angels that Isaiah saw and the four faces and four wings that Ezekiel saw, the sages agreed that two wings were lost when the Temple was destroyed. The suggestion was made that the loss of two wings exposed the angels' legs to Ezekiel's view.

> The Rabbis say: those with which they cover their legs, as it says: "Their legs were a straight leg" [Ezek 1:7]. Now, if it was not [the wings covering the legs] that were reduced, how would he [Ezekiel] have known? [But] perhaps they were revealed and he saw them. Because if you do not say this, [consider:] "As for the likeness of their faces: There was a human face" [Ezek 1:10]. Then they [the wings over their faces] were reduced as well? Rather, it was revealed and he saw it. Here too, they were revealed and he saw them. Now, that! It is well and fine, it is proper etiquette to uncover one's face before one's master. It is not proper etiquette to uncover one's leg before one's master. (*BT*, Hagigah 13b)

The final sentence of this passage explained Maimonides' understanding of the sages' motivation in placing restrictions on the teaching of *Arayot*, the Account of the Beginning, and the Account of the Chariot. It was a question of good manners in honoring the Creator.

THE ACCOUNT OF THE BEGINNING

Maimonides openly stated that the Account of the Beginning and the Account of the Chariot pertained to physics and metaphysics, as these topics were defined by the Greek philosophic tradition. "The Account of the Beginning is identical with natural science, and the Account of the Chariot with divine science" (*Guide* I: Introduction; p. 6). Modern scholars have not known what to make of Maimonides' claims. Davidson (2005) wrote:

> Maimonides was ... convinced that the contents of science and philosophy are integral to the rabbinic worldview and that rabbinic religion not only permits but mandates the study of philosophy. He was certain—bizarre though it may sound to us—that a highly valued, and no less highly obscure, subject of nonlegal scriptural and rabbinic study called the "account of the chariot" is identical with the philosophic science of metaphysics. A page or

two after identifying the account of the chariot as the science of metaphysics, he quotes a talmudic statement to the effect that the legal give and take of experts in rabbinic dialectic is "a small thing," while the account of the chariot is a "major thing." (p. 107)

Davidson concluded that Maimonides "is saying in so many words that the ancient rabbis themselves rated metaphysics as of greater value than rabbinic dialectic," but he failed to inquire in what sense physics and metaphysics might be taken that made them subject to prohibition.

Maaseh Bereshith, the "Account of the Beginning," concerns the creation of the world in Genesis 1:1. The word *maaseh* has two distinct meanings. It means "account, story, narrative." It also means "work, deed." *Bereshith* is the first word of Scripture. It is usually translated as "in the beginning" or "genesis." According to Maimonides, when God created the world, God also created time. There was no beginning in the sense of a beginning within a pre-existing matrix of time, in which one could conceive of there having been any kind of anything before the genesis, including time. The chapters that begin with the word *bereshith* are an account of that genesis. The Account of the Beginning means the work of creating the universe. It also means the account of the creation of the universe out of nothing.

Let us explore Maimonides' interpretation of Genesis 1:1 (Bakan, 1991, pp. 48–49). Maimonides used the verse as scriptural authority for his understanding of angels by interpolating a philological teaching of Rabbi Akiva. In connection with a different verse, Rabbi Akiva had taught that the Hebrew word *et*, which indicates the accusative, should be read as the preposition "with." The biblical verse is conventionally understood to mean, "In the beginning God created the heaven and the earth." Maimonides commented as follows:

> Among the things you ought to know is the fact that the *Sages* have explicitly stated in a number of passages that the word *et* figuring in his words, *et ha-shamayim ve-et ha-aretz* ["the heaven and the earth"], has in that verse the meaning: with. They mean by this that He created together with the heavens all that is in heaven and together with the earth all that is in the earth [i.e., the intellects]. (*Guide* II:30; p. 350)

Maimonides asserted that we read the Hebrew word *et* in the text of Genesis 1:1 as a preposition meaning "with." The word *et* can mean "with," but the usual interpretation of Genesis 1:1 treats it in its other sense as a grammatical marker that indicates that the following noun is the object of the verb. According to Maimonides, however, the phrase *et ha-shamayim ve-et ha-aretz* is to be understood to mean, not "the heaven and the earth," but "*with* the heaven and *with* the earth." This interpretation of *et* transforms what are ordinarily considered objects of the verb into prepositional phrases.

Maimonides indicated a reading of the text that makes no immediate sense. He implied that the sages read Genesis 1:1 to mean, "In the beginning God created with the heaven and with the earth." Such a reading would make heaven and earth co-creators with God. It would not imply, as Maimonides elsewhere claimed, that God created heaven and earth with their respective contents.

What is the meaning of Maimonides' apparent inconsistency? Maimonides created a puzzle and left his reader to work out the correct solution. It is clear that the puzzle was intentional because it also occurs in the Talmud. Concerning the translation of the Septuagint, the Old Greek translation of the Bible, the Talmud stated:

> There was an incident with King Ptolemy, that he gathered seventy-two elders of Israel and placed them in seventy-two houses, and he did not reveal to them why he had gathered them. He then visited each one of them, and said to them, "Write for me [that is, in Greek] the Law of Moses your teacher." The Holy One, Blessed is He, placed counsel in each of their hearts and all of them arrived at a common decision [about the translation]. And they wrote for him, "In the beginning God created" (*BT*, Megillah 9a).

The Talmudic passage continued with several further examples of the independent agreement of the seventy-two translators. Implicit in the narrative is the expectation that each of the biblical passages whose translations were praised might plausibly have been translated in another manner. Maimonides' discussion of the word *et* invited the reader to consider the exegesis that the Septuagint had successfully avoided.

Maimonides' explication of the meaning of *et* in Genesis 1:1 left the sentence without an apparent object to its verb. However, the noun that precedes the adverbial phrases can be grammatically read as either the subject or the object of the verb. Because Hebrew verbs always imply pronouns when they occur in the absence of nouns, the word *bara*, "created," can mean "he created"; and the word *Elohim*, "God" can be understood, without doing violence to the grammar of the sentence, as the object of the verb rather than as its subject. Instead of the conventional reading "In the beginning God created the heaven and the earth," the first verse of Scripture can be read as "In the beginning He created *Elohim* with the heaven and with the earth." By this change, the word *Elohim* ceases to be a name for God and instead means something that is part of the created universe and differs from its Creator. Maimonides elsewhere remarked that "every Hebrew knows that the term *elohim* is equivocal, designating the deity, the angels, and the rulers governing the cities" (*Guide* I:2; p. 25).

Interestingly, precisely this reading of Genesis 1:1 occurs in *Sefer HaBahir*, the oldest extant text of the kabbalah. The *Bahir* dates to the last quarter of the twelfth century (Scholem, 1954), making it exactly contemporary with Maimonides' publications of his *Commentary on the Mishnah*, *Mishneh Torah*, and *Guide of the Perplexed*. Paragraph 8 of the *Bahir* states:

Rabbi Boi said: What of the scripture, "From the world I was set up, from the head <before the earth>" [Prov 8:23]? ... The Torah said, "I pre-existed the head of the world, as it is said, "From the world I was set up, from the start." And lest you say that the earth was before it, it goes on to teach before the earth. As it is said, "In the beginning He created God" [Gen 1:1]. And what did He create? The necessities of the All, and afterwards "God" [Gen 1:1]. And what is written subsequently? "The heaven and the earth" [Gen 1:1].

Maimonides' reading of Genesis 1:1 was neither idiosyncratic nor unacceptably outlandish in the views of his contemporary esotericians.

Maimonides, who no more than hinted at the reading that the *Bahir* boldly asserted, approached the topic indirectly when he stated that Onqelos may have understood the word *Elohim* to mean "angel." "In my opinion it is also possible that Onqelos interpreted [*Elohim*] as signifying an angel" (*Guide* I:27; p. 58). The reader of Maimonides' subtext was to correlate the *Guide*'s dispersed references to the word *Elohim* with the use of the term in the Account of the Beginning. The result is a reading of *Elohim* in Genesis 1:1 as a collective designation of the angels, which is to say, the Aristotelian forms or intellects. For Maimonides, both the matter and the forms or processes that constitute the universe and regulate what transpires within it were created at the instant of creation, when the celestial and terrestrial realms were created together with the *Elohim*.

Maimonides' understanding of physics in terms of matter and form that divide into intelligences, forms in celestial matter, and forms in terrestrial matter, was a medieval commonplace. Since he elsewhere explained that Aristotelian forms were what the Bible called angels, his use of esoteric literary techniques in connection with Genesis 1:1 did not pertain to a secret of the law. His cryptic formulation was presumably intended to provide novices with practice in deciphering esoteric writing, so that they might learn his literary methods and be able to apply them to rare passages whose solutions he did not provide.

It is also significant that the first chapter of the *Guide* comments on Genesis 1:26. Maimonides asserted that the doctrine of the corporeality of God rested on a misunderstanding of the verse, "Let us make man in our image, after our likeness" (*Guide* I:1; p. 21). For his purpose at the beginning of the *Guide*, he might have cited any biblical verse that employed the word *zelem*, "image," before we went on to introduce the concept of forms in clarification of the term. His citation of Genesis 1:26 was not casual, however. Employing the esoteric literary technique of dispersion, Maimonides returned to the verse midway through the *Guide*, where he explicitly stated:

> Our Law does not deny the fact that He, may He be exalted, governs that which exists here through the intermediation of the angels. Thus there is the

text of the Sages with reference to the dictum of the Torah: *Let us make man in our image* [Gen 1:26], and its dictum: *Come, let us go down* [Gen 11:7], which dicta are in the plural. (*Guide* II:6; pp. 262–263)

Because Maimonides interpreted the word *elohim* in Genesis 1:1 as a plural noun that referred to the angelic intelligences, the biblical verse, "In the image of *elohim* He created him," referred to the creation of the human intellect in reflection of the angelic intelligences. As Maimonides had explained in the *Mishneh Torah*, human beings alone are capable of apprehending the incorporeal entities in the universe with the special intellect with which people are endowed.

> The text, 'Let us make man in our image, after our likeness' . . . means that man should have a form that knows and apprehends intellectual beings that are devoid of matter, such as the angels which are forms without substance, so that [intellectually] man is like the angels. (*BK*, *Laws of the Fundamental Principles of the Torah*, IV:8; p. 39a)

In this way, Maimonides solved the exegetical problem of the plural subject in Genesis 1:26, "Let us make man in our image, after our likeness." The plurality referred to the angels, not to their Creator.

We begin to reach the secret of the Account of the Beginning when we extend Maimonides' line of thought about angels to the further biblical statement, "Male and female he created them" (Gen 1:27).

> Among the things on which you ought to reflect carefully is the fact that it mentions the creation of man in the *six days of the Beginning* and says: *Male and female created He them* [Gen 1:27]. It then concludes its account of the creation, saying: *And the heaven and the earth were finished, and all the host of them* [Gen 2:1]. Then it makes a new start regarding the creation of Eve from Adam. (*Guide* II:30; p. 355)

Maimonides treated Genesis 1:27 as a chapter heading. He mentioned it, but said nothing more in its regard. The literary position of the reference, immediately prior to the conclusion of Maimonides' passage, indicated its importance. Understanding its secret concluded the Account of Creation.

What was Maimonides leaving unsaid? Let us consider the sexuality of angels before attempting to understand what Maimonides intimated by associating their sexuality with Eve's creation from Adam. Maimonides' phrasing in the previous passage was ambiguous. It can support the sort of literal reading that Leo Strauss made:

> That passage suggests to the vulgar mind more strongly than any other biblical passage that God is corporeal in the crudest sense. . . . Literally understood, that saying might be thought to mean that man is the image of God because he is bisexual or that the Godhead contains a male and a female element that generate 'children of God' and the like. Maimonides

does not discuss the implication which was stated, for it is one of the secrets of the Torah and we are only at the beginning of our training. (Strauss, 1963, pp. xxvi, xxviii)

Strauss rightly recognized the concern of Maimonides' secrets with sexuality, but he failed to appreciate that Maimonides insisted on the incorporeality of God both openly and secretly. Maimonides did not secretly attribute sexual dualism to the Creator. By making his reader go to the trouble of deciphering Genesis 1:1 and 1:26 as references to angels, Maimonides made it possible for them to interpret Genesis 1:27 "of their own understanding" as a further reference to angels. Maimonides intimated that the sexual dualism of human beings reflected a dualism that pertained to angels.

Holding fast to Maimonides' definition that "the angels . . . are forms without substance," let us examine his view that sexual metaphors are appropriate to form and matter.

> Matter . . . is always receptive and passive, if one considers its essence, and is not active except by accident. Form, on the other hand, is in its essence always active, as has been made clear in the books on natural science, and is passive only by accident. (*Guide* I:28; p. 61)

In keeping with matter's receptivity to form, Maimonides remarked that Plato and his predecessors "concealed what they said about the first principles and presented it in riddles . . . [and] designated Matter as the female and Form as the male" (*Guide* I:17; p. 43). Importantly, Maimonides' citation misrepresented Plato's position in a manner that suited Maimonides. In the *Timaeus* 51A, Plato had described the Receptacle, which was sometimes understood to signify Matter, as a Mother (Pines, 1963, p. lxxvi). Maimonides differed from Plato in treating the sexuality of matter as a metaphor. He allowed that matter was receptive, hence figuratively female, but he did not credit matter with the generative function of a mother.

Further developing the sexual metaphor, Maimonides explained the narrative of Proverbs 7:6–21 as an allegory of the sublunar realm of matter and form. The story of the "married harlot" told of the seduction of a young man by a woman whose husband had gone off on a trip. Maimonides pointed out the significance of this story as a moral lesson, but he also stated that Solomon "likens matter . . . to a harlot who is also a married woman. In fact his entire book is based on this allegory." Maimonides fulfilled his promise, reverting to the metaphor of the married harlot much later in the *Guide*, directly after completing his exposition of the chariot vision of Ezekiel. He wrote:

> How extraordinary is what Solomon said in his wisdom when likening matter to a married harlot, for matter is in no way found without form and is consequently always like a married woman who is never separated from a man and is never free. However, notwithstanding her being a married

> woman, she never ceases to seek for another man to substitute for her husband, and she deceives and draws him on in every way until he obtains from her what her husband used to obtain. This is the state of matter. For whatever form is found in it, does but prepare it to receive another form. And it does not cease to move with a view to putting off that form that actually is in it and to obtaining another form; and the self-same state obtains after that all passing-away and corruption or deficiency are due solely to matter. (*Guide* III:8; pp. 430–431)

We suggest that the sexual imagery that Maimonides employed metaphorically in reference to the relations of form and matter was to be interpolated in reading his remarks concerning the creation of Adam and Eve. Here we reach a portion of the Account of the Beginning where Maimonides hinted at, but did not explain, his intention.

He began by referring to a narrative in Genesis Rabbah VII that concerned the creation of Eve:

> Adam and Eve were created together, having their backs joined, and ... this being was divided and one half of it, namely, Eve, taken and brought up to [Adam].... It also confirms their union by saying: And shall cleave unto his wife, and they shall be one flesh [Gen 2:24]. (*Guide* II:30; pp. 355–356)

Maimonides here made no interpretation of the separation of Eve from Adam. He offered no chapter headings. He drew the reader's attention to selected aspects of the biblical story, but he provided no clues regarding their meaning. We are left on our own to attempt a figurative interpretation in keeping with what we know of Maimonides' thinking. The story of Adam and Eve in Genesis 2:4–3:24 conceals a secret of the law. It is not to be read literally, but is instead to be deciphered. How did Maimonides understand it?

Maimonides provided a hint when he mentioned a rabbinic narrative that linked the separation of Eve from Adam with the separation of the waters above and below the firmament on the second day of creation. According to the sages, when God created the world, He did not complete the work of the second day of creation. Maimonides explained:

> It is not said regarding the work of the second day that it was good.... The best [explanation] ... about this is their saying that this was so because the work of the water had not been terminated. To my mind also the reason in question is very clear.... But there is something hidden, as you will see, with regard to the firmament and the thing above it, which is called water.... If ... the matter is considered according to its inner meaning and to what was truly intended, it is most hidden ... it was necessary for it to be one of the concealed secrets so that the vulgar should not know it. (*Guide* II:30; p. 353)

Maimonides pointed out that the declaration "that it was good" is not to be found in the scriptural account of creation on the second day. Maimonides accepted the explanation, given by some of the sages, that the absence of the evaluation "that it was good," which was said of the first, third, fourth and fifth days (Gen 1:4, 9, 12, 18, 21, 25), meant that the work of the second day was not completed on that day, and so could not be evaluated. Maimonides also asserted that he had a clear concept in mind, and he implied that he was being obscure deliberately. The topic was evidently restricted. He provided a hint, however, when he said that it concerned "the firmament and the thing above it, which is called water."

Maimonides expected his reader to be aware that the rabbinic midrash went on to remark that God pronounced the sixth day, when Adam and Eve were created, as "very good" (Gen 1:31). This phrasing led the sages to conclude that the creation of Adam and Eve coincided with the completion of the creation of the waters and the firmament. How may this midrash be interpreted as a clue to a secret of the law?

In his discussion of Genesis 1:7, where the waters divide above and below the firmament, Maimonides designated the original water as "a certain common matter, which it names water" (*Guide* II:30; p. 352). Its identification as water was nominal. "That which is above the firmament is called water in name only and ... it is not the specific water known to us" (*Guide* II:30; p. 353). Maimonides elsewhere referred in passing to "the rational faculty—I mean the intellect, which is the hylic intellect" (*Guide* I:72; p. 190). This phrasing contains the unique reference in the *Guide* to the Platonic concept of *hylé* or primal matter. Like the Neoplatonic concept of overflow, it should be treated in an Aristotelian sense as a metaphor. Its use indicated that, for Maimonides, common matter was intelligible, a theoretical postulate rather than a physical quiddity. It was, in short, an angelic form.

With the understanding that the common water was "hylic" intellect, that is, angelic intelligence in general, we may examine Maimonides' discussion of the division of the waters.

> Among the things you ought to know is that the words, *And He divided between the waters* [Gen 1:7], and so on, do not refer merely to a division in place in which one part is located above and one below, while both have the same nature. The correct interpretation of these words is that He made a natural division between both of them—I mean with regard to their form—making one part, that which He first calls water, into one particular thing by means of the natural form with which He invested it, and bestowing upon the other part a different form, that latter part being water proper. Hence it says: *And the gathering of the waters He called Seas* [Gen 1:10] In this way it makes it clear to you that first *water* of which it is said, *over the face of the waters*, is not the water that is in the seas. (*Guide* II:30; p. 352)

Given that the division was natural rather than spatial, and that part of it was accomplished "by means of the natural form with which He invested it," we may infer that Maimonides was hinting at a categorical distinction between intellect and form. The figurative references to "water proper ... the water that is in the seas" instantiated the further category, matter. Maimonides stated: "The firmament itself was produced from water; as [the sages] say: The middle group congealed" (*Guide* II:30; p. 352; citing Genesis Rabbah, IV). The rabbinical derivation of earth from water or, more precisely, the solid state of matter from its fluid state, served Maimonides as a means to hint at the concept of matter in general.

Maimonides did not indicate how he imagined that intellect divided into form and matter. His metaphoric use of the Neoplatonic concept of "overflow" allowed readers to interpolate a Neoplatonic process of emanation, but his own thinking was almost certainly a variant of strict Aristotelianism. His attribution of the seas to "a different form" suggests a possible line of reasoning. Although the divine creation of form, matter, and intelligence occurred simultaneously, the biblical narrative attributes a temporal sequence among them as a figurative representation of their logical relation to each other. The creation of the intelligible ideas of form and matter was part of the creation of angelic intelligences; the implementation of these ideas through the creation of formed matter was logically secondary, although temporally simultaneous.

Let us now consider the story of Eve's separation from Adam, whose mention Maimonides' juxtaposed with the story of the separation of the waters and congealing of the firmament. The structural parallels between the two biblical narratives suggests that Maimonides regarded both stories as parables that shared the same meaning. For Maimonides, both biblical narratives concerned the common matter of intellect that underlies both forms and matter. If this construction of Maimonides' intention is correct, the subtext of the story of the creation of Eve from Adam's rib tells us nothing that we do not already know. It is a variant way of conveying the same subtext as the parable of the division of the waters and the congealing of the firmament. What was novel in the story of Adam and Eve was the *manifest* content of the parable: the sexualization of form and matter as Adam and Eve, and the phallic motif of Adam's rib. Was it the manifest sexuality of the narrative, and not its philosophically coherent subtext, that led Maimonides to surround its discussions with constraints?

Maimonides' discussion of Adam and Eve continued with explicit attention to the sexual content of the narrative through the remark that Scripture "confirms their union by saying: And he shall cleave unto his wife, and they shall be one flesh" (*Guide* II:30; p. 356). Maimonides implied that the union of form and matter was analogized to marriage and sexual union. Implicitly, the aspect of creation that was incomplete on the second day, but was completed on the sixth, was the union of form and matter that was analogized to sexual coitus and the conception of a child through whom "they shall be one flesh."

Maimonides confirmed that his meaning was sexual in the course of a discussion of the biblical penalty for Sabbath violation.

> Perhaps it has already become clear to you what is the cause of the Law's establishing the Sabbath so firmly and ordaining *death by stoning* for breaking it. The Master of the prophets has put people to death because of it. It comes third after the existence of the deity and the denial of dualism. (*Guide* II:31; p. 359)

The passage contains a riddle. In what sense does the Sabbath come third? Maimonides seems outwardly to be addressing priority or importance, but he is secretly intimating that the Sabbath comes third in a logical syllogism. If one affirms the existence of God, who is One, and one therefore denies dualism, what is one to make of the duality of the water and the firmament? Or the duality of Adam and Eve? Even though prophets expressed abstractions by using sexual metaphors, the vulgar would insist on thinking anthropomorphically and conclude that God created souls in a sexual manner. Further, they would presume a dualism, since two gods are necessary, a male and a female god, in order to create sexually and give birth to souls. Maimonides nevertheless stated that the figures were not to be understood as a pair of deities. Dualism was to be denied. The male and female figures were instead to be understood in a fashion consistent with the performance of marital obligations on the Sabbath.

Maimonides expressed the same secret of the Sabbath through yet another esoteric phrasing. Genesis 2:2 states, "And on the seventh day the *Elohim* finished that work that they had done, and the *Elohim* rested on the seventh." The corresponding phrasing in Exodus 3:17 employs two verbs, *shabbat vayyinaphash*. These terms are conventionally understood to mean "he rested and was refreshed." Maimonides stated, however, that the second verb was to be understood differently:

> As for the verb *vayyinaphash* [Exod 31:17], it is a passive form deriving from the word *nephesh* [*soul*]. Now we have already made clear the equivocality of the term *soul* and have explained that it may have the meaning of purpose and volition. Accordingly it means that His purpose was perfected and all His will realized. (*Guide* I:67; p. 162)

The biblical verb *vayyinaphash* means "he was refreshed"; but, by deriving it from *nephesh*, "soul," Maimonides implied a reading that should be translated "he ensouled." Interestingly, the reading that Maimonides only intimated was openly asserted in Paragraph 39 of the *Bahir*:

> as it is written, "And on the seventh day, He rested [*shabbat*] and he ensouled" [Exod 31:17]." What is "and he ensouled"? It teaches that the

Sabbath day sustains all souls, as it is said, "[Sabbath] and he ensouled."
Another matter. It teaches that all souls are from there, as it is said, "and
He ensouled."

Scholem (1987, p. 155) remarked that the *Bahir* treated the verb as though it meant "there was soul-making." Maimonides read the word the same way. For Maimonides, the creation of a soul upon the sexual conception of a child on Sabbath completed God's work of creation. "His purpose was perfected and all His will realized."

Maimonides explained the Account of the Beginning as a series of allegories that pertained to the relations of incorporeal ideas and their activities as forms when conjoined with matter. At the same time, Maimonides' secrecy regarding the Account of the Beginning provided his readers with need to engage in the type of exegesis that Maimonides thought appropriate to dreams and visions of prophecy. The Account of the Beginning contained a dualistic doctrine, but the dyad was angelic rather than divine. There were not "two authorities," God and Metatron. Aher had had no valid reason for his apostasy. The *heiros gamos*—sacred marriage—of form and matter was celebrated both in the story of Adam and Eve and in the Talmud's requirement of the commemoration of their consummation of the work of creation through Jews' performance of marital union on Friday evenings. Knowledge of the secret dualism did not mitigate the danger of the material. Perplexity was still possible.

What resolved perplexity over the Account of the Beginning was Maimonides' reading of the Sabbath as third. Though all existence could be traced to a marriage of form and matter, existence could not be made to account for the conception of a child. The form and matter that made up the child's body had prior existence in the parents' bodies as seed and nutriments—we would today correct medieval biology and say sperm and ovum. However, the form of the child was an entirely new and unprecedented creation—a soul unique to the child and newly created for each child—whose synergistic coming-into-being attests to a Creator who demonstrably transcends form and matter when engaged in the creation of souls. The secret of the Sabbath proved that dualism was created. It concerned form and matter. God was unequivocably one. The Account of the Beginning was a question of physics. It did not reach to the topic of metaphysics.

MAIMONIDES ON SEXUALITY

Because modern readers often confuse sexual imagery with prurience, it is important to appreciate the mood of Maimonides' interest in sexual imagery. Maimonides used sexual metaphors freely in contexts other than scriptural exegesis. In a letter that he wrote to Rabbi Jonathan ha-Kohen of Lunel, he used a series of sexual metaphors to describe his relationship with the law.

Before I had been formed in the belly, the Law knew me, and before I came forth out of the womb, she had sanctified me for her study ... and dedicated me to disperse her fountains abroad.... She is my loving hind, the bride of my youth, whose love ravished me ... since I was a young man.... Many strange and foreign women have nevertheless become rival wives to her: Moabites, Edomites, Sidonites, Hittites. The Lord ... knows that I took these other women in the first instance only in order to serve as perfumers, cooks and bakers for her (my true bride), and to show the peoples and the princes her beauty, for she is exceedingly fair to behold. Still, her conjugal rights were diminished ... because my heart was divided into many parts. (Twersky, 1980, p. 40)

Maimonides' student, Joseph ibn Aknin, used sexual imagery allegorically in a letter to Maimonides that expressed his dissatisfaction with the presentation of Aristotelian philosophy by the Muslim philosopher Ibn Rushd.

Some time ago your beloved daughter, the beautiful and charming Kimah, obtained grace and favour in my sight, and I betrothed her unto me in faithfulness, and married her in accordance with the Law, in the presence of two trustworthy witnesses, viz., our master Abd-allah and Ibn Rushd. But she soon became faithless to me; she could not have found fault with me, yet she left me and departed from my tent. She does no longer let me behold her pleasant countenance or hear her melodious voice. You have not rebuked or punished her, and perhaps you are the cause of this misconduct. Now, 'send the wife back to the man, for he is'—or might become—'a prophet; he will pray for you that you might live,' and also for her that she may be firm and steadfast. If, however, you do not send her back, the Lord will punish you. Therefore seek peace and pursue it; listen to what our Sages said: 'Blessed be he who restores to the owner his lost property'; for this blessing applies in a higher degree to him who restores a man his virtuous wife, the crown of her husband. (Friedländer, 1904, pp. xxiv–xxv)

The ease that these private letters display in their recourse to sexual images indicates the milieu in which Maimonides composed the *Guide*. Sexual images were commonplace, explicit, and unremarkable. Some were intended metaphorically, and others allegorically, in both cases as means to express ideas that were not at all sexual. As expressions of abstract concepts, they were innocuous, appropriate, and effective. Given Maimonides' comfort with sexual images, we may appreciate his sensitivity to their occurrence in biblical and rabbinic texts.

At the same time, sexual images directly engage the appetitive faculty and play a notable role in psychopathology. For Maimonides, the appetitive faculty was the seat of emotions, sexual desire among them. Sexuality was not a theme that a physician of the soul could responsibly avoid. One of the difficulties that

Maimonides had in writing the *Guide* was to expound on the meaning of the sexual representation of God by the prophets in Scripture without violating the Mishnah's restrictions on the discussion of the Account of the Beginning. He wanted to resolve perplexity by teaching the inner meaning or latent content of the imagery, but the sexual modesty of the sages obliged him to do so without describing the outer meaning, the manifest content. Rabbinical tradition had risked both the idolatry of corporeal conceptions of God and the promotion of perplexity, along with the consequent moral misconduct, rather than engage in immodest speech regarding sexuality. Maimonides abided by the modesty of the tradition, but he struggled with it. His writing was consequently a kind of duplex. It had to refer to the sexual in the representation of God on the one hand, and it had to negate the sexuality on the other. In keeping with the Mishnah, it could not discuss the sexuality publicly. It could be explicit, however, in its discussions of the allegorical meanings of sexual images that it could not openly describe. These constraints explain much that is obscure in the *Guide*. Maimonides used all manner of occasion to intimate the sexual aspects of visions of prophecy, but he spoke openly and in detail only of the inner, nonsexual meaning of the imagery—imagery that he declined to describe!

THE ACCOUNT OF THE CHARIOT

By *Maaseh Merkabah*, the Account of the Chariot, the Talmud referred to the vision of the glory of God enthroned on the chariot that begins the book of the prophet Ezekiel. The Talmud forbade its explanation to "one, save that he were wise, and understanding of his own knowledge." The Talmud also related that when the sages decided which books to include in the Bible, they debated excluding Ezekiel from the canon. One rabbinical authority, Hanahiah ben Hezekiah, asserted that the words in Ezekiel contradicted the words of the law in connection with *hashmal* (*BT*, Hagigah 13a). The consensus included the text in the Bible, but considered its understanding to be potentially dangerous. The Talmud told of a child who was reading the Book of Ezekiel in his teacher's house when he grasped the meaning of the word *hashmal*. A fire burst out of the word and consumed him (*BT*, Hagigah 13a).

Maimonides treated the Account of the Chariot as a narrative whose interpretation divided it into three portions: "there were . . . three apprehensions, that of the *wheels*, that of the *living creatures*, and that of the *man*, who is above the *living creatures*" (*Guide* III:5; p. 425). The three visions occurred in the text of Ezekiel in the sequence: living creatures, wheels, and man. Maimonides recorded a difference of opinion among the sages as to the extent of the secrecy of the first two visions.

> The *Sages of the Mishnah* . . . said that it is permissible to teach the first two apprehensions only, I mean the apprehension of the *living creatures* and

that of the *wheels*, whereas only *the chapter headings* may be taught with regard to the third apprehension, that of the *hashmal* and of what is connected with it. However, *our holy Rabbi* believes that all three apprehensions are called the *Account of the Chariot* and that with respect to none of them may anything other than *the chapter headings* be taught. . . . There is also a difference of opinion among the Sages about whether it is permissible for it [the third vision] to be alluded to in any way through teaching— I mean to say through the transmission of the chapter headings—or whether it is not permissible in any way that an allusion be made to the teachings of this third apprehension, though it be only through the chapter headings; but he who is a wise man will understand in virtue of his own intelligence. (*Guide* III:5; pp. 425–426)

In keeping with the more stringent standards, Maimonides provided chapter headings for the first two visions and left his readers entirely on their own to interpret the third vision. Let us proceed directly to the third vision.

Forbidden to provide chapter headings with regard to Ezekiel's third vision, Maimonides indicated his interpretation of the vision by drawing attention to specific features of the vision's description in Scripture. For example, he contented himself with a single enigmatic statement about the enthroned man.

The likeness of a man that was on the throne and that was divided, is not a parable referring to Him, who is exalted above all composition, but to a created thing. Accordingly the *prophet* himself says: *This was the appearance of the likeness of the glory of the Lord* [Ezek 1:28]. Now *the glory of the Lord* is not the Lord. (*Guide* III:7; p. 430)

Most of Maimonides' remarks concerning the figurative portion of the third vision pertained to the image of the throne. It too was a created thing: "As for the *throne of glory* belonging to the created things, the Sages state this expressly, but in a strange manner. For they say that it was created before the creation of the world" (*Guide* II:26; p. 331).

In his lexicon at the beginning of the *Guide*, Maimonides explained that the concept of the throne had, through metonymy, become synonymous with the concepts of light and glory.

Throne [*kisse*]. Originally the meaning given to this word in the Hebrew language was that it was the term designating the throne . . . the throne became an existent thing indicative of the grandeur, the high rank, and the great dignity of him who was thought worthy of it, the *Sanctuary* was called a *throne*, because of its indicating the grandeur of Him who manifested Himself therein and let His light and glory descend upon it. Thus Scripture says: *Thou throne of glory, on high from the beginnings* [Jer 17:12], and so on. (*Guide* I:9; p. 34)

According to Maimonides, people spoke of the throne when they meant the glory. In a similar fashion, people today may speak of the White House when meaning the American president.

In a further passage that identified the throne with the glory, Maimonides cited Onqelos for identifying both images with the concept of the *Shekhinah*, "Presence" or "Indwelling."

> Now as for the dictum: *And there was under his feet, as it were, a work of the whiteness of sapphire stone* [Exod 24:10]. The interpretation of Onqelos is, as you know, as follows. He considers that the third person suffix, "his," in the words *his feet* refers to God's *throne*; accordingly he translates: *And under the throne of His glory.* . . . [Onqelos] referred the term *throne* to *His glory*, I mean to the *Indwelling*, which is a created light. Similarly he renders in his *translation* the verse: *For my hand upon the throne of the Lord* [Exod 17:16], as: *From God whose Indwelling is on the throne of glory.* And in a similar way you find on the tongue of the whole nation the words: *the throne of glory.* (*Guide* I:28; p. 60)

Maimonides' description of the Presence as "a created light" referred presumably to the light that God created on the first day of creation (Gen 1:3) in advance of the light cast by the celestial bodies that God created on the fourth day. The created light was a figurative image whose meaning Maimonides mentioned in passing in the course of a discussion of the term "glory."

> *The glory of Y.H.V.H.* is sometimes intended to signify the created light that God causes to descend in a particular place in order to confer honor upon it in a miraculous way: *And the glory of Y.H.V.H. abode upon Mount Sinai, and [the cloud] covered it* [Exod 24:16], and so on. (*Guide* I:64; p. 156)

When the term "glory" referred to the created light, it signified the Presence "that God causes to descend in a particular place in order to confer honor upon it in a miraculous way." Maimonides elsewhere expressed the concept more fully. "*In Thy light do we see light* [Ps 36:10] has the . . . meaning . . . that through the overflow of the intellect that has overflowed from Thee, we intellectually cognize, and consequently we receive correct guidance, we draw inferences, and we apprehend the intellect" (*Guide* II:12; p. 280). Interpreting "His Indwelling—I mean His created light" (*Guide* I:25; p. 55) as a figurative reference to an angelic intelligence, we may understand the Presence as an intellectual process that manifests in a physical location in the universe—"a particular place"—and, by doing so, serves "to confer honor upon it" by imparting a numinous quality to it. The experience of a natural phenomenon as numinous or holy was "miraculous," but in a fashion that was consistent with the general miracle of nature. There is no indication that Maimonides referred to a supernatural intervention within nature. It was a question of perceiving the inherent and natural holiness of a created thing.

Maimonides stated that the vision of the divided man was "the ultimate perception" that Ezekiel attained. "The apprehension of the form of the divided man of which it is said: *From the appearance of his loins and upward, and from the appearance of his loins and downward* [Ezek 1:27]—is the ultimate perception and the highest of all" (*Guide* III:5; p. 426). If we have understood Maimonides correctly up to this point, we may infer that "the ultimate perception and the highest of all" that was represented figuratively by the enthroned man was no other than the Active Intellect. The division of the man in two, like the distinction between the man and the throne, had the same allegorical significance as the division of the primal waters and the separation of Eve from Adam in the Account of the Beginning. The paired ideas of matter and form were products of the one Intellect.

Maimonides asserted, however, that the Account of the Chariot discussed metaphysics. What secret of the law did he attribute to the text of Ezekiel? In commenting on the verse, "And upon the likeness of the throne was a likeness as the appearance of a man" (Ezek 1:26), Maimonides cited a rabbinical saying.

> The comprehensive dictum to which we have alluded is their dictum in *Bereshith Rabbah* [xxviii], which reads: *Great is the power of the prophets; for they liken a form to its creator. For it is said: And upon the likeness of the throne was a likeness as the appearance of a man.* They have thus made clear and manifest that all the forms apprehended by all the prophets in *the vision of prophecy* are created forms of which God is the Creator. And this is correct, for every imagined form is created. (*Guide* I:46; p. 103)

Maimonides then proceeded to compare the greatness of the enthroned glory with the case of a rabbi who performed the act of *halizah* alone and at night. Performing the *halizah* in this manner is outrageous. The *halizah* is a commanded public humiliation of a man who refuses to marry his childless brother's widow. A public ritual is performed in which she is to "loose his shoe from off his foot and spit in his face" before denouncing him before the community (Deut 25:9). Despite the outrageousness of the rabbi, circumventing the purpose of the law by observing it secretly and privately, another rabbi is said to have declared, "How great is his strength ... how great is his power!" Maimonides commented that it was characteristic of the rabbis to "speak in this way when they express appreciation of the greatness of something said or done, but whose appearance is shocking" (*Guide* I:46; p. 103). The comparison implied that Maimonides recognized both the outrageousness and the legitimacy of Ezekiel's recourse to the image of the enthroned glory. The association with *halizah* also intimates that the imagery is to be understood in some manner that is explicitly sexual. In this context, we may immediately read the citation from Ezekiel 1:26 as sexual double entendre. "And upon the likeness of a 'throne' was a likeness as the appearance of a man." If Ezekiel's circumspect description of the appearance of a man sitting on a throne was equivalent to a secret performance of *halizah*, what Ezekiel had avoided describing had been a vision of a man and a woman in sexual union.

Maimonides' implicit reading of Ezekiel's third vision was consistent with a passing remark in the Talmud. Rabbi Joshua and Rabbi Yosi the Priest were expounding the Account of the Chariot to each other when "the skies thickened with clouds and something like a rainbow appeared amidst the clouds, and ministering angels were gathering and coming to hear, like people who gather and come to see the merrymaking before a groom and bride" (*BT*, Hagigah, 14b). The comparison of the two angels with merrymakers at a wedding implied that the Account of the Chariot concerned a groom and a bride. The Talmudic narrative also implied that the two rabbis, whose meditations on Scripture induced visionary experiences of their own, themselves beheld imagery whose content was marital.

People do have dreams and visions in which they imagine people and other anthropomorphic beings engaged in sexual activities. Maimonides intimated that even a prophet such as Ezekiel might have such a vision. Considerations of modesty had led Ezekiel to employ euphemisms whose sexual double entendre would be lost on children but self-evident to sexually active adults. Ezekiel's example, in making the explicit sexuality of his vision a topic of public reticence and secrecy, stood as precedent for the sages, who permitted the text to be read but forbade its public discussion. The constraints of modesty surrounding human sexuality were responsible for the restrictions. There was nothing unnatural, scandalous, or in any sense objectionable about having such a vision, providing that its public discussion was modestly avoided and its explicit sexuality was privately interpreted as a metaphor. The sexuality of the manifest content of the vision was problematic, however, because it aroused the affective faculty and might lead to perplexity and immoral conduct. Recourse to esotericism was appropriate because the metaphoric meaning could not be explained without reference to the explicitly sexual manifest imagery that expressed it.

Maimonides interpreted related scriptural passages in a consistent manner. Discussing the vision of God's throne that Moses, Aaron, and the elders of Israel saw in Exodus 24:10, Maimonides remarked on its translation into Aramaic by Onqelos. Summarizing Onqelos' interpretation, Maimonides stated: "The final end of the matter consists in the rejection of the doctrine of the corporeality of God. He does not explain to us what they apprehended and what is intended by this parable" (*Guide* I:28; p. 60). In noting Onqelos' procedure, Maimonides intimated that the Account of the Chariot was to be approached in a similar fashion. The imagery of Ezekiel's vision was not to be stated explicitly, but its correct interpretation depended on "the rejection of the doctrine of the corporeality of God."

Because Maimonides followed rabbinical tradition in crediting Moses with the authorship of the Pentateuch, he allowed that the sexual imagery in the Pentateuch might be taken to indicate that Moses too had visions whose imagery was sexual.

> You may believe that the great station attained by [Moses] was indubitably, in its entirety, a vision of prophecy . . . [and] that this ocular apprehension also occurred in the vision of prophecy as is stated with respect to *Abraham:* "*Behold a smoking furnace and a flaming torch that passed.*" (*Guide* I:21; p. 51; citing Gen 15:17)

By truncating the quotation from Genesis 15:17, Maimonides emphasized its sexual allusions. The smoking furnace and the flaming torch were euphemisms for female and male genitalia.

Continuing to make our way without the benefit of chapter headings, we may ask what was at stake for Maimonides in the sexuality that he inferred in the Account of the Chariot. Unlike the sexual concerns of the *Ayarot* and the gender issues in the Account of Creation, the presence of sexuality in the texts of Ezekiel 1 and 8:1–4 was not at all obvious. Most readers of the Bible never imagine—indeed, may reject as far-fetched and mistaken—any reading of sexual double entendre into scriptural accounts of the enthroned glory. Are we to believe that Maimonides and, according to him, the sages agreed with both the medieval kabbalah and psychoanalysis in reading sexuality into these passages? What was there about the Account of the Chariot that persuaded a critically minded rationalist like Maimonides that these passages had necessarily to be read in a sexual way?

Once the reader formulates the question, an answer may be discovered in explicit statements within the *Guide*. Maimonides expounded the first two visions that comprise the Account of the Chariot as a cosmology, but much earlier in the *Guide* he twice mentioned briefly that his cosmology was simultaneously an anthropology.

> Know that it was not because of all that we have mentioned in comparing the world as a whole to a human individual that it has been said about man that he is a small world. . . . This is because of that which is a proprium of man only, namely, the rational faculty—I mean the intellect, which is . . . something that is not to be found in any of the species of living beings other than man. (*Guide* I:72; p. 190; see also pp. 191–192)

Rabbinical teachings endorsed the late antique idea of the human being as a microcosm. The Talmud stated: "He who destroys one soul in Israel is as if he had destroyed the whole world" (*BT*, Sanhedrin, 37). Maimonides neither cited nor paraphrased the sages on this point. He simply affirmed the concept of the "little world" and went on to make his point about the position of reason. We may treat the passages' unexplained relevance to the main concerns of the *Guide* as instances of Maimonides refraining from even so little as a chapter heading.

The concept of the human microcosm can signify that the physical, chemical, and organic processes in the human being are the same processes that operate throughout the universe. It can be and for Maimonides was an exclusively scientific concept. It was also something more. Because Maimonides regarded Ezekiel's vision as a cosmology that was analogous to an anthropology, his discussion collapsed in a direction that could only be regarded as sexual. What was only allegorically sexual about the cosmos was literally sexual as it applied to the microcosm, because human beings are sexual creatures. Shortly before Maimonides likened Ezekiel 1:26 to a secret performance of *halizah*, he openly asserted that "we have no intellectual cognition of our bringing somebody other than us to existence except through *mubashara* [sexual intercourse]" (*Guide* I:46; p. 99). Just as angels cannot be imagined without metaphors that are corporeal, so the divine creation of a human being, the coming into being of a person, cannot be conceptualized without metaphors that are procreative and coital.

Elsewhere, in the course of a discussion of creation out of nothing, Maimonides made the same point obliquely by using the example of sexual conception to illustrate a subsidiary concept.

> In the case of everything . . . which is generated after not having existed . . . the nature of that particular thing after it has attained its final state . . . is different from its nature when it is being generated and is beginning to pass from potentiality to actuality. . . . For example, the nature of the feminine seed . . . is different from the nature of this seed as it exists in the state of pregnancy after it has encountered the masculine sperm. (*Guide* II:17; p. 294)

The inner meaning of the coital symbolism of the Account of the Chariot pertained, then, not to the human role in bringing a child into being, but to God's role in doing so. God's creation of a child is not a sexual act, but the imaginative faculty resorts to sexual imagery in order to portray divine creation in a vision of prophecy. Creation out of nothing is something that the human mind cannot grasp as it does other things. How can one represent creation out of nothing? There are various conditions in life in which the idea of creation out of nothing comes to our attention. It especially comes when we watch how a child comes into being and we consider that nothing existed before; it also occurs when someone whom we love dies and we have to be reconciled to an existence in which that person has returned to nothing. The creation out of nothing cannot be represented in a normal and rational manner. What the mind can do, however, is grasp it through a metaphor, the metaphor of sexuality, whereby human beings act to bring other human beings into existence.

Maimonides' theory of metaphor anticipated the contemporary understanding. The philosopher Suzanne K. Langer (1957) remarked that abstract concepts are often first attained in mythic modes of thought, that is, mental images, and only secondarily replaced by discursive thought, expressed in verbal abstractions. Historians of science established that scientific discoveries are often attained in the form of metaphors that may or may not be revised to become analogs, heurisms, and models (Barbour, 1974; Hesse, 1970; Leary, 1990; Leatherdale, 1974; MacCormac, 1976). The metaphors, analogs, or models are not limited to single images or symbols, but involve a capacity for "logical analogy" (Langer, 1957) or "imaginative rationality" (Lakoff & Johnson, 1980, p. 193). These discussions of the place of metaphor in scientific discovery were developed into a general theory of metaphor by George Lakoff and Mark Johnson (1980, 1999), a philosopher and a literary scholar, who argued that an enormous part of everyone's thought consists of metaphors that have their basis in bodily experiences. Metaphor, in this sense of the term, is not a literary device but a procedure of thought, a relation that some thoughts have to other thoughts. Our bodily experiences furnish a basic store of mental images that are used in two ways: literally, as concrete ideas that concern the body and its activities, and metaphorically, as ways of conceptualizing abstractions. Perceptible phenomena can be thought about and discussed nonmetaphorically, but metaphor is a sine qua non for abstract thought (Lakoff, 1993, p. 205; Thomas, 1969, pp. 25, 31–32). Time, life, causation, and many other realities, or aspects of them, cannot be conceptualized without the use of metaphor.

Maimonides' appreciation that some abstract concepts can be expressed only in metaphor had enormous implications for theology. It radically altered Maimonides' concept of imagination. Because unenlightened approaches to mental images resulted in idolatry, the sages had limited access to the Account of the Beginning and the Account of the Chariot. Continuing their policy, Maimonides explicitly condemned *Sefer Shiur Komah*, which discusses the features and size of the divine body, but he otherwise avoided mentioning the very existence of esoteric visionary literature, even though it included texts that were titled *Beraita de-Ma'aseh Bereshit* and *Ma'aseh Merkabah* (Idel, 1990, p. 34). At the same time, Maimonides' theory of metaphor facilitated novel options. Idolatry was not integral to images, but had instead to do with ways that images were sometimes treated. An image that was idolatrous when treated concretely or literally might be no less than necessary to the metaphoric expression of theological truth. The aniconic tradition that stems from the Second Commandment did not pertain to metaphors. Although the unenlightened were best to avoid imagery in general, the philosophically learned could safely and lawfully make esoteric use of mental images once they were devoted to a negative theology that necessitated the treatment of images as metaphors.

Maimonides' concern to convey the secret of the law that he was not permitted to explain except to someone "wise, and ... understanding of his own knowledge" led him to disperse the esoteric teaching in a variety of manners throughout the Guide. The idea that childbearing has metaphoric use in reference to the divine act of creation may also be detected, for example, in Maimonides' discussion of the term *yalod*, "to bear children."

> *To bear children* [*yalod*].... Now none of the children of [Adam] born before [Seth] had been endowed with true human form, which is *the image of Adam and his likeness* referred to in the words: *the image of God and His likeness*. As for Seth, it was after [Adam] had instructed him and procured him understanding and after he had attained human perfection that it was said of him: *And [Adam] begot [a son] in his own likeness, after his image* [Gen 5:3]. (*Guide* I:7; pp. 32–33)

Scripture's use of the phrase "in his own likeness, after his image" provided Maimonides with an opportunity to place God's act of creating Adam in parallel with Adam's act of begetting Seth. Because the passage was concerned to explain the meanings of the term *yalod*, rather than the terms for image and likeness, Maimonides implied that the concept of childbearing had metaphoric use in reference to creation out of nothing.

Further duplicating his esoteric message, Maimonides went so far as to intimate that the emission of *hashmal* from the enthroned glory symbolized orgasm. He stated:

> Among the things to which your attention should be drawn belongs his dividing *the likeness of the man that was on the throne*; the upper part of the likeness being *as the color of hashmal* and the lower as the appearance of fire. They [the sages] have explained that the word *hashmal* is composed of two notions, *hash* and *mal* [*Hagigah*, 13a–b]; this means, of the notion of rapidity, indicated by *hash*, and of that of cutting, indicated by *mal*, the intention being to combine through a simile two separate notions regarding the two sides, above and below. (*Guide* III:7; pp. 429–430)

The esotericism of this passage was complex. The division of the man above and below into *hashmal* and fire was not further developed. Instead, Maimonides changed his topic to the division of the word *hashmal* into the two terms *hash* and *mal*. He suggested that the terms indicated a rapid cutting motion, that is, a sawing back and forth, that we are to appreciate as a simile that concerns "two separate notions regarding the two sides, above and below." Implicitly, the likeness of the man on the throne was engaged in coitus, sawing back and forth in his seat.

Maimonides provided what may be yet a further reference to procreation in the following remark about the opening verse of the book of Ezekiel.

> To the whole of things requiring investigation belongs the tying of the apprehension of the Chariot to a year, a month, and a day, and also to a place. This is something the significance of which ought to be sought. It should not be thought that this is a matter without significance. (*Guide* III:7; p. 428)

Maimonides instructed us to discover a meaning in the date and place of Ezekiel's visions. He was referring to precise information that Ezekiel provided. The time was the thirtieth year, the fourth month, and the fifth day of the month, and the place was by the river Kebar (Ezek 1:1). Maimonides provided no further explicit information concerning the first verse of Ezekiel. In conformance with the restrictions on teaching the Account of the Chariot, he supplied a literal "chapter heading" and left the reader "who is wise and . . . understanding of his own knowledge" to puzzle out the meaning on his own.

Let us apply the hermeneutics that Maimonides recommended for the interpretation of prophecy. Consider the date: year 30, month 4, and day 5. Everyone who is familiar with Hebrew knows that in Hebrew numbers may be written out in full as words or they may be represented in abbreviated fashion by letters. The number 30 is represented by the letter *lamed*, which sounds like an English L; the number 4 is represented by the Hebrew letter *dalet*, which sounds like a D; and the number 5 is represented by the letter *heh*, which sounds like an H. Because Hebrew is written without vowels, the three letters constitute the word *LeiDaH*, which in Hebrew means birth—as an act—or, perhaps better, birthing—as a process. Next consider the place: the river Kebar. The technique of rearranging the order of the word's letters allows us to entertain the word *KeRuB* as an anagram of the place name *KeBaR* in Ezekiel 1:1. *KeRuB* is the word "cherub," a word that Maimonides explained elsewhere in the *Guide* as "a human being of tender age" (*Guide* III:1; p. 417; citing *BT*, Hagigah, 13b). Putting together these hints, we are brought to understand how Maimonides might have the reader understand the meaning of the first verse of Ezekiel. When Ezekiel saw the figure of a man who was seated on the throne of glory and emitting radiation from his waist downward, what he saw was a vision of prophecy that portrayed both coitus and *leidah kerub*, the birthing of a human being of tender age, the creation of a human soul (see also Bakan, 1991, pp. 110–111).

Maimonides' position was that the prophet apprehended God's creating in sexual imagery because sexuality is useful for representing creation out of nothing (*Guide* I:46, p. 99). The method of negation was important to Maimonides because, in the method of negation, one strips away these corporeal features, allowing the concept of the creation out of nothing to be left as a residue. Speaking of a list of verbs in his lexicon in Book I, Maimonides says of them, "There is no doubt that when corporeality is abolished, all these predicates are likewise abolished" (*Guide* I:26, p. 57).

Maimonides' claim that "we have no intellectual cognition of our bringing somebody other than us to existence except through *mubashara* [sexual intercourse]" (*Guide* I:46; p. 99) explains the sense in which he equated the Account of the Chariot with metaphysics. *Arayot* concerned prohibited sexual acts. The Account of the Beginning concerned sexual images that allegorized ideas that could also be discussed in discursive language. The Account of the Chariot again concerned sexual images, but these were metaphors that expressed concepts that could not be expressed in any other manner. Interpretation of the Account of the Beginning required a prophet to be a philosopher, but interpretation of the Account of the Chariot exceeded the reach of philosophy alone. The rabbinic saying, "The Law speaks in the language of human beings," described a necessity of human thought and speech. Anthropomorphism cannot be avoided. Metaphysics cannot be conceptualized without recourse to anthropomorphism.

The Account of the Chariot illustrated Maimonides' claim that, through imagination, the mind can achieve concepts that cannot be grasped by the rational faculty alone. Philosophers were wrong when they limited actualization to the rational faculty. Prophecy depends on the additional actualization of the imagination. The Account of the Chariot used the imagery of coitus to express the concept of creation out of nothing, an intelligible that could not be conceptualized without recourse to metaphor. Prophets similarly used their imaginations to reach toward the essence of God. Maimonides distinguished between knowing the existence of God and reaching toward the essence of God. "There is an immense difference between guidance leading to a knowledge of the existence of a thing and an investigation of the true reality of the essence and substance of that thing" (*Guide* I:46; p. 97). Philosophers might be able to demonstrate the *existence* of God, but they could not reach beyond the existence toward the *essence* of God. Philosophy included studies and meditations on the sciences and the development of an argument from design. Prophecy began with apprehensions of the angelic forms and continued through the sense of God's presence. The sense of presence that Maimonides cultivated was an anthropomorphic imagination through which he communed with God, while God remained transcendent of his imagination.

CONCLUSIONS

The Talmud restricts the discussion of three biblical passages as "secrets of the law." The sexual misdemeanors of Leviticus 18 may be taught only to two students at a time; Genesis 1–3 to only one student at a time; and Ezekiel 1 only to a student who knows its meaning on his own. Maimonides asserted that the Account of the Beginning (Genesis 1–3) concerned physics, and the Account of the Chariot (Ezekiel 1) concerned metaphysics. When Maimonides' esoterically written discussions of the secrets are decoded, the Account of the

Beginning proves to use sexual dualism, including but not limited to Adam and Eve, as an allegorical way of discussing the relation of form and matter. The Account of the Chariot uses the motif of the sexual conception of a child as a metaphor for expressing creation out of nothing. These and analogous interpretations of sexual imagery, in both Scripture and the tale of the four who entered Paradise, were therapeutic interventions for dealing with appropriate cases of perplexity. The two interpretations enabled people to fulfill the commandments of belief in the existence and unity of God. Interpretation of the Account of the Beginning addressed the theological error of dualism, while interpretation of the Account of the Chariot pertained to the theological error of corporeal conceptions of God. These interpretations of the secrets of the law addressed imagination's seduction of the affective faculty by permitting inappropriate emotions to be detached from the biblical imagery and replaced with appropriate emotions.

SIX

Maimonides' Psychotherapy Client Population

MAIMONIDES' CURE OF SOULS began with the traditional philosophical equation of immorality, mental illness, and ignorance, but added to it the biblical concepts of free will, voluntarily induced ignorance (repression), and psychogenic paralysis and blindness (hysterical conversion symptoms). To cure perplexity, Maimonides prescribed rational mysticism, which began with a philosophic understanding of natural science, proceeded to a theological argument from design, and so arrived at a knowledge of God's existence and unity. Further meditations on the presence of God produced the love and fear of God. The fear sometimes took intense form as a guilty mystical death. The love sometimes developed into bliss or passionate love that coincided with an immediate sense of the *Shekhinah*. The tropes of death, resurrection, eternal life, and the world to come alluded to these rational mystical experiences.

Like any other religious practice, rational mysticism could precipitate perplexity regarding the understanding of religion. Perplexity ranged in intensity from mild puzzlement to acute spiritual crises. To counter perplexity, Maimonides recommended the rational interpretation of mental imagery through the treatment of the images as symbols. Drawing on traditional rabbinical secrets, Maimonides emphasized the abandonment of sexual images following their allegorical interpretations. However, he acknowledged that some sexual images were unavoidable, and he drew attention to their metaphoricity.

The client population that Maimonides treated by these means may be inferred from several pages that he devoted to close arguments against practices of asceticism that Jews were performing to "imitate the followers of other religions" (*Eight Chapters* iv; p. 64). Maimonides referred presumably to Muslim Sufis and, to a lesser extent, Christian solitaries and monks. He began by allowing that ascetic practices can usefully be employed as correctives of opposite tendencies.

> When, at times, some of the pious ones deviated to one extreme by fasting, keeping nightly vigils, refraining from eating meat or drinking wine, renouncing sexual intercourse, clothing themselves in woolen and hairy garments, dwelling in the mountains, and wandering about in the wilderness, they did so, partly as a means of restoring the health of their souls . . . and partly because of the immorality of the townspeople. (*Eight Chapters* iv; p. 62)

The pious were imitated, however, by others who imagined that extreme practices, which were permissible only as correctives of opposite extremes, were virtuous and permissible under all conditions.

> When the ignorant observed saintly men acting thus, not knowing their motives, they considered their deeds of themselves virtuous, and so, blindly imitating their acts, thinking thereby to become like them, chastised their bodies with all kinds of afflictions, imagining that they had acquired perfection and moral worth, and that by this means man would approach nearer to God, as if He hated the human body, and desired its destruction. It never dawned upon them, however, that these actions were bad and resulted in moral imperfection of the soul . . . those who are spiritually well, but have recourse to remedies, will undoubtedly become morally ill. (*Eight Chapters* iv; pp. 62–63)

Maimonides maintained that Jewish law required none of the excesses. "The perfect Law which leads us to perfection . . . recommends none of these things" (p. 63). Not only did the law "aim at man's following the path of moderation" (p. 63), but it explicitly prohibited excessive self-denial.

> The Law even warns us against these practices, if we interpret it according to what tradition tells us is the meaning of the passage concerning the Nazarite, "And he (the priest) shall make an atonement for him because he hath sinned against the soul." The Rabbis ask, "Against what soul has he sinned? Against his own soul, because he has deprived himself of wine." Is this not then a conclusion *a minori ad majus*? If one who deprives himself merely of wine must bring an atonement, how much more incumbent is it upon one who denies himself every enjoyment. (*Eight Chapters* iv; p. 63)

Further to support his argument, Maimonides cited a passage in the Palestinian Talmud where the rabbis "greatly blame those who bind themselves by oaths and vows, in consequence of which they are fettered like prisoners. The exact words they use are, 'Said Rabbi Iddai, in the name of Rabbi Isaac, "Dost thou not think that what the Law prohibits is sufficient for thee that thou must take upon thyself additional prohibitions?"'" (*Eight Chapters* iv; p. 66; citing JT, Nedarim, 9:1).

Maimonides' concern with the problem of asceticism provided him with an opportunity to address the more subtle, more frequent, and no less debilitating extremism of excessive fastidiousness. Maimonides insisted that the mean was to be achieved not fastidiously but flexibly, with frequent departures on both sides of the mean. "The saintly ones were not accustomed to cause their dispositions to maintain an exact balance between the two extremes, but deviated somewhat, by way of [caution and] restraint, now to the side of exaggeration, and now to that of deficiency" (*Eight Chapters* iv; p. 60). Not only were the saints untroubled about minor deviations from the mean, but they also undertook minor deviations as correctives of inadvertent lapses. "The moral man will constantly examine his characteristics, weigh his deeds, and daily investigate his psychic condition; and if, at any time, he finds his soul deviating to one extreme or another, he will immediately hasten to apply the proper remedy, and not suffer an evil aptitude to acquire strength . . . by the constant repetition of that evil action which it occasioned" (p. 67).

Like Maimonides' discussion of asceticism, his concern with fastidiousness in maintaining the mean addressed what he regarded as a moral defect. In the context of his recommendation of desensitization as a therapeutic technique, his treatment of scrupulosity as a sin implied an effort to address anxiety that distorted religious behavior into a compulsive caricature of wholesome religion. (For modern views of scrupulosity, see Mora, 1969; Weisner & Riffel, 1960).

Adherence to the mean was not a straightforward matter. Referring to the Sages' categories of the *tsaddik*, "righteous man," and the *hasid*, "saint" (Scholem, 1972), Maimonides explained that the emotional life of each character type differed. He began by presenting philosophers' perspective on the topic.

> Philosophers maintain that though the man of self-restraint performs moral and praiseworthy deeds, yet he does them desiring and craving all the while for immoral deeds, but, subduing his passions and actively fighting against a longing to do those things to which his faculties, his desires, and his psychic disposition excite him, succeeds, though with constant vexation and irritation, in acting morally. The saintly man, however, is guided in his actions by that to which his inclination and disposition prompt him, in consequence of which he acts morally from innate longing and desire. Philosophers unanimously agree that the latter is superior to, and more perfect than, the one who has to curb his passions, although they add that it is possible for such a one to equal the saintly man in many regards. (*Eight Chapters* vi; p. 75)

Maimonides did not approve of saintliness, but instead condemned it as an excess or extremism that was inconsistent with the mean enjoined by the law.

> Whoever is particularly scrupulous and deviates somewhat from the exact mean in disposition, in one direction or the other, is called a saint. For example, if one avoids haughtiness to the utmost extent and is exceedingly humble, he is termed a saint, and this is the standard of saintliness. If one only

departs from haughtiness as far as the mean, and is humble, he is called wise—and this is the standard of wisdom. And so with all other dispositions. The ancient saints trained their dispositions away from the exact mean towards the extremes; in regard to one disposition in one direction; in regard to another in the opposite direction. This was superrogation. We are bidden to walk in the middle paths which are the right and proper ways, as it is said, "and thou shalt walk in His ways" (Deut. 28:9). (*BK, Laws Relating to Moral Dispositions and to Ethical Conduct* I:5; pp. 47b–48a)

In keeping with his endorsement of self-restraint in observation of the mean, Maimonides noted that the Talmudic sages recognized the same emotional attitudes toward virtue as did philosophers and saints, but the sages evaluated the dispositions oppositely.

> The Rabbis ... consider him who desires iniquity, and craves for it (but does not do it) more praiseworthy and perfect than the one who feels no torment at refraining from evil; and they even go so far as to maintain that the more praiseworthy and perfect a man is, the greater is his desire to commit iniquity, and the more irritation does he feel at having to desist from it. (*Eight Chapters* vi; p. 76)

To account for the different points of view without discrediting philosophy, Maimonides noted that the philosophers were addressing the circumstances of "things which all people commonly agree are evils, such as the shedding of blood, theft, robbery, fraud, injury to one who has done no harm, ingratitude, contempt for parents" (p. 77). The sages also found themselves unconflicted regarding the desirability of *mishpatim* or rational laws, whose value was self-evident. The rabbinical teachings about conquering desire pertained instead to *huqqim* or ceremonial laws. "When ... the Rabbis maintain that he who overcomes his desire has more merit and a greater reward (than he who has no temptation), they say so only in reference to laws that are ceremonial prohibitions" (p. 77). It cannot be otherwise, because "were it not for the Law, they would not at all be considered transgressions" (p. 77).

These considerations imply that it is not possible to know whether an emotional attitude is appropriate or inappropriate without prior knowledge as to whether a particular commandment is a *mishpat* or a *hoq*, a rational law or a ceremonial one. The difference between the two is not always self-evident. As examples of ceremonial laws, Maimonides cited a rabbinical teaching:

> Man should not say, "I do not want to eat meat together with milk; I do not want to wear clothes made of a mixture of wool and linen; I do not want to enter into an incestuous marriage," but he should say, "I do indeed want to, yet I must not, for my father in Heaven has forbidden it." (*Eight Chapters* vi; p. 76)

The ceremonial character of the prohibitions of mixing meat and milk or wool and linen is self-evident, but Maimonides also counted incest as a ceremonial prohibition. He regarded the desire for incest as natural, and saw no guilt in the desire itself. "The Rabbis say that man should permit his soul to entertain the natural inclination for these things, but that the Law alone should restrain him from them" (p. 77). At the same time, long habituation in a ceremonial law could so train the emotions that they became unreliable guides toward truth. Many Jews find the prospect of eating meat along with milk to be revolting, wearing a mixture of wool and linen unaesthetic, and incest utterly abhorrent. It is not possible to know through introspection whether a desire is natural or educated, and whether a prohibition is ceremonial or rational. There could be no dispensing, in Maimonides' view, with an education in theology and law. The diseases of the soul affected the emotions of the appetitive faculty, but they might have their etiology in the perplexity to which the rational faculty was liable. "As regards the *rational* faculty . . . I maintain that observance and transgression may also originate in this faculty, in so far as one believes a true or a false doctrine, though no action which may be designated as an observance or a transgression results therefrom" (*Eight Chapters* II; p. 48).

Maimonides' approach to ceremonial laws was psychologically astute. A person who makes a conscious decision to refrain from a desired action can feel empowered, enjoy positive self-esteem, and be content, whereas a person who feels obliged to refrain from the same action may feel helpless, suffer negative self-regard, be unhappy, and engage in the rationalization that the action is not desirable. Maimonides recommended avoiding the rationalization, admitting the desire, mastering it, and enjoying the positive effects of feeling one's sense of agency.

In the *Mishneh Torah*, Maimonides discussed a further circumstance when therapy of the appetitive faculty was contingent on the health of the rational faculty. There were exceptions, he stated, to the doctrine of the mean. Pride and anger were to be avoided on all occasions.

> There are some dispositions in regard to which it is forbidden merely to keep to the middle path. They must be shunned to the extreme. Such a disposition is pride. The right way in this regard is not to be merely meek, but to be humble-minded and lowly of spirit to the utmost. . . . Anger too, is an exceedingly bad passion, and one should avoid it to the last extreme. One should train oneself not to be angry even for something that would justify anger. (*BK, Laws Relation to Moral Dispositions and to Ethical Conduct* II:3; p. 48b)

The knowledge that pride and anger were to be shunned did not arise from the appetitive faculty. Like the doctrine of the mean, knowledge of exceptions to it was an achievement of the rational faculty. The soul's health depended on the accord of the appetitive faculty with the rational faculty, whose knowledge depended in turn on its avoidance of perplexity.

Maimonides' concerns with asceticism and fastidiousness suggest that his client base consisted primarily of high-functioning neurotics. His cure of souls was ineffective with populations that were unable to achieve the love and fear of God. Not only children but adults of various temperaments are unable to complete the education necessary to perfect their moral and rational qualities.

> The moral virtues are a preparation for the rational virtues, it being impossible to achieve true, rational acts—I mean perfect rationality—unless it be by a man thoroughly trained with respect to his morals and endowed with the qualities of tranquillity and quiet . . . many people who have received from their first natural disposition a complexion of temperament with which perfection is in no way compatible. Such is the case of one who . . . cannot refrain from anger, even if he subjects his soul to a very stringent training. This is also the case of one . . . in whom the seminal vessels abundantly generate semen. For it is unlikely that such a man, even if he subject his soul to the most severe training, should be chaste. Similarly you can find among people rash and reckless folk. . . . Perfection can never be perceived in such people. And to make an effort for their benefit in this matter is pure ignorance on the part of him whose makes the effort. (*Guide* I:34; pp. 76–77)

Maimonides maintained that in addition to chronic, characterological vices of temperament, a variety of adverse moods might function as impediments to prophecy. Like every other bodily faculty, imagination functioned imperfectly whenever it "grows tired, is weakened, and is troubled. . . . Accordingly you will find that the prophecy of the prophets ceases when they are sad or angry, or in a mood similar to one of these two. You know their [the sages'] saying that *prophecy does not descend [during a mood of] sadness or of languor*" (*Guide* II:36; p. 370; citing *Chapters of Rabbi Eliezer*, xxxviii).

When Maimonides' comments on eligibility for his cure of souls are gathered together, they prove self-contradictory. A person had to possess moral virtues before rational virtues could be achieved, rational virtues before the love and fear of God could be achieved, and the love and fear of God before moral virtues could be achieved. Who then was able to be cured? The circularity of Maimonides' multiple claims suggests once again that his psychotherapy was only supportive. He offered a practice of meditation that was routinely psychohygienic. Because mystical experiences sometimes spontaneously accomplish conflict resolution, some people who engaged in Maimonides' rational mysticism may have found that their experiences were more deeply transformative. In other cases, the meditations may have produced heightened perplexity—including spiritual emergencies—that could be resolved through the type of theological interpretation that Maimonides provided. The likelihood of accidentally triggering conflict resolution may have been significantly increased by the self-selection of the client population that could successfully use Maimonides' methods in order to experience a sense of Presence. Because they had to be high functioning in order to achieve the desired meditative experiences, many were high-enough functioning to be able to profit from them. Maimonides had neither technique nor theory, however, by which to encourage mystical experiences to develop into conflict resolutions. It was a question of standing under a tree in the hope that lightning would strike. It was not sailing a kite into a storm cloud. Nevertheless, it was enough clinical success often enough for Maimonides to call it a cure of souls that justified his discussion of the secrets of the law.

Importantly, Maimonides made no claims regarding the possibility of characterological change. He subscribed to the majority rabbinical view that religion obligates a lifelong experience of conflict. The conflict pertained to humanity's natural endowment. The twin inclinations to do good and to do evil were both to be included when fulfilling the obligation to "love the Lord your God with all your heart and with all your soul and with all your might" (Deut 6:5). Fishbane (1994) explained:

> One possibility, urged by the sages, is for the true devotee to sublimate base instincts to divine ends. The clash of opposing *yetzers* [inclinations] would of course still remain, but the negative effects of the evil inclination would be overcome. Such a religious psychology strikingly softens the stern duality of two opposing *yetzers* and suggests the possibility of self-mastery. (p. 5)

Through self-mastery, the rabbis held, it was possible for any Jew to attain righteousness. It was necessary only to make oneself fulfill all of the observances of the law. Scholem (1991) explained:

> The righteous person, who seeks to meet the demands of the Torah, is caught in a never-ending struggle with his Evil Urge, which rebels against these demands; he must constantly wage battle with his own nature. But even this struggle between the Good Urge and the Evil Urge, in which he emerges as the "hero who conquers his own drive," never goes beyond the demands placed upon every human being. (p. 91)

From the late Second Temple period, Judaism had also known a second standard. Scholem (1991) characterized it as follows:

> The *Hasid* . . . the pious man is the extraordinary type . . . the *Hasid* carries out not only what is demanded of him, that which is good and just in the eyes of the Law, but goes beyond the letter of the Law. . . . He demands nothing of his fellow, and everything of himself. Even when carrying out a prescription of the Law, he acts with such radical exuberance and punctiliousness that an entire world is revealed to him in the fulfillment of a commandment, and an entire lifetime may be needed to carry out just one commandment properly. (p. 90)

Rabbinical sources provide no indication that anyone could voluntarily develop into a *hasid*; Maimonides followed the majority interpretation of *hasidut* as a practice of asceticism, of which rabbinical tradition disapproved (Fraade, 1987). It is clear, however, that a minority view conceptualized *hasidut* as an unconflicted life. In *Sifrei Deuteronomy* 32, a midrash suggested that the noun *lebabekha*, "your heart," be read as two words, *leb bakh*, "heart in you." Fishbane (1994) commented:

> In this way Moses is made to urge the people to love God . . ." with your whole heart . . . the explication . . . follows: "that your heart not be divided [*haluq*] toward God." From this it would seem that the instruction is to love God with a perfect service and not be conflicted. The divided self must be brought in line, for the One God demands all one's heart. (p. 5)

Reduction or resolution of mental conflict, leading to increased psychic integration, is the goal of successful psychoanalysis. Some rabbis knew that the phenomenon existed, but none knew how to produce it. Had Maimonides aimed to produce psychic integration, we may be assured that he would have cited the appropriate rabbinical precedents and made his position clear. As it was, he kept to the majority opinion, characterized *hasidut* as asceticism, and considered it inappropriate.

Maimonides' failure to associate *hasidut* with conflict resolution cautions against overvaluation of certain trends in his writings that point toward a liberal approach to Jewish ceremonialism. To account for the existence of *huqqim*, Maimonides proposed that God had resorted to a "ruse" that tolerated the devotions consequent of idolatrous beliefs, providing only that the customs and rites were devoted to God, rather than to idols.

> As at that time [of Moses] the way of life generally accepted and customary in the whole world and the universal service upon which we were brought up consisted in offering various species of living beings in the temples in which images were set up, in worshipping the latter, and in burning incense before them. . . . His wisdom, may He be exalted, and His gracious ruse, which is manifest in regard to all His creatures, did not require that He give us a Law prescribing the rejection, abandonment, and abolition of all these kinds of worship. For one could not then conceive the acceptance of [such a Law], considering the nature of man, which always likes that to which it is accustomed. . . . Therefore He, may He be exalted, suffered the above-mentioned kinds of worship to remain, but transferred them from created or imaginary and unreal things to His own name, may He be exalted, commanding us to practice them with regard to Him, may He be exalted. . . . Through this divine ruse it came about that the memory of *idolatry* was effaced and that the grandest and true foundation of our belief—namely, the existence and oneness of the deity—was firmly established,

while at the same time the souls had no feeling of repugnance and were not repelled because of the abolition of modes of worship to which they were accustomed and than which no other mode of worship was known at the time. (*Guide* III:32; pp. 526–527)

The natural world, according to Maimonides, demonstrated "the deity's wily graciousness and wisdom. . . . Similarly the deity made a wily and gracious arrangement with regard to . . . the living beings that suck. For when born, such individuals . . . cannot feed on dry food. Accordingly breasts were prepared for them so that they should produce milk. . . . Many things in our Law are due to something similar" (*Guide* III:32; p. 525).

Consistent with his view that *huqqim* have only a pedagogical function, Maimonides asserted that meditation was the only necessary act of worship.

> To come near to this true deity and to obtain His good will, nothing is required that is fraught with any hardship whatever, the only things needed being *love of Him and fear of Him* and nothing else. For these two are . . . the end of divine worship: *And now, Israel, what doth the Lord thy God require of thee, and so on.* (*Guide* III:29; p. 518)

Maimonides was severely criticized by his contemporaries for his assertion that the "laws concerning sacrifice and repairing to the temple were given only for the sake of the realization" of the fundamental principle of divine unity (*Guide* III:32; p. 530). Maimonides should, however, be taken at his word. Maimonides saw the commanded sacrificial rituals as providing a transition to a religion totally free of idolatry. The commanded sacrifices were concessionary to old ways of worship, which they constrained enough to allow the new forms of worship to emerge. The implicit end, which emerged historically with the fall of the Second Temple of Jerusalem in 70 C.E., was the removal of sacrifice as a mode of worship altogether. Possibly Maimonides saw a wholly rational Judaism, engaging in worship of the heart as its only obligatory act of worship, as a future hope for the messianic era. If so, such an intellectual apprehension would have been only a theoretic possibility for Maimonides. He never suspended his own observance of the *huqqim*, and his failure to understand *hasidut* as conflict resolution attests to the sincerity of his embrace of psychic conflict for both himself and his contemporaries.

Maimonides' cure of souls neither aimed at nor dependably produced psychotherapeutic changes of the type and extent that Freud established as the goal of psychoanalysis. At the same time, Maimonides took several decisive steps toward the invention of psychoanalysis. He placed the concept of psychotherapy on the Western intellectual agenda, replaced ignorance with resistance as the problem needing correction, and prioritized the interpretation of imaginations, including sexual images, as the vehicle of cure. In all, Maimonides expanded the theory and technique of moral reform to a point that verged on, but finally stopped short of the dismantling of resistance that Freud (1914b) made a defining feature of psychoanalysis. Maimonides' systematic interpretation of corporeal and sexual images as having incorporeal and nonsexual meanings neglected to address the persisting emotional sources of the imagery. He sought to keep imagination from contaminating the affective faculty, but he had no means beyond behaviorism to address the affective faculty directly. He offered a masterful supportive psychotherapy, but it was not an uncovering technique.

CONCLUSIONS

The client population for Maimonides' cure of souls may be inferred from his discussions of asceticism and fastidiousness as moral defects. He opposed aspirations to saintliness and advocated the moderation of the mean. He followed majority rabbinical tradition in recommending a life of inner conflict, in which natural desire ran counter to ceremonial obligation. His technique was a very sophisticated form of supportive psychotherapy, but it accomplished little more. He was able to detach inappropriate affects from mental imagery, but he had no program for addressing affective disorders themselves. He presumably had success chiefly with high-functioning neurotics.

SEVEN

Convergences of Maimonides and Freud

MAIMONIDES HAD ALL the pieces that were necessary to devise an uncovering psychotherapy, but he never assembled the pieces into an effective depth psychology. His interest in imagery ended with the insight, "The Law speaks in the language of human beings." He took no interest in the particular contents of the images that he regarded as allegories and metaphors. He brought people to awareness of their imaginations or "transferences onto God" (Merkur, 2009), but he did not interpret the content of the transferences beyond the generic ideas of anthropomorphism and wholesome love and fear. The reorganization of Maimonides' contributions into an uncovering technique awaited the innovations of Freud. Where Maimonides regarded imagery as symbolic expressions of concepts, Freud additionally shared the Romantic understanding that imagery always has a nonmetaphoric content that expresses a truth of its own (Thalmann, 1972). Because Freud analyzed what Maimonides discarded, Freud gained unprecedented access to the unconscious.

FREUD'S ACCESS TO MAIMONIDES

Freud was assuredly indebted to Maimonides through the general, nonspecific heritage of the kabbalah, Renaissance esotericism, and German Romanticism. The seed of psychoanalysis was contained in Maimonides' cure of souls. Hasidism may have been an important conduit of Maimonides' legacy. Freud's great-grandfather Ephraim and grandfather Shlomo were rabbis in the town of Tysmienica, in Galicia, where Freud's father Jacob was born in 1815. Jewish life in Tysmienica was then completely dominated by rabbinic and Hasidic leaders, and Jacob Freud was a well-educated product of its milieu (Aron, 1957, pp. 286–288). He would certainly have been personally acquainted with at least some of Maimonides' legal writings and possibly also with philosophical conceptions, such as the Active Intellect, that had been adopted by some sects of Hasidism (Nachman, 1990, pp. 253, 259–263; Nachman, 1993, p. 23; Nathan, 1973, p. 143). Jacob Freud abandoned the Hasidism of his upbringing by the time of his second marriage, in a Reform Jewish ceremony, to Malke Amalie Nathanson. He is nevertheless the person most likely to have conveyed to his son one of the few teachings that scholars feel secure in attributing to the historical Rabbi Israel Baal Shem Tov, the eighteenth century founder of Eastern European Hasidism. The Baal Shem Tov's disciple, Rabbi Jacob Joseph of Polonoye, wrote:

> I heard a convincing argument said in the name of my teacher [the Baal Shem Tov]. It concerned the strange thoughts (*mahshavot zarot*) which come to man in the midst of his prayer.... They appear in order to be repaired and elevated. The strange thought which appears one day is different from that of another day. [The Baal Shem Tov] taught that one must pay close attention to this matter. I learned from him how to repair the strange thoughts even if they are about women. One should elevate them and make them cleave to their source, the [*Sefirah*] *Hesed*. (As cited in Ariel, 1988, p. 179).

In meditation, a *tikkun*, literally, "repair, healing," may require no more than the overcoming of discordant thoughts by their linkage to the meditations. For example, a person who was engaging in meditation might suddenly experience an unbidden sexual fantasy. To abandon the meditations and pursue the fantasy was considered sinful. Jews were traditionally enjoined to push such fantasies out of their thoughts. The Baal Shem Tov uniquely proposed that Jews not bring their meditations to a halt, but instead accept the fantasies and weave them into their ongoing meditations. Hasidim were to reinterpret the fantasies by allegorizing them. By treating sexual fantasies as allegories, for example, of the relation of God to the *Shekhinah*, which kabbalists considered feminine, sexual fantasies could be "elevated" to a metaphysical level that was congruent with the meditations that the fantasies interrupted. In this manner, the evil of the fantasy's manifest content would be transformed into good; the fantasy, which had threatened to interrupt the ecstasy, would instead be made to further it.

Merkur (1994) suggested that the Baal Shem Tov's distinctive teaching about the handling of sexual fantasies promoted an attitude of tolerance that Jacob Freud may have communicated to his son, not as a religious teaching, but by way of advice to an adolescent concerning the management of his sexual fantasy life. In the present context, we emphasize that the Baal Shem Tov's teaching was a kabbalistic adaptation of Maimonides' program for the interpretation of anthropomorphisms.

Did Maimonides also influence Freud more directly? Freud did not refer to Maimonides, but his silence is not conclusive. We know that Freud zealously promoted psychoanalysis as a natural science and sometimes went to astonishing lengths in order to disavow Jewish influences on his work. For example, although Freud publically claimed and the official biographies all state that his was a completely secular household that paid no attention to Jewish traditions of any kind, A. A. Brill (1940) reminisced that when Freud was in America in September 1909 to lecture at Clark University, "he sent a *Rosh Hashana* good wishes cable to his wife and family in Vienna" (p. 160). Another misrepresentation is more telling. After Abraham Roback (1929) had boasted of Freud in a book on *Jewish Influence in Modern Thought*, Freud wrote Roback, "I have never learned or spoken Yiddish" (Roback, 1957, pp. 30, 34). Yiddish was nevertheless Freud's mother tongue. According to Theodor Reik, who knew Freud's mother Amalia "when she was an old lady" and summered at Bad Ischl, near Salzburg, "she did not speak in high German but Galician Yiddish" (Freeman, 1971, pp. 80, 85). Freud's lie was not only gratuitous, but its extravagance suggests that it was counterphobic. If so, it asserted the very opposite of what Freud feared was the truth: that Roback was right, and psychoanalysis was a profoundly Jewish innovation.

Freud's parents were part of the great migration of Jews out of the ghettos in Eastern Europe, entering into the main streams of Western civilization, socially, occupationally, educationally, and so forth. Judaism was in great ferment, and Maimonides' rationalism grew in significance because it helped Jews to find their way to modernity. In parallel with, and possibly inspired by, the revival of interest within the Roman Catholic Church in the nineteenth century in the philosophy of St. Thomas Aquinas, whose Aristotelianism facilitated the church's adjustment to modern science, there was considerable interest in Western intellectual circles in Maimonides' *Guide*, on which Aquinas had drawn (Burrell, 1988). At about the middle of the nineteenth century, interest in the work by non-Jewish philosophers was revived as a result of a new translation into French by Solomon Munk. Subsequently, it was translated into almost all European languages.

In addition to the burst of scholarship on the *Guide* that was associated with the universities, a religious interest in the *Guide* developed among Jews moving into the mainstream of Western intellectual life. The *Guide* was available to Freud in French, German, and English translations, the latter by Scheier and Friedländer. Some of the convergences between Freud and Maimonides concern materials that are found only in Maimonides' *Eight Chapters*. Maimonides composed the *Eight Chapters* as a preface to his commentary on *Pirke Avoth*, "Chapter of the Fathers," an ethical treatise in the Mishnah that is often printed as a separate volume. Maimonides' *Eight Chapters* enjoyed a similar status. Either as a commentary on *Pirke Avoth* or on its own, *Eight Chapters* was available to Freud in German translations that were published in 1798, 1804, 1809, 1863, and 1876. There were as well a French translation of 1811 and an English version of 1834–35 (Gorfinkle, 1912, p. 33).

Maimonides' influence on liberal Judaism was conveyed to Freud as part of his religious schooling as a child. Religious education was compulsory in

Austrian schools, and Freud was schooled in Judaism from his first year at the Volksschule through his last year at the Gymnasium. During his elementary schooling, Freud was taught privately; but at the Leopoldstädter Communalgymnasium, which Freud attended from 1865 until 1873, he was taught, at least in his final years (1870–73), by Samuel Hammerschlag, who was both a member of the faculty of the Gymnasium and a leader within the Kultusgemeinde, a Jewish organization that coordinated and supervised Jewish education throughout Vienna (Rainey, 1971, pp. 51–64). Hammerschlag's curriculum for the year 1868–69 has been preserved. The seventh and eighth classes, which Freud would have attended in 1871–73, included "History of the Jews: From the Completion of the Talmud through Maimonides," and "History of the Jews: From Maimonides to the End of the Seventeenth Century" (Rainey, 1971, pp. 69, 71–72). The curriculum was a liberal one that presented the prophets and Maimonides as precursors of Lessing, Kant, Schiller, and Goethe (Ater, 1992, p. 227). Freud was deeply influenced by Hammerschlag and retained him as a lifelong friend, visiting him in his home and sometimes borrowing money from him during his medical school years. Freud published a glowing obituary of Hammerschlag upon his death in 1904 (Rainey, 1971, pp. 65–67).

At the University of Vienna, Freud concentrated on scientific and medical studies that were preparatory for his intended career as a neurologist. He made an exception, however, of six separate credits in philosophy, which he took with Franz Brentano (Merlan, 1945, 1949), who was a leading Aristotelian scholar of the period. In letters to his friend Eduard Silberstein, Freud (1990) mentioned the topics of three of the courses: "selected metaphysical problems . . . a text by Mill on the utilitarian principle," and "the existence of God" (pp. 66–70). When Freud and a classmate wrote Brentano some objections to his arguments about God's existence, they were invited to his home on two occasions that Freud mentioned in his letters (pp. 94–95). Freud referred to Brentano's concept of God as an "airy existence" (p. 71), and Brentano's published lectures *On the Existence of God* support Freud's verdict. Brentano (1987) dismissed negative theology because "there is no real difference between such agnosticism and utter atheism" (p. 47), advanced the concept of incorporeal intelligibles in connection with what he called "the psychological proof" of the existence of God" (pp. 290–301), and presented as Aristotelian an argument for God as "the first, directly necessary cause" (pp. 315–330). Brentano notwithstanding, his argument is not derived from Aristotle but is instead a compromise between the unmoved mover of Aristotle and the necessary existent of Ibn Sina. Brentano gave the impression of greater originality than his arguments possessed by mentioning neither Ibn Sina nor Maimonides, who had depended on Ibn Sina. The omission at least of Ibn Sina cannot have been due to oversight. In *The Psychology of Aristotle: In Particular His Doctrine of the Active Intellect*, Brentano (1977) reviewed and considered the medieval positions of Ibn Sina, Ibn Rushd, and Aquinas, none of whom classicists ordinarily trouble to read (p. x). At a minimum, we may trust that Brentano exposed Freud to ideas such as those found in his public lectures. By bringing Freud, let us say, to the ideas of intelligibles and the Active Intellect, Brentano made it possible for Freud to move in intellectual spaces similar to those that Maimonides moved in, giving him a sense of science that was broader than that of Brücke, from whom Freud learned physical determinism.

Brentano was assuredly familiar with the name of Maimonides, whom Aquinas had termed *the Rabbi* as though no other bore mention. It is also possible that he had himself consulted Maimonides' *Guide*. Brentano was evidently aware of the rabbinic tradition that allowed that God was an agent in connection with every human birth. He claimed that what he was writing was "in the spirit of Aristotle" when he stated:

> The intellectual part of man must be infused into the fetus by the deity. Thereby the development of the fetus into an actual human body will reach its consummation. For since the human soul cannot exist without the intellectual part, while the human body is what it is only through the human soul, it follows that the human body becomes a *human* body and that an actual new man is generated only at the moment when the deity unites the intellectual part with the body into one substance. It is thus through a direct act of God that the intellectual part is produced from nothing and that the corporeal part is given its character as a human body. (Brentano, 1977, pp. 134–135)

The doctrine that God infuses the human soul into the body was Talmudic. Its presentation by Maimonides included the detail, credited by Brentano to "the spirit of Aristotle," that the distinctively human component of the soul was the intellectual faculty. May we assume that Freud, having learned about Maimonides from Hammerschlag in 1871–1873, and acquiring an introduction to Aristotelian philosophy from Brentano beginning in the fall of 1874, would have conversed about the *Guide*, if not with Brentano, then certainly with Hammerschlag? From 1873 onward, Hammerschlag served as the librarian of the Kultusgemeinde (Rainey, 1971, p. 68) and could easily have put a copy of the *Guide* in Freud's hands.

Freud may also have picked up an understanding of Maimonides from others around him who were probing the thought of Maimonides anew because they saw things in Maimonides that were desirable for changes in Judaism. It is possible that Freud's father Jacob might have introduced him to the work of Maimonides in a casual conversation at the dinner table. Again, Josef Breuer, who was Freud's closest and most trusted friend between 1883 and 1886, and co-authored *Studies in Hysteria* (1895) with Freud, was assuredly conversant with the name, reputation, and perhaps also the work of Maimonides. Josef Breuer's father Leopold had earned his living as a teacher of religion in the Viennese Jewish community (Oberndorf, 1953, p. 65).

Leopold Breuer wrote the introductory text book on Judaism that Freud studied as a child with Samuel Hammerschlag (Diller, 1991, p. 72). Although the Breuers were liberal Jews, Josef Breuer was a member of the burial society, the *Hevra Kadishah*, "Holy Fellowship," from 1873 until his death in 1925. Ordinarily, a *Hevra Kadishah* was a voluntary organization within a Jewish community whose duties included washing the dead, dressing their bodies for burial, keeping vigil over the corpse, and performing the burial in strict accord with Jewish ritual observance. Medical men, such as Josef Breuer, were often recruited for their knowledge of anatomy. The Viennese community's *Hevra Kadishah* was somewhat unusual, in combining a benevolent society and study group with the conventional burial functions (Klein, 1985, pp. 58, 82; Rice, 1990, pp. 102–103). If Breuer attended the study groups, he would have encountered different opinions of Maimonides on many occasions over the years.

Freud also had daily contact with other Jews who were in between traditional Jewish culture and Western culture. His first public lectures on dreams were given to Jews. From 1895 onward, Freud was a member of the B'nai Brith Society, a Jewish club or lodge whose social and cultural gatherings he attended on alternate Tuesdays. He both heard lectures and occasionally gave them. For example, he lectured on "Dreams" to his B'nai Brith lodge on December 7 and 14, 1897, and on Zola's *La Fécondité* on April 27, 1900. On May 2, 1896, Freud lectured on dreams to a young audience in the *Jüdisch-Akademische Lesehalle*, "Jewish Academic Reading Hall" (Jones, 1953, pp. 330, 355). We may reasonably assume that Freud was comprehensible to at least some members of his B'nai Brith audiences, and that some of his fellow members engaged him in intellectual conversations that he found interesting. It is inconceivable that none of them were familiar with Maimonides. Maimonides' project in the *Guide* was too near that of Freud for it not to have been drawn to his attention in the Jewish intellectual subculture in Vienna. It is almost impossible that someone would not have said to him something to the effect: "You are interested in interpreting dreams? Then you must read Maimonides, who interpreted the writings of the prophets in Scripture as dreams, and showed how to interpret them."

DREAM INTERPRETATION

A systematic comparison of Maimonides and Freud may begin with the *Guide*'s recognition as a work on the interpretation of the dreams and visions of prophets. It is a medieval precursor of Freud's *Interpretation of Dreams* (1900). The *Guide* claims to be a commentary on "certain terms" and "very obscure parables" in the books of the prophets other than Moses (*Guide* I:Introduction; pp. 5–6), but the *Guide*'s literary genre should not be confused with its purpose. Maimonides claimed that the prophecy of prophets other than Moses occurred exclusively through dreams and visions. God "has informed us of the true reality and quiddity of prophecy and has let us know that it is a perfection that comes in a dream or in a vision" (*Guide* II:36; p. 370). As a result, the *Guide* constituted a medieval treatise on the interpretation of dreams and visions.

Both Freud and Maimonides regarded the content of the vision or dream as the result of mental work. We see this in Maimonides in his fundamental formulation of the essence of prophecy: "Know that the true reality and quiddity of prophecy consist in its being an overflow . . . toward the rational faculty in the first place and thereafter toward the imaginative faculty" (*Guide* II:36, p. 369). In Freud, the formulaic was represented in two major chapters of *The Interpretation of Dreams*: Chapter V, entitled "The Material and Sources of Dreams," and Chapter VI, "The Dream Work."

Freud (1900) recognized that waking experiences contribute a "day residue" to dreams that form subsequently during sleep. Maimonides similarly indicated that "a matter that occupies a man greatly—he being bent upon it and desirous of it—while he is awake and while his senses function, is the one with regard to which the imaginative faculty acts while he is asleep when receiving an overflow of the intellect corresponding to its disposition" (*Guide* II:36; p. 370).

According to Maimonides, the mental work of prophecy involved two of the soul's faculties in a manner that was consistent with the process that Freud called the dream work. In the case of dreams, there was an overflow "toward the rational faculty in the first place and thereafter toward the imaginative faculty" (*Guide* II:36; p. 369). The formation of visions observed the same sequence. The imagination, Maimonides explained, retained "things which are perceived by the senses, combining things, and imitating them" (*Guide* II:36; p. 370). Freud (1900) proposed a similar division between the rational and imaginative elaborations of the day residue. He maintained that the preconscious, a subdivision of the secondary process that performs rational thought, formulates the latent dream content, which the dream work, produced by the primary process, converts into imagery, fashioning the dream.

Maimonides maintained that visions and dreams have both external and internal meanings. The words of the prophets were not to be understood literally. Only "an ignorant or heedless individual might think that [the texts] possess only an external sense, but no internal one" (*Guide* I:Introduction; p. 6). The prophetic writings instead made use of equivocal expressions.

> The prophets use in their speeches equivocal words and words that are not intended to mean what they indicate according to their first signification, the word being mentioned because of its derivation. For instance the words *maqqel shaqed* [*a rod of an almond tree*] are used because from this indication one may go on to the words that follow: *Shoqed 'ani*, and so on [I watch over]. (*Guide* II:29; pp. 347–348)

Maimonides also claimed that the rabbinic sages both interpreted the prophets correctly and perpetuated the prophets' orientation to their visions and texts. Rabbinic narratives often had either to be read as having both external and internal meanings or they had to be dismissed as idiocy.

> If . . . a perfect man of virtue should engage in speculation on them [the Midrashim], he cannot escape one of two courses: either he can take the speeches in question in their external sense and, in so doing, think ill of their author and regard him as an ignoramus—in this there is nothing that would upset the foundations of belief; or he can attribute to them an inner meaning, thereby extricating himself from his predicament and being able to think well of the author whether or not the inner meaning of the saying is clear to him (*Guide* I:Introduction; p. 10).

In composing various passages in his writings in an esoteric literary style, Maimonides emulated the prophets and sages. His distinction between the literal and hidden senses of prophetic parables also compares with one of the fundamental premises of Freud's dream theory, the distinction between the manifest dream content on the one hand and the latent dream thoughts on the other. Freud (1900) wrote, "It is only necessary to take notice of the fact that my theory is not based on a consideration of the manifest content of dreams but refers to the thoughts which are shown by the work of interpretation to lie behind dreams. We must make a contrast between the *manifest* and the *latent* content of dreams" (p. 135).

Freud privileged the latent dream thoughts, which he argued to be verbal in content, over the imagery of the manifest dream content. For Maimonides too, words were superior to images. In his discussion of Onqelos' Aramaic translation of Scripture, Maimonides stated that "there is a great difference between that which is said to happen *in a dream* or *in the visions of the night*, [or] that which is said to happen *in a vision* and *apparition*, and that which is said without qualification: *And the word of the Lord came unto me, saying*, or, *And the Lord said unto me*" (*Guide* I:27; p. 58). Further, in the course of interpretation, Maimonides allowed the conversion of images into words in order to reach the meaning. Freud employed the same procedure in psychoanalysis. In Chapter VI of *The Interpretation of Dreams*, Freud spelled out the process of dream generation from the latent to the manifest. Maimonides noted the inevitability of constraints on ideas' representation by imagery. "The mental representation of the action of one who is separate from matter is very difficult [just as] the mental representation of the existence of one who is separate from matter . . . the imagination cannot represent to itself an existent other than a body or a force in a body" (*Guide* II:12; p. 279). Freud (1900) generalized that "considerations of representability" were a regular feature of the dream work. Freud's further discussions of the dream work, involving condensation and displacement, may be treated as an advance beyond Maimonides.

Like Freud, Maimonides approached dream interpretation with a principle that was quite contrary to one commonly associated with good scholarship. Both Maimonides and Freud interpreted by violating context. Although it is a principle of good scholarship to attribute meaning to a word in accordance with the way that that word occurs in its context, Maimonides recommended something quite different. Maimonides provided a virtual lexicon of selected biblical words in Part I of the *Guide*. For each word he indicated a number of meanings that the word can have. He maintained that the true meaning of the word was often something that was not the meaning seemingly intended by the context. He wrote: "Some of these terms are equivocal.... Other are derivative.... Others are amphibolous terms, so that at times they are believed to be univocal and at other times equivocal." The lexicon served as a kind of handbook for two things—for identifying words that were critical in Scripture and for helping in their interpretation out of their apparent context by pointing to alternative meanings.

For Maimonides, the interpretation of dreams, prophetic visions, Scripture, and rabbinic narratives proceeded by making inferences from the external meanings concerning internal meanings. Toward that task Maimonides offers a number of recommendations. First, there were two kinds of dreams. In some dreams, the internal meaning was contained in the theme of the vision or dream. These dreams were parables. More difficult to interpret were dreams that Maimonides called composites. In them, separate meanings were woven together into a whole, and their interpretation required separation and separate decoding. The first steps in the identification of the internal meaning of a composite dream were to recognize the fact that it was composite and to deal with its parts separately. To exemplify his approach, Maimonides cited a passage that narrated Jacob's dream: "And behold a ladder set up on the earth and the top of it reached to heaven; and behold the angels of God ascending and descending on it. And behold the Lord stood above it" (Gen 28:12–13). Maimonides' advice was to break up the passage. He wrote that "every word occurring in this parable refers to an additional subject in the complex of subjects represented by the parable as a whole" (*Guide*, I:Introduction; pp. 12–13). Maimonides divided the passage into seven parts and asserted that each part referred to a different subject. He stated that the word "ladder" indicated one subject, "set up on the earth" a second, "and the top of it reached to heaven" a third, "and behold the angels of God" a fourth, "ascending" a fifth, "and descending" a sixth, and "And behold the Lord stood above it" a seventh (*Guide*, I:Introduction, pp. 12–13). A composite vision or a dream warranted a major deviation from the common principle of identifying meaning. The common principle for the identification of obscure meaning was to carefully identify the questionable item in its context and to use that context as a guide to interpretation. Here, however, the plain meaning of the vision or dream obscured the internal meanings and had to be overcome if the internal meanings were to be interpreted. The imaginative process of vision and dreammaking imposed, as it were, an artificial context that had to be ignored if the deeper sense was to be uncovered.

Maimonides' procedure in interpreting composite dreams corresponded exactly to the method of interpretation that Freud advocated in *The Interpretation of Dreams*. Freud (1900) wrote: "We must take as the object of our attention ... not the dream as a whole but the separate portions of its content.... I put the dream before [a patient] cut up into pieces [and have him] give me a series of associations to each piece.... [T]he method of dream-interpretation which I practice ... employs interpretation *en detail* and not *en masse*; [the method] regards dreams from the very first as being of a composite character, as being conglomerates of [different] psychical formations" (pp. 103–104).

Like Freud, Maimonides included wordplays among the varieties of interpretation that he made of prophetic symbols. The rebus was one type of wordplay. In a rebus, a picture of an eye might be used to represent the word "I." Maimonides said that the prophets "see things whose purpose it is to point to what is called to attention by the term designating the thing seen because of that term's derivation or because of an equivocality of terms. In that case the action of the imaginative faculty consists in occasioning the appearance of a thing designated by an equivocal term, through one of whose meanings another can be indicated" (*Guide* II:43; p. 392). He cited an example from the Book of Amos, where the prophet's vision of *qayits*, "summer fruit," was followed by a verbal prophecy that used the identically spelled, cognate word *qets*, "end." "Similarly *Amos* saw *klub qayits* [*a basket of summer fruit*], so that he should infer from it the end of the period. It accordingly says: *Ba' haq-qets* [*The end is come*]" (*Guide* II:45; p. 392).

Maimonides also included anagrams among the wordplays that occurred in prophecies. An anagram is a word made from the same letters of another word by changing the order of the letters. "Stranger than this is the intention aroused through the use of a certain term whose letters are identical with those of another term; solely the order of the letters is changed; and between the two terms there is in no way an etymological connection or a community of meaning" (*Guide* II:43; p. 392). He offered the examples of *hoblim*, meaning "ravagers," and *bohalam*, "loathing," which are unrelated etymologically but spelled with the same Hebrew letters. "I mean from the term hoblim, their repugnance for the Law and the repugnance of God for them. However, this meaning can only be derived from hoblim through changing the order of the [letters], 'ha,' ... 'ba' and ... 'lam'" (*Guide* II:43; p. 393).

Maimonides also anticipated Freud in allowing interpretations through wordplays. Commenting on Daniel 10:6, "And his body was like *tarshish*," Maimonides interpreted the last word as one might hear it spoken. It is read on a page as one word, but when it is spoken it can be heard as *tar*, meaning "two," plus *shish*, meaning "six." Because two sixths are equal to one third,

Maimonides interpreted Daniel 10:6 as a cosmological allusion that was consistent with his claim that "All created things are divided into three parts: the separate intellects, which are angels; the second, the bodies of the spheres [heaven]; the third, first matter—I mean the bodies subject to constant change, which are beneath the sphere" (*Guide* II:10; p. 273).

THE PRIVILEGED PLACE OF SEXUALITY

The Talmud's discussion of dream interpretation included several examples in which dreams had sexual meanings (Bakan, 1958; Lorand, 1957), and Maimonides accorded sexuality a privileged place in visions of prophecy. For Maimonides, sexual symbolism that signified the creation out of nothing was exemplified by the chariot vision of Ezekiel. Not only Ezekiel, but merkabah mystics and kabbalists had visions or dreams that contained images of divine sexual intercourse. Maimonides treated the sexual symbolism in prophecy as one of the secrets of the law and followed Plato in referring to form and matter as male and female.

Images of sexual intercourse fall under the heading of what Freud (1918, p. 51) called "primal scenes." Freud found that these fantasies existed quite commonly. The fantasied events, parental intercourse, seduction by an adult, and being threatened by castration may appear as memories, according to Freud, but they are very largely facilitated by what he described as "phylogenetic endowment." Sometimes they corresponded to actual events, but "if they are withheld by reality, they are put together from hints and supplemented by phantasy." Freud (1916–17) wrote that in these fantasies:

> The individual reaches beyond his own experience into the primaeval experience at points where his own experience has been too rudimentary. It seems to me quite possible that all the things that are told to us in [psycho]analysis as phantasy—the seduction of children, the inflaming of sexual excitement by observing parental intercourse, the threat of castration (or rather castration itself)—were once real occurrences in the primaeval times of the human family, and that children in their phantasies are simply filling the gaps in individual truth with prehistoric truth. I have repeatedly been led to suspect that the psychology of the neuroses has stored up in it more of the antiquities of human development than any other source. (pp. 370–371)

The kabbalah followed Maimonides in according a privileged place to sexual imagery. Where, however, Maimonides had treated the imagery as metaphor, the kabbalah created a myth of universal sexuality (Scholem, 1954). By reifying the symbolism, the kabbalah replaced the sexual metaphors of matter and form with a literal belief that all existent things manifest masculinity, femininity, or their union. Freud's (1905) extension of the concept of sexuality psychologized the kabbalah's universalization of sexuality, reasserting a psychological perspective that was consistent with Maimonides.

Maimonides' willingness to place the secrets of the law before the public violated rabbinical scruples. In his legal writings, however, Maimonides provided great license for the respect to suspension of rabbinic law when indicated by medical reasons. We have suggested that Maimonides' therapeutic intention was his warrant for deviating from the rabbinic injunction with respect to concealing the secrets of the Law. Maimonides hoped to relieve suffering that was caused by perplexity, and the medical context of the *Guide* was integral to its candor regarding sexuality. Freud also prioritized medical ethics over conventional concerns for sexual modesty.

It is possible that Freud was first exposed to the Jewish mystical tradition in the form of the kabbalah and came to Maimonides only later. The letters that Freud wrote his friend Wilhelm Fliess between 1887 and 1904 refer at intervals to the ideas that he was developing at the time of writing. Freud seems to have been working with his extended concept of sexuality from a very early period. Draft A, enclosed with a letter dated December 18, 1892, presents the thesis: "No neurasthenia or analogous neurosis exists without a disturbance of the sexual function" (Freud, 1895, p. 38). Freud attributed hysteria to sexuality in his published work soon afterward, in connection with Breuer's cathartic method of hypnotherapy (Breuer & Freud, 1893; Freud, 1894). He must have been interpreting latent sexual meanings in neurotic symptoms prior to February 7, 1894, when he wrote to Fliess: "You are right—the connection between obsessional neurosis and sexuality is not always all that obvious. I can assure you that in my case 2 (urinary urgency), it was not easy to find either, someone who had not searched for it as single-mindedly as I did would have overlooked it" (Freud, 1985, p. 66). The letter implies that Freud had earlier written Fliess that sexuality also underlay obsessional neurosis, yet Fliess had difficulty discerning the evidence. The exchange implies that Freud was interpreting latent sexual content in materials that were not manifestly sexual, as is consistent with Bakan's (1958) hypothesis of his initial inspiration by the Jewish mystical tradition.

A few months later, Freud added the concept of mental conflict. On May 21, 1894, he wrote that "*conflict* coincides with my viewpoint of defense," which is to say, repression (Freud, 1985, p. 66).

On July 24, 1895, Freud dreamed the first dream that he interpreted completely using the method of analysis that he was to publish in *The Interpretation of Dreams* (1900). He wrote Fliess: "Clinically, it all fitted together long ago, but the psychological theories I needed were arrived at only very laboriously" (Freud, 1985, p. 134). Freud had evidently been interpreting dreams well before he "grasped the general principle" (p. 419) that "dreams are motivated by wish fulfillment" (p. 140). Schur (1966, p. 47) suggested that "Freud may have been attempting for the first time . . . the systematic application of free association to every single element of the manifest dream, after which he connected these associations until a meaningful trend emerged." Public lectures on dreams to a Jewish youth group and the Bnai Brith followed in 1896 and 1897 (Freud, 1985, pp. 185, 290).

On December 6, 1896, Freud wrote of the "rearrangement" of memory traces "in accordance with fresh circumstances" (p. 207). Six months later, on May 2, 1897, his self-analysis was under way and he recognized that the reworking of memories permitted neurosis to originate at a later time than the events contained in memory. "The fantasies stem from things that have been *heard* but understood *subsequently*, and all their material is of course genuine" (p. 239). On September 21, 1897, Freud announced the crucial breakthrough. He had abandoned his belief that neuroses are caused by pathogenic events. In May 1896, he had regarded masturbation as the cause of neurosis (p. 175), but he had since fixed on the sexual seduction of children. Now he renounced the idea of an actual physical event. Because the unconscious was unable to distinguish truth and fiction, neurosis could be attributed to pathogenic fantasies, of which only a portion reflected actual events (p. 264). "In the collapse of everything valuable, the psychological alone has remained untouched. The dream [book] stands entirely secure" (p. 266). With this decisive change in his orientation from neurology to psychology, Freud arrived at the point at which Maimonides' distinctive approach to the interpretation of sexual imagery departed from the kabbalists' approach, and he concurred with Maimonides.

Freud developed his cure of souls almost immediately thereafter. Less than five weeks later, on October 27, 1897, he announced his understanding of resistance and, with it, the therapeutic action of psychoanalysis.

> Resistance, which finally brings the [analytic] work to a halt, is nothing other than the child's former character, the degenerative character, which developed or would have developed as a result of those experiences that one finds as a conscious memory in the so-called degenerative cases, but which here is overlaid by the development of repression. I dig it out by my work; it struggles; and the person who initially was such a good, noble human being becomes mean, untruthful, or obstinate, a malingerer—until I tell him so and thus make it possible for him to overcome this character. In this way resistance has become something actual and tangible to me, and I wish that instead of the concept of repression I already had what lies concealed behind it as well. (p. 274)

This letter reported clinical work that Freud was doing with patients; but he had implicitly discovered the therapeutic sequence through his self-analysis: resistance, interpretation of character, disclosure of bad character as fantasy. The attention to character, in addition to fantasy, was the crucial innovation that allowed Freud's technique to surpass Maimonides by moving beyond supportive psychotherapy into psychoanalysis.

SOCIOCULTURAL CONFLICT MODEL

The topics of dream interpretation and universal sexuality have been common to all branches of the Jewish mystical tradition since Maimonides' era. They indicate Freud's debt to Judaism, but not necessarily to Maimonides. Further points of convergence between Maimonides and Freud are otherwise unparalleled.

One of Freud's main ideas, which he discussed extensively, was the necessity of conflict between civilization and instinctual gratification. Freud (1927, p. 7) wrote, for example, that "every civilisation must be built up on ... renunciation of instinct." He announced his original arrival at the concept in a letter to Fliess dated May 31, 1897.

> The horror of incest (something impious) is based on the fact that, as a result of communal sexual life (even in childhood), the members of a family remain together permanently and become incapable of joining with strangers. Thus incest is antisocial—civilization consists in this progressive renunciation. Contrariwise, the "superman." (Freud, 1985, p. 252)

Maimonides held to a similar opinion. He stated: "To the totality of purposes of the perfect Law there belong the abandonment, depreciation, and restraint of desires.... [M]ost of the lusts and licentiousness of the multitude consist in an appetite for eating, drinking, and sexual intercourse" (*Guide* III:33, p. 532).

Freud (1939) said that ethics are justified rationally in part "by the necessity for delimiting the rights of society as against the individual, the rights of the individual as against society, and those of individuals as against one another" (p. 122). Maimonides found the justification of the law not so much in the will of God, but in the benefit that the law conferred to human beings.

> The Law as a whole aims at two things: the welfare of the soul and the welfare of the body. As for the welfare of the soul, it consists in the multitude's acquiring correct opinions.... As for the welfare of the body, it comes about by the improvement of their ways of living one with another. This is achieved through two things. One of them is the abolition of their wronging each other. This is tantamount to every individual among the people not being permitted to act according to his will and up to the limits of his power, but being forced to do that which is useful to the whole. The second thing consists in the acquisition by every human individual of moral qualities that are useful for life in society so that the affairs of the city may be ordered. (*Guide* III:27; p. 510)

In Maimonides' view, intellect was the particular psychological function that constrained moral conduct. In commenting on the condition of people who may attain to the world to come, Maimonides cited Psalm 32:9: "Be not as the horse or as the mule, which have no understanding; whose mouth must be held in with bit and bridle." Unlike the horse and mule, a human being is able to exert self-control. "With man, the influences which restrain him are his control of self. When a man achieves human perfection it restrains him from doing those things which are called vices ... it urges and impels him toward those things which are called virtues" (*Helek*, p. 216). Freud (1927, p. 51) wrote similarly of "the desired primacy of the intelligence over the life of the instincts," and named "the psychological ideal, the primary of the intelligence" (p. 48).

Maimonides and Freud converged in their view that the common injunctions with respect to sexual behavior are conventional. They do not have their basis in human nature. They are generated socially and imposed on the individual. Maimonides stated: "The disapproval of the uncovering of the private parts is a generally accepted opinion, not a thing cognized by the intellect" (*Guide* III:8, p. 434). Again, Maimonides did not hold with the widely shared view that what is "natural" is also legislative or licensing. He disagreed with the assumption that somehow all natural tendencies comprise some kind of imperative or permission. He instead maintained that the purpose of the Law was in many instances precisely to counteract what was done "naturally." Taking guidance from instruction, a person should aim to have control over "natural" impulses and tendencies, and do what has to be done in order to reduce them. On this point there was a major convergence between Maimonides and Freud. For Freud (1930, 1939), "instinctual renunciation" was the key to understanding both civilization and psychopathology.

Maimonides strongly indicated the importance of admitting to inappropriate desire. He distinguished between admitting desire and acting on it when doing so was inappropriate. Maimonides wrote that the sages "command that man should conquer his [inappropriate] desires, but they forbid one to say, 'I, by my nature, do not desire to commit such and such a transgression.' ... [A man] should not say, 'I do not want ...' but he should say, 'I do indeed want to, yet I must not'" (*Eight Chapters* vi; p. 76). The admission to inappropriate desire was also a fundamental part of psychoanalysis. Both Maimonides and Freud were deeply opposed to the Christian principle that identified sin in thought with sin in conduct, as in "whosoever looketh on a woman to lust after her hath committed adultery with her already in his heart" (Mt 5:28).

Above all other natural desires that were prohibited by external social pressures, Maimonides counted the desire for incest. As we have seen, Maimonides followed rabbinic custom in distinguishing two classes of biblical precept. "Those commandments whose utility is clear ... as in the case of the prohibition of killing and stealing ... are called *mishpatim* ... and those whose utility is not clear to the multitude are called *huqqim*" (*Guide* III:26; p. 507). Maimonides indicated that because the reasons for having *huqqim* were not patent, the only way that one could know that these acts are prohibited is by having been instructed about them. "Were it not for the Law, they would not at all be considered transgressions. Therefore, the Rabbis say that man should permit his soul to entertain the natural inclination for these things, but that the Law alone should restrain him from them" (*Eight Chapters* vi, p. 77). He also cited Rabbi Simeon ben Gamliel who said: "Man should not say, 'I do not want to eat meat together with milk; I do not want to wear clothes made of a mixture of wool and linen, I do not want to [engage in incest],' but he should say, 'I do indeed want to, yet I must not, for my father in heaven has forbidden it'" (*Eight Chapters* vi; p. 76). The narrative is notable for its inclusion of the prohibition of incest among the examples of *huqqim*. Rabban Simeon ben Gamliel had differed from the rabbinical consensus, expressed in the Babylonian Talmud, Yoma 67b, that classified incest among the *mishpatim*. By citing the dissenting view, Maimonides made it his own. Maimonides allowed that incest was in the category of *huqqim*, the natural desires that the law prohibited for the sake of society.

Maimonides regarded incest as a primary human desire. He said that when Scripture stated that there was "weeping in their families" (Num 11:10), it meant that they were weeping over the injunctions against incest (*Mishneh Torah, Kedushah*, 22:18). In his codification of the laws pertaining to incest, Maimonides held as exemplary the conduct of the sage who asked his disciples, "Warn me to beware of my daughter, warn me to beware of my daughter-in-law" (*Mishneh Torah, Kedushah*, 22:20). The open acknowledgment of the desire for incest was seen by Maimonides as a way of managing the incest problem.

The prescription of allowing the soul to entertain the inclination for incest consciously, but certainly not engaging in incestuous conduct, was also a central feature of Freud's program of psychoanalysis. In Freud's formulation, the Oedipus complex consisted of the desires for incest and patricide, and neurosis involved a failure to renounce and resolve the two desires. Freud considered the admission to incestuous desire a necessary condition of psychotherapeutic change.

THEORIES OF PATHOLOGY AND THERAPY

Maimonides, we have seen, began with the Socratic attribution of wrongdoing to ignorance, interpolated Jewish concepts of free will, and arrived at the concept that wrongdoing produces mental illness because it accomplishes a voluntary loss of knowledge. Once lost, ignorance becomes involuntary. Maimonides cited the text of Isaiah to illustrate his theory.

> Make the heart of this people fat,
> and their ears heavy,
> and shut their eyes;

> lest they see with their eyes,
>   and hear with their ears,
> and understand with their hearts,
>   and turn and be healed
> (*Eight Chapters* viii; p. 97; citing Is 6:10).

Maimonides similarly understood the relation between wrongdoing and the psychogenic losses of other normal functions, such as paralysis in the case of Jereboam and blindness in the case of the Sodomites. He also applied his theory to the interpretation of the biblical story of the fall of Adam. He maintained that the functioning of the intellect became impaired as a consequence of Adam's disobedience, so that "he was punished by being deprived of that intellectual apprehension" (*Guide* I:2; p. 25). For Maimonides, the loss of intellect or correct knowledge was the vehicle of being cut off from God, that is, not being able to be in touch with God. He regarded the phenomenon as self-induced. "It is clear that we are the cause of this *hiding of the face*, and we are the agents who produce this separation" (*Guide* III:51; p. 626).

Maimonides' concept of sin followed in consequence. For Maimonides, observance of the law protected the normal freedom of the will, while *averah*, transgression, entailed its loss. Violating the commandments was dysfunctional. To sin was to act in a manner that caused loss of the normal ability to choose one's own conduct. It also caused a loss of insight into one's involuntary condition.

Freud advanced closely similar ideas about mental illness. Freud (1923a) described the freeing of a patient's will as a goal of psychoanalysis. In making the unconscious conscious, psychoanalysis sets out "to give the patient's ego *freedom* to choose one way or the other" (p. 50). Freud (1914b, p. 16) referred to his concept of repression as "the corner-stone on which the whole structure of psycho-analysis rests," and for many years wavered in his estimation of whether it was voluntary or involuntary. In his final view, he regarded repression as an involuntary consequence of trauma, an automatic reaction of the psychic mechanism to helplessness, that overcomes mental paralysis by excluding the traumatic ideas from conscious thought (Freud, 1926). However, Freud's early writings agreed more closely with Maimonides by implicitly attributing repression to conscious opposition to instinct. Consistent with this implication, when Freud (1923a) first explicitly articulated his superego model, by which the child's identifications with the parents and their values serves to internalize societal restraints on instinct, he used the term "repression" in its connection. However, only a few months later, Freud (1923b) revised his position. For the remainder of his life, he distinguished between two inhibiting phenomena, attributing repression to the ego but conscience and value judgment to the superego. Repression keeps ideas from becoming conscious. Conscience admits ideas to consciousness, but then judges them.

The replacement of repression by conscience is one of the implicit goals of psychoanalytic treatment.

Interestingly, both Freud's psychological studies under Charcot in Paris and his earliest psychological publications (Freud, 1893) involved cases of hysterical paralysis and hysterical blindness, the two syndromes that Maimonides noted in *Eight Chapters*. Freud also studied the seeming suspension of voluntary control that occurs in hypnosis when he became expert in Breuer's cathartic method of therapy (Breuer & Freud, 1895). Freud named his own procedure "psychoanalysis" in the late 1890s, when he replaced hypnotic suggestion with free association as a means to access involuntary processes in the unconscious. Moving beyond Maimonides, Freud saw a causal connection between repression and neurotic symptoms. His description of neurosis in terms of inhibition, fixation, and repetition compulsion articulated his understanding of the dynamic relation between repressed materials and pathological symptom formation. The symptoms of neurosis were returns of the repressed in symbolic forms.

For Maimonides, losses of volition were cumulative. The loss of voluntary action included the loss of understanding and produced a loss of the ability to engage in repentance. "Likewise does God withhold man's ability to use his free will in regard to repentance" (*Eight Chapters* viii; pp. 95–96). Because ignorance prevented repentance, the therapeutic task was to overcome ignorance. Due, however, to the involvement of the imagination and the appetitive faculty, a merely intellectual education, consistent with traditional Aristotelianism, was not adequate. It did not suffice to *know*, it was necessary also to *understand*. In citing Isaiah 6:10 in the *Eight Chapters*, Maimonides quoted the classical biblical expression of the curative power of understanding: "lest they . . . understand with their hearts, and turn and be healed" (*Eight Chapters* viii; p. 97; citing Is 6:10). Understanding permitted the voluntary act of *teshuvah*, "returning" to God, and the healing associated with it.

To promote understanding, Maimonides recommended a medieval practice of rational mysticism. Bakan (1966b) counted psychoanalysis as a contemporary practice of rational mysticism. Certainly free association should be recognized as a form of meditation. In his first discussion of the technique, Freud (1900) wrote:

> As we fall asleep, 'involuntary ideas' emerge . . . [and] change into visual and acoustic images. . . . In the state used for the analysis of dreams and pathological ideas, the patient purposely and deliberately abandons this activity and . . . the involuntary thoughts which now emerge . . .—and here the situation differs from falling asleep—retain the character of ideas. *In this way the 'involuntary' ideas are transformed into 'voluntary' ones.* (p. 102; Freud's italics)

With these words, Freud explained that free association is performed during an alternate state of consciousness that resembles the hypnagogic state between waking and sleeping. The patient is asked to report verbally whatever the contents of consciousness may be. The act of speaking aloud tends to suppress spontaneously arising imagery through their preconscious translation into spontaneously arising verbal equivalents. Freud's discussion implied that the imagery persisted preconsciously and provided a foundation for the therapeutic effects of free association.

To further clarify the procedure of free association, Freud added the following passage in the 1909 edition of *The Interpretation of Dreams*.

> The adoption of the required attitude of mind towards ideas that seem to emerge 'of their own free will' and the abandonment of the critical function that is normally in operation against them seem to be hard of achievement for some people. The 'involuntary thoughts' are liable to release a most violent resistance, which seeks to prevent their emergence. If we may trust that great poet and philosopher Friedrich Schiller, however, poetic creation must demand an exactly similar attitude. In passage in his correspondence with Körner—we have to thank Otto Rank for unearthing it—Schiller (writing on December 1, 1788) replies to his friend's complaint of insufficient productivity: 'The ground for your complaint seems to me to lie in the constraint imposed by your reason upon your imagination. I will make my idea more concrete by a simile. It seems a bad thing and detrimental to the creative work of the mind if Reason makes too close an examination of the ideas as they come pouring in—at the very gateway, as it were. Looked at in isolation, a thought may seem very trivial or very fantastic; but it may be made important by another thought that comes after it, and, in conjunction with other thoughts that may seem equally absurd, it may turn out to form a most effective link. Reason cannot form any opinion upon all this unless it retains the thought long enough to look at it in connection with the others. On the other hand, where there is a creative mind, Reason—so it seems to me—relaxes its watch upon the gates, and the ideas rush in pell-mell, and only then does it look them through and examine them in a mass.—You critics, or whatever else you may call yourselves, are ashamed or frightened of the momentary and transient extravagances which are to be found in all truly creative minds and whose longer and shorter duration distinguishes the thinking artist from the dreamer. You complain of your unfruitfulness because you reject too soon and discriminate too severely.'
>
> Nevertheless, what Schiller describes as a relaxation of the watch upon the gates of Reason, the adoption of an attitude of uncritical self-observation, is by no means difficult. Most of my patients achieve it after their first instruction. I myself can do so very completely, by the help of writing down my ideas as they occur to me. (Freud, 1900, pp. 102–103)

Maimonides' procedure of *hitbonenut*, which meditates on God's purpose for oneself, requires an attitude of objective self-observation, where free association involved "an attitude of uncritical self-observation." Both procedures were meditations on autobiography. In other respects the differences were substantial. *Hitbonenut* was oriented toward decisions on future actions, free association toward the understanding of the past. Freud had patients associate freely partly in order to manifest memories and fantasies that they could not understand and partly to enable them to arrive at self-understanding that he termed "insight." Of all of the things that a psychoanalyst may say to a patient, none is more important than interpretation, because interpretation alone can catalyze the patient's self-understanding, which is to say, insight. Due to the curative power of insight, Freud discouraged analysts from intervening whenever a patient's free associations led spontaneously to insight. When analysts do choose to speak, they favor interpretations of the patients' transference, or experience of the analysts as behaving similarly to their parents, because insight is most needed, dramatic, and potentially curative when imaginative projections are maximally vivid and intense.

In a little appreciated passage, Freud (1933) acknowledged the close proximity of psychoanalysis to mysticism.

> It is easy to imagine . . . that certain mystical practices may succeed in upsetting the normal relations between the different regions of the mind, so that, for instance, perception may be able to grasp happenings in the depths of the ego and in the id which were otherwise inaccessible to it. It may safely be doubted, however, whether this road will lead us to the ultimate truths from which salvation is to be expected. Nevertheless it may be admitted that the therapeutic efforts of psycho-analysis have chosen a similar line of approach. Its intention is, indeed, to strengthen the ego, to make it more independent of the super-ego, to widen its field of perception and enlarge its organization, so that it can appropriate fresh portions of the id. Where id was, there ego shall be. It is a work of culture—not unlike the draining of the Zuider Zee. (pp. 79–80)

Freud denied that mystical experiences arrive at ultimate truths that are salvific. He instead encouraged a view of mysticism as a technique whose effects compare with psychoanalysis in accomplishing not supernature but "a work of culture." Like psychoanalysis, mysticism can provide increased access to the hidden sources of emotional life.

A lesser point of convergence between Maimonides and Freud may be seen in the Hebrew word *teshuvah*, ordinarily translated as "repentance," which literally means "return." Maimonides' model conceptualized repentance as a return from anthropomorphic and possibly idolatrous imagination to rational and emotionally wholesome belief in God. Freud's goal of making the unconscious conscious was similarly a concept of return: a return of repressed materials to consciousness that permitted consciousness to return from fantasy to reality.

PSYCHIC REALITY

For Maimonides, the interpretation of prophecy depended on the ability to distinguish the real from the imaginary. He wrote: "I do not consider that you might confuse intellectual representation with imagination and with the [reproduction] of an image of a sense object by the imaginative faculty" (*Guide* II:2; p. 254). Freud (1911, p. 222) referred to the "reality principle" and "reality-testing" as conditions of consciousness that made possible the recognition of dreams' manifest incoherence.

For Maimonides, all of the reports of the prophets other than Moses were visions and dreams. But they were no less "real" for being visions and dreams. Imagination could bring one to mental content that contained information that was superior to the thinking of the rational faculty alone. Through imagination, the mind could reach to things that could not be attained by reason alone. There are important differences between Maimonides and Freud on this point, but an ascription of reality to fantasy was similarly to be found in Freud's approach. For example, in musing over the question of how to deal with the truthfulness of patients' childhood memories, Freud (1916–17) stated: "It will be a long time before we can take our proposal that we should equate phantasy and reality and not bother to begin with whether the childhood experiences under examination are the one or the other. Yet this is clearly the only correct attitude to adopt towards these mental productions." Speaking of memories that were only fantasies, he stated, "It remains a fact that the patient has created these phantasies for himself, and this fact is of scarcely less importance for his neurosis than if he had really experienced what the fantasies contain. The phantasies possess psychical as contrasted with material reality, and we gradually learn to understand that in the world of the neuroses it is psychical reality which is of the decisive kind" (p. 368).

Freud systematically distinguished between fantasy and reality and postulated the impossibility of avoiding a series of developmentally appropriate fantasies in childhood, including the primal scene, the Oedipus complex, and the family romance. Neurosis was characterized, according to Freud, by a failure to outgrow the fantasies. Freud's therapeutic project involved identifying the fixated fantasy, analyzing the transference in order to demonstrate to the patient that the fantasy was a fantasy, and so enable the patient to recognize and resolve the infantilism. Freud's clinical technique flowed from the importance that he ascribed to fantasy in human thought.

For Maimonides, too, the basic human problem was a consequence of mistaking fantasy for reality. In Maimonides' view, all perplexity, all errors in theology, and all idolatry stemmed from the reification of imagination. Perplexity arose when dreams and visions of prophecy were treated literally. They were instead to be interpreted as parabolic blends of intellect and imagination that were in harmony with nature. Maimonides' therapeutic project began by demonstrating the necessary existence, unity, and utter simplicity of God, which precluded his possession of attributes and made God unknowable. Having established the logical necessity of a negative theology, Maimonides provided insight into the condition of perplexity by disclosing positive theologies as fantasies.

UNDERSTANDING ON ONE'S OWN

In the Jewish mystical tradition, esoteric teaching was done on a one-to-one basis. The obligation was set forward in the mishnah to the Talmud, Hagigah 11b. The Accounts of the Beginning and the Chariot were to be taught only to a single student at a time. Learning the Account of the Chariot was restricted to one "wise, and ... understanding of his own knowledge." The task consisted, in a sense, of coming to understand what one already potentially knew. The teacher was to expound only enough to promote the self-understanding of the student, and even chapter headings might not be conveyed for its final portions.

The convergence with Freud's method was precise. The fundamental rule of psychoanalysis was the patient's pledge to truthfully say whatever thoughts entered the patient's stream of consciousness. By associating freely, and reporting the associations aloud, the patient became aware of the patient's own knowledge. The task of the psychoanalyst was to facilitate the patient's process of "understanding of his own knowledge." In classical technique, the exposition by the psychoanalyst was minimal. The project in the psychoanalytic hour was precisely that of the patient coming to understand consciously what he or she already knew unconsciously. Whatever confrontations, interpretations, support, and teaching an analyst might do, it was the patient's growth in self-understanding that was Freud's goal.

THE UNCONSCIOUS

Both Maimonides and Freud entertained the concept of the unconscious. In *The Psychology of Aristotle* (1977), Brentano observed that "the assumption of an unconsciously acting intellectual power, analogous to the unconscious powers of the bodily part, was in fact a necessity for Aristotle ... it is none other than the active intellect [*nous poietikos*] which is active before all thought, since it is the active principle of intellectual cognition" (p. 50). In Maimonides' view, the Active Intellect caused ideas that did not exist within the human mind, whose existence were only potential, to become actual within a prophet's rational faculty. "That which brings intellect into existence is an intellect, namely, the Active Intellect" (*Guide* II:4; p. 258). In addition, Maimonides extended Aristotle's concept of the unconscious by attributing prophecy to an overflow of the Active Intellect, first to the rational faculty, and second to the imagination. Since conscious experience of a vision of prophecy was limited to the end result of this process, not only the Active Intellect, but also the rational and imaginative faculties were credited with unconscious operations in Maimonides' system.

In Freud's model of the psyche, the formation of latent dream thoughts was attributed to the preconscious, which performed rational thinking outside consciousness. The conversion of the latent dream thoughts into dream imagery was attributed to the unconscious. Although Freud seldom referred to it, he also postulated a mental process that corresponded to the Active Intellect. In *Moses and Monotheism* (1939), Freud asserted that "Human beings found themselves obliged in general to recognize 'intellectual [geistige]' forces—forces . . . which cannot be grasped by the senses" (p. 114). This sentence acknowledged Freud's belief in the intellectual aspect of reality that Aristotle's concept had sought to address.

In *Future of an Illusion*, Freud (1927, p. 53) stated that "the voice of the intellect is a soft one, but it does not rest till it has gained a hearing." He admitted that "our god *Logos* is perhaps not a very almighty one" (p. 54) but he placed his hopes in its effectiveness.

> Our god, *Logos*, will fulfill whichever of these wishes nature outside us allows, but he will do it very gradually, only in the unforeseeable future, and for a new generation of men. He promises no compensation for us, who suffer grievously from life . . . in the long run nothing can withstand reason and experience (p. 54).

Freud's personification of *Logos* was notable. Aristotle had maintained that "it is the *logos* which is a thing's essence or nature" (*Parts of Animals*, I i 642a); and *logos*, "word" or "idea," had been the Stoics' and Middle Platonists' term for the Aristotelian *nous*, "Active Intellect." Maimonides had asserted that Jewish tradition, from the Bible onward, had personified the Active Intellect as an angel. Freud's personification of *Logos* conformed with the same literary convention.

For Maimonides, the act of understanding of one's own knowledge involved the Active Intellect, the process that caused potentiality to turn into actuality both in the mind and in the external world. Freud expressed an equivalent concept when he described psychoanalysis as making the unconscious conscious.

For both Maimonides and Freud, the unconscious and its manifestations were inalienably sexual. In Maimonides' view, the Active Intellect was an intellectual process that was continually engaged in universal processes of generation and corruption. Its unceasing fitting and refitting of forms to matter was conceptualized most naturally in anthropomorphic, sexual terms. Maimonides' explication of the vision of Ezekiel as coital imagery that symbolized the process of creation out of nothing identified the enthroned glory as a symbolic representation of the Active Intellect engaging in generation and corruption.

In *Three Essays on the Theory of Sexuality*, in which Freud (1905) extended the concept of sexuality to include foreplay as well as coitus, and the oral, anal, and Oedipal (phallic) erotism of childhood in addition to adult genitality, he developed the view that thought as a whole is a sublimation, that is, a process of metaphorization, of the varieties and aspects of sexuality. For both Maimonides and Freud, the noetic was predicated on the sexual, through extrapolation and metaphorization from it.

VIEWS OF JUDAISM

The convergences of Maimonides and Freud extended to their views of Judaism. Where Freud (1913) described God as "the exalted father," a projection of the child's attitude to the father, Maimonides conceptualized biblical language similarly. Quoting the Talmudic saying, "The Law speaks in the language of human beings," Maimonides identified projection as a general source of biblical anthropomorphisms and theological error. He also described the process of projection in close detail. One instance pertained to interpersonal contexts: "If a man ... alleges that certain families and individuals are of blemished descent and refers to them as bastards—suspicion is justified that he himself may be a bastard ... whosoever blemishes others projects upon them his own blemish" (*Mishneh Torah, Kiddushin*, 19:17). Elsewhere Maimonides indicated that a proneness to anger was the great character defect of Moses. Not only was it an intrinsic vice, but it had two very negative effects for the people. Moses' anger was sinful because it encouraged others to indulge their anger. It was also the basis of the people's attribution of the characteristic of anger to God. According to Maimonides, when the people saw Moses becoming angry, they inferred that God was angry with them, too. "When Moses said or did anything [the people] subjected his words or actions to the most searching examination ... when they saw that he waxed wrathful, they said of Moses that ... his anger resulted from his knowledge that God was angry with them" (*Eight Chapters* iv; p. 68). Moses' anger misled the people to believe that God could be angry, and that the attribute of anger was properly ascribable to God. The projection of anger onto God was a theological error, an anthropomorphism, and an idolatry.

Maimonides was also critical of mere religious observance by "ignoramuses who observe the commandments" (*Guide* III:51, p. 619), and he asserted that the *Guide* was not addressed to them. "It is not the purpose of this Treatise ... to teach those who have not engaged in any study other than the science of the Law—I mean the legalistic study of the Law. For the purpose of this Treatise ... is the science of Law in its true sense" (*Guide* I:Introduction; p. 5). He rejected the claim that Judaism rests on received tradition alone (*Guide* III:31; p. 524). He insisted that a correct understanding of Jewish tradition rests on "the science" or systematic philosophy of the law. It requires a selective use of received tradition, based on a critical awareness of the theory that makes Judaism coherent philosophically as a way of life. Freud made a similar point using modern language. Freud (1913) conceptualized the development of intellectual culture in three epochs: ages of magic, religion, and science. Religion, founded on the anthropomorphic projection of parental gods, was a group neurosis (Freud, 1927) or, worse, a group psychosis (Freud, 1930).

Both Freud and Maimonides sought to understand Judaism as the historical product of earlier religious development. The idea that the Jewish religion is something progressively developmental is already provided in Scripture. Abraham discovered the existence of God long before Moses was even born. Moses later added societal commandments to the contents of Abraham's personal religion. Maimonides followed the Scriptural line of thought. However, he added the notion that Abraham was brought up in the Sabian religion, and that it was the move beyond Sabianism that characterized Abraham's contribution. Maimonides wrote: "It is well known that the Patriarch Abraham was brought up in the religion and the opinion of the Sabians ... they consider the ... sun as the chief deity. ... Abraham ... differed from the people and declared that there is a Maker besides the sun" (*Guide* III:29; p. 514).

Like Maimonides, Freud viewed the Jewish religion as a progressive development out of earlier and more primitive religion. Freud adopted an evolutionary perspective in *Totem and Taboo* (1913), when he discussed the emergence of religion out of magic. In *Moses and Monotheism* (1939), Freud discussed the development of Judaism out of religion in general. Here Freud reversed his general pessimism about religion and wrote in admiration of the Jewish achievement. He suggested that the abstract concept of God was derived from concrete images of God through a "triumph of intellectuality over sensuality or, strictly speaking, an instinctual renunciation" (p. 119). Freud remarked that "all such advances in intellectuality have as their consequence that the individual's self-esteem is increased" (p. 115). The particular religion out of which Jewish monotheism emerged, according to Freud, had been a devotion to the sun—in this case not Sabianism as Maimonides attributed to the era of Abraham, but the Egyptian worship of the sun god Aton in the era of Moses. Even this disagreement is lessened, when it is remembered that Maimonides addressed Abraham's solitary achievement while Freud addressed Moses' social achievement as a public educator. Freud wrote, "The religion of Moses ... forced upon the people an advance in intellectuality" (p. 123). And again, "[The] turning from the mother to the father points ... to a victory of intellectuality over sensuality—that is, an advance of civilization, since maternity is proved by the evidence of the senses while paternity is a hypothesis, based on an inference and a premise" (p. 114). In this way, Freud, like Maimonides, placed the intellectual as the ultimate goal of his technique of personal development and traced the historical origin of his point of view to the emergence of Jewish monotheism.

PROPHETIC AMBITION

The question is often raised about how Freud understood his relationship to Judaism. Like Einstein, Freud served on the Board of the Hebrew University of Jerusalem, but Jewish interests and Jewish identity were not major concerns. Freud generally admitted only limited connections to Judaism. However, in 1926, when illness kept Freud from attending his B'nai Brith lodge brothers' celebration of his seventieth birthday, he wrote to them:

> What bound me to Jewry, was (I am ashamed to admit) neither faith nor national pride ... plenty of other things ... make the attractiveness of Jewry and Jews irresistible.... Because I was a Jew I found myself free from many prejudices which restricted others in the use of their intellect; and as a Jew I was prepared to join the Opposition and to do without agreement with the 'compact majority.' (Freud, 1941, pp. 273–274)

Freud's statement, "Because I was a Jew I found myself free from many prejudices which restricted others in the use of their intellect," anticipated his thesis in *Moses and Monotheism* (1939) that Moses' opposition to idolatry made possible an advance of the intellect to which Jews have been indebted ever after. Freud counted himself among the beneficiaries of Moses' achievement. He counted himself in the Jewish tradition that he believed descended authentically from Moses.

The 1930 preface to the Hebrew translation of Freud's *Totem and Taboo* contains the statement: "The author hopes ... that he will be at one with his readers in the conviction that unprejudiced science cannot remain a stranger to the spirit of the new Jewry" (Freud, 1913, p. xv). The expression "new Jewry" implied that Freud regarded with favor the Enlightenment and Reform movements of Judaism that were taking place all around him, and he hoped that science could not "remain a stranger" to its spirit. Freud's hope corresponded exactly to the position of Maimonides, who similarly understood that the received tradition of Judaism required correction through its embrace of science and philosophy.

Like Maimonides, Freud hoped to reform Judaism. Much of Freud's work was directed toward nullifying the effects of the tyrannical and arbitrary father figures that are carried in the mind. These he explicitly identified with the figure of Moses in the Judeo-Christian tradition. Indeed, in *Moses and Monotheism* he proposed the interesting theory that hostility to Jews was due to the association, in the mind of the anti-Semitic person, of Jews with Moses, and thus with the law as a yoke imposed by tyranny. Freud's project was to dissociate the Jews from this negative figure of Moses by making them out to be the chief victims of Moses rather than his representatives.

It is arguable that Maimonides' lifelong project equally shared these two characteristics, that science not be a stranger to the Jews, and the Jews somehow remove the arbitrary and tyrannical features from the law of Moses. In his intense effort to promote psychotherapy through rational mysticism, Freud offered a contemporary version of the project of Maimonides. Maimonides had a unified understanding of Judaism, based on reason, that conceptualized it historically as a natural religion, based in natural theology, that had universal significance. Freud similarly aspired to transform rational mysticism into a universal practice.

It is interesting that both Freud and Maimonides had lifelong preoccupations with Moses. For both of them, Moses was understood, in Freud's phrase, as the "law-giver." For Maimonides, the prophecy of Moses consisted of the 613 commandments of the Law and the preservation of the authentic legacy of Moses was the explicit concern of Maimonides' life's work. For Freud (1939), Moses was the paradigmatic tyrannical father figure. And yet Freud (1914a) strangely wrote a very different article about Michelangelo's statue in Rome. He sat in front of the statue for long hours, allowing himself to have fear and terror as though he were at Sinai. He engaged in a bizarre struggle to determine what the statue meant, in the sense not of Michelangelo's intentions, but Moses'. He came to a final conclusion that Moses, while in wrath and rising to strike, contained his wrath.

Psychoanalysts have long been aware that Freud identified with Moses. They have assumed that the identification was metaphoric, that Freud saw himself founding psychoanalysis as Moses had founded Judaism. One may wonder, however, whether the identification was not literal, whether Freud did not see himself continuing the historical project of Moses and Maimonides, to defeat idolatry and give to the world the rational mysticism that Judaism essentially is and ought to be. This would be a religion that takes full cognizance of human subjectivity and relativity, but at the same time stays grounded in rationality and stresses the enhancement of human consciousness free from the blinding and paralysis of repression.

CONCLUSIONS

Nonsexual, metaphysical interpretations of sexual imagery became a mainstay of the kabbalah following the publication of Maimonides' *Guide* and were assigned an explicitly therapeutic function in the teachings of Rabbi Israel Baal Shem Tov, the founder of Hasidism. Freud's father Jacob had been a Hasid and may have mediated Maimonides' teaching to his son, perhaps in connection with advice concerning the management of his fantasy life. Freud was introduced to Maimonides as part of his religious education in Gymnasium. Maimonides' key psychological texts, the *Eight Chapters* and the *Guide*, were both available to Freud in German and other European translations; Franz Brentano, his philosophy professor at the University of Vienna, was an expert in the psychology of Aristotle. Freud's use of dream interpretation and the privileged place he assigned to sexual symbolism were common to Talmudic tradition, as well as both Maimonides and the kabbalah, but further convergences with Maimonides were unique. Both Freud and Maimonides attributed mental conflict to the opposition of inborn desire with rational social conduct. Both identified mental illness with involuntary inhibition. Both discussed hysterical paralysis and hysterical blindness as paradigmatic instances of inhibition. Both regarded therapy as a gain in freedom. Both had theories of the unconscious. Both regarded the recovery of lost understanding as the key to therapy. Both prescribed self-reflective meditations (*hitbonenut*, free association) that aimed at the achievement of insight into the self. Both practiced interpretation as the therapist's major contribution. Both attributed psychic reality to imagination. Intriguingly, both identified with Moses.

Some of the convergences between Maimonides and Freud may be traced to shared circumstances. Both were Jews, who were indebted both to the Bible and to rabbinical teachings about dream interpretation, which referred prominently to sexual motifs. Both Maimonides and Freud participated in the systemic male chauvinism of their cultures. Both were physicians who took concern with psychogenic ailments, and both enjoined their patients to engage in rational meditations as a means of cure.

In replacing ignorance with imagination as the cause of mental illness, Maimonides introduced the paradigm of psychotherapy to which Freud was heir, possibly through both German Romanticism and East European Hasidism. In other respects, the convergences between Maimonides and Freud are better explained if we assume that Freud read both the *Eight Chapters* and the *Guide*. Their views agree in important places. They also differ in places, but many of the differences prove on close examination to include crucial points of convergence. They often shared an appreciation of a problem even when they differed concerning its solution. Each of them had a certain glimpse of truth. Each was in touch with rational mysticism, an intellectual practice that for a variety of reasons has not been too visible in history but is valuable for coping with the questions.

Even when their views differed, in studying their works carefully there is something to learn and build on concerning the therapeutic questions that they addressed. Supportive psychotherapies are not all of a single type. Maimonides' cure of souls was an insight-oriented approach to sublimation that has much to recommend it. As Freud explained in 1909 to Oskar Pfister, who was both a psychoanalyst and a Lutheran pastor:

> The permanent success of psycho-analysis certainly depends on the coincidence of two issues: the obtaining of satisfaction by the release of tension, and sublimation of the sheer instinctual drive ... we generally succeed only with the former. ... In your case ... [patients] are ready for sublimation, and to sublimation in its most comfortable form, namely the religious. ...

Our public, no matter of what racial origin, is irreligious, we are generally thoroughly irreligious ourselves and, as the other ways of sublimation which *we* substitute for religion are too difficult for most patients." (Freud & Pfister, 1963, p. 16)

Again in 1910, Freud wrote Pfister: "Things are easier for you than for us physicians, because you can sublimate the transference on to religion and ethics" (Freud & Pfister, 1963, pp. 39–40).

Maimonides' cure of souls may be considered a valuable adjunct to psychoanalysis for patients who find its religious commitments congenial. Although the two therapies differ, they are complementary.

References

Alexander, Franz and French, Thomas Morton. (1946). *Psychoanalytic therapy: Principles and application.* New York: Ronald Press.

[al-Farabi]. (1961). *The Fusul al-Madani (aphorisms of the stateman) of al-Farabi* (Ed. & Trans. D. M. Dunlop). Cambridge: Cambridge University Press.

Altmann, Alexander. (1936). Maimonides' attitude toward Jewish mysticism. In Alfred Jospe (Ed.), *Studies in Jewish thought: An anthology of German Jewish scholarship* (pp. 200–218). Detroit: Wayne State University Press, 1981.

———. (1969). Saadya's theory of revelation: Its origin and background. *Studies in Religious Philosophy and Mysticism.* Plainview, NY: Books for Libraries Press.

———. (1972). Maimonides' "four perfections." *Israel Oriental Studies* 2:15–23.

Ariel, David S. (1988). *The mystic quest: An introduction to Jewish mysticism.* Northvale, NJ: Jason Aronson.

Aristotle. (1984). *The complete works of Aristotle: The revised Oxford translation,* 2 vols. Ed. Jonathan Barnes. Princeton, NJ: Princeton University Press.

Aron, Willy. (1957). Notes on Sigmund Freud's ancestry and Jewish contacts. *Yivo Annual of Jewish Social Science* 11:286–95. New York: Yivo Institute for Jewish Research.

Ater, Moshe. (1992). *The man Freud and monotheism.* Jerusalem: Magnes Press, The Hebrew University.

Bahya Ben Joseph Ibn Paquda. (1973). *The book of direction to the duties of the heart* (Trans. Menahem Mansoor with Sara Arenson & Shoshana Dannhauser). London: Routledge & Kegan Paul.

Bakan, David. (1958). *Sigmund Freud and the Jewish mystical tradition.* Princeton, NJ: D. Van Nostrand.

———. (1966a). *The duality of human existence: Isolation and communion in Western man.* Boston: Beacon Press.

———. (1966b). Science, mysticism, and psychoanalysis. *Catholic Psychological Record* 4:1–9. Reprinted in *On method: Toward a reconstruction of psychological investigation* (pp. 139–149). San Francisco: Jossey-Bass, 1969.

———. (1971). *Slaughter of the innocents: A study of the battered child phenomenon*. San Francisco & London: Jossey-Bass.

———. (1979). *And they took themselves wives: The emergence of patriarchy in Western civilization*. San Francisco: Harper & Row.

———. (1989). Contributions to the history of psychology: LIII. Maimonides' "Freudian" theory of prophecy. *Psychological Reports* 64:667–675.

———. (1991). *Maimonides on prophecy: A commentary on selected chapters of* The Guide of the Perplexed. Northvale, NJ: Jason Aronson.

Barbour, Ian G. (1974). *Myths, models, and paradigms: A comparative study in science and religion*. New York: Harper & Row.

Bin Tufail, Abu Bakr Muhammad. (1982). *The journey of the soul: The story of Hai bin Yaqzan* (Trans. Riad Kocache). London: Octagon Press.

Bion, Wilfred R. (1962). *Learning from experience*. Northvale, NJ: Aronson, 1994.

———. (1963). *Elements of psycho-analysis*. New York: Basic Books.

———. (1967). *Second thoughts: Selected papers on psycho-analysis*. London: William Heinemann; reprinted London: Karnac Books, 1984.

Blumenthal, David R. (1977). Maimonedes' intellectualist mysticism and the superiority of the prophecy of Moses. *Studies in Medieval Culture* 10 (1977), 51–68; rpt. in David R. Blumenthal (Ed.), *Approaches to Judaism in medieval times* (pp. 27–51). Chico, CA: Scholars Press, 1984.

———. (1980). On the study of philosophic mysticism. In Baruch M. Bokser (Ed.), *History of Judaism: The next ten years* (pp. 81–92). Chico, CA: Scholars Press.

———. (1988). Maimonides: Prayer, worship, and mysticism. In David R. Blumenthal (Ed.), *Approaches to Judaism in medieval times, vol. III* (pp. 1–16). Atlanta: Scholars Press.

———. (1999). Philosophic mysticism: The ultimate goal of medieval Judaism. http://www.js.emory.edu/BLUMENTHAL/PhilMyst.html. Reprinted in David R. Blumenthal, *Philosophic mysticism: Studies in rational religion* (pp. 115–127). Ramat Gan, Israel: Bar-Ilan University Press, 2006.

———. (2006). Maimonides' philosophic mysticism. In *Philosophic mysticism* (pp. 128–151).

Brentano, Franz. (1977). *The psychology of Aristotle: In particular his doctrine of the active intellect* [1867] (Ed. & trans. Rolf George). Berkeley: University of California Press.

———. (1987). *On the existence of God: Lectures given at the Universities of Würzburg and Vienna (1868–1891)* (Ed. & trans. Susan F. Krantz). Dordrecht, Boston, & Lancaster: Martinus Nijhoff.

Breuer, Joseph, & Sigmund Freud. (1893). On the psychical mechanism of hysterical phenomena: Preliminary communication. In *The standard edition of the complete psychological works of Sigmund Freud, Vol. 2* (pp. 1–17). London: Hogarth Press, 1955.

——— . (1895). *Studies on hysteria*. In *The standard edition of the complete psychological works of Sigmund Freud, Vol. 2*. London: Hogarth Press, 1955.

Brill, Abraham Arden. (1940). Reflections, reminiscences of Sigmund Freud. *Medical Leaves* 3:18–29. Reprinted in Hendrik M. Ruitenbeek (Ed.), *Freud as we knew him* (pp. 154–169). Detroit: Wayne State University Press, 1973.

Buber, Martin. (1965). *Between man and man*. New York: Macmillan.

Burrell, David B. (1988). Aquinas's debt to Maimonides. In Ruth Link-Salinger (Ed.), *A straight path: Studies in medieval philosophy and culture. Essays in honor of Arthur Hyman* (pp. 37–48). Washington, DC: Catholic University of America Press, 1988.

Capps, Donald. (1971). Hartmann's relationship to Freud: A reappraisal. *Journal of the History of the Behavioral Sciences* 6:162–175.

Chernus, Ira. (1982). *Mysticism in rabbinic Judaism: Studies in the history of Midrash*. Berlin & New York: Walter de Gruyter.

Cleary, Tom S., & Shapiro, Sam I. (1995). The plateau experience and the postmortem life: Abraham H. Maslow's unfinished theory. *Journal of Transpersonal Psychology* 27(1):1–23.

Corbin, Henry. (1972). *Mundus imaginalis* or the imaginary and the imaginal. *Spring 1972*, 1–18.

Davidson, Herbert A. (1963). Maimonides' *Shemonah Peraqim* and Alfarabi's *Fusul al-Madani*. *Proceedings of the American Academy for Jewish Research* 31:33–50.

——— . (1992). *Alfarabi, Avicenna, & Averroes, on intellect: Their cosmologies, theories of the active intellect, & theories of human intellect*. New York & Oxford: Oxford University Press.

——— . (2005). *Moses Maimonides: The man and his works*. Oxford: Oxford University Press.

Diller, Jerry Victor. (1991). *Freud's Jewish identity: A case study in the impact of ethnicity*. Rutherford: Fairleigh Dickinson University Press; London & Toronto: Associated University Press.

Drob, Sanford L. (2000a). *Kabbalistic metaphors: Jewish mystical themes in ancient and modern thought*. Northvale, NJ, & Jerusalem: Jason Aronson.

——— . (2000b). *Symbols of the Kabbalah: Philosophical and psychological perspectives*. Northvale, NJ, & Jerusalem: Jason Aronson.

Elior, Rachel. (2004). *The three temples: On the emergence of Jewish mysticism* (Trans. David Louvish). Oxford & Portland, OR: Littman Library of Jewish Civilization.

Fakhry, Majid. (1971). Three varieties of mysticism in Islam. *International Journal for the Philosophy of Religion* 2/4:193–207.

Fauteux, Kevin. (1994). *The recovery of self: Regression and redemption in religious experience*. New York: Paulist Press.

Fishbane, Michael. (1994). *The kiss of God: Spiritual and mystical death in Judaism*. Seattle: University of Washington Press.

Fraade, Steven D. (1987). Ascetical aspects of ancient Judaism. In Arthur Green (Ed.), *Jewish spirituality: From the Bible through the Middle Ages* (pp. 253–288). New York: Crossroad.

Freeman, Erika. (1971). *Insights: Conversations with Theodor Reik.* Englewood Cliffs, NJ: Prentice-Hall.

Freud, Sigmund. (1966). *The standard edition of the complete psychological works of Sigmund Freud*, 24 vols. (Ed. James Strachey, with Anna Freud, Alix Strachey, & Alan Tyson). London: Hogarth Press. (Hereafter cited as *Standard edition*.)

———. (1893). Some points for a comparative study of organic and hysterical motor paralyses. *Standard edition*, 1:160–172. London: Hogarth Press, 1966.

———. (1894). The neuro-psychoses of defence. *Standard edition*, 3:45–61. London: Hogarth Press, 1962.

———. (1900). The interpretation of dreams. *Standard edition*, 4–5:1–625. London: Hogarth Press, 1958.

———. (1905). Three essays on the theory of sexuality. *Standard edition*, 7:130–243. London: Hogarth Press, 1953.

———. (1911). Formulations on the two principles of mental functioning. *Standard edition*, 12:218–226. London: Hogarth Press, 1958.

———. (1913). Totem and taboo: Some points of agreement between the mental life of savages and neurotics. *Standard edition*, 13:1–161. London: Hogarth Press, 1958.

———. (1914a). The Moses of Michelangelo. *Standard edition*, 13:211–238. London: Hogarth Press, 1958.

———. (1914b). On the history of the psycho-analytic movement. *Standard edition*, 14:7–66. London: Hogarth Press, 1957.

———. (1916–17). Introductory lectures on psycho-analysis. *Standard edition*, 15–16:9–463. London: Hogarth Press, 1961–63.

———. (1918). From the history of an infantile neurosis. *Standard edition*, 17:7–133. London: Hogarth Press, 1955.

———. (1923a). The ego and the id. *Standard edition*, 19:12–59. London: Hogarth Press, 1961.

———. (1923b). Remarks on the theory and practice of dream interpretation. *Standard Edition*, 19:109–121. London: Hogarth Press, 1961.

———. (1926). Inhibitions, symptoms, and anxiety. *Standard edition*, 20:87–172. London: Hogarth Press, 1959.

———. (1927). The future of an illusion. *Standard edition*, 21:5–56. London: Hogarth Press, 1961.

———. (1930). Civilization and its discontents. *Standard edition*, 21:64–145. London: Hogarth Press, 1961.

———. (1933). New introductory lectures on psycho-analysis. *Standard edition*, 22:5–182. London: Hogarth Press, 1964.

———. (1939). Moses and monotheism: Three essays. *Standard edition*, 23:6–137. London: Hogarth Press, 1964.

———. (1941 [1926]). Address to the Society of B'Nai B'rith. *Standard Edition*, 20:273–274. London: Hogarth Press, 1959.

———. (1985). *The complete letters of Sigmund Freud to Wilhelm Fliess 1887–1904* (Trans. & Ed. Jeffrey Moussaieff Masson). Cambridge: Belknap Press of Harvard University Press.

———. (1990). *The letters of Sigmund Freud to Eduard Silberstein 1871–1881* (Ed. Walter Boehlich, Trans. Arnold J. Pomerans). Cambridge: Harvard University Press.

Freud, Sigmund, & Pfister, Oskar. (1963). *Psychoanalysis and faith: The letters of Sigmund Freud and Oskar Pfister* (Eds. Heinrich Meng & Ernst L. Freud). New York: Basic Books.

Friedländer, M. (Trans.). (1904). Introduction. In Moses Maimonides. *The guide for the perplexed* (2nd ed.). Reprinted New York: Dover, 1956.

Fromm, Erich. (1939). Selfishness and self-love. *Psychiatry* 2:507–523.

Galston, Miriam. (1990). *Politics and excellence: The political philosophy of Alfarabi*. Princeton, NJ: Princeton University Press.

Gorfinkle, Joseph I. (ed.). (1912). *The eight chapters of Maimonides on ethics (Shemonah Perakim): A psychological and ethical treatise*. New York: Columbia University Press; reprinted New York: AMS Press, 1966.

Grof, Christina, & Grof, Stanislav. (1990). *The stormy search for the self: A guide to personal growth through transformational crisis*. Los Angeles: Jeremy P. Tarcher.

Grof, Stanislav, & Grof, Christina (Eds.). (1989). *Spiritual emergency: When personal transformation becomes a crisis*. Los Angeles: Jeremy P. Tarcher.

Hadot, Pierre. (2002). *What is ancient philosophy?* (Trans. Michael Chase). Cambridge & London: Belknap Press of Harvard University Press.

Halbertal, Moshe. (2007). *Concealment and Revelation: Esotericism in Jewish thought and its philosophical implications* (Trans. Jackie Feldman). Princeton & Oxford: Princeton University Press.

Haq, Syed Nomanul. (1994). *Names, natures and things: The alchemist Jabir ibn Hayyan and his kitab al-Ahjar* (Book of Stones). Dordrecht, Boston, & London: Kluwer Academic Publishers.

Hartmann, Heinz. (1958). *Ego psychology and the problem of adaptation*. New York: International Universities Press.

Havens, Joseph. (1968). *Psychology and religion: A contemporary dialogue*. Princeton, NJ: D. Van Nostrand.

Heath, Peter. (1992). *Allegory and philosophy in Avicenna (Ibn Sina): With a translation of the book of the Prophet Muhammad's ascent to heaven*. Philadelphia: University of Pennsylvania Press.

Heschel, Abraham Joshua. (1982). *Maimonides: A biography*. (Trans. Joachim Neugroschel.) New York: Farrar Straus Giroux.

———. (1996). *Prophetic inspiration after the prophets: Maimonides and other medieval authorities* (Ed. Morris Faierstein). Hoboken, NJ: Ktav.

Hesse, Mary. (1970). *Models and analogies in science*. Notre Dame: Notre Dame University Press.

Hodgson, M. G. S. (1960). Batiniyya. In H. A. R. Gibb, J. H. Kramers, E. L,vi-Provencal, & J. Schacht (Eds.), *The Encyclopaedia of Islam*, Volume I (2nd ed.) (pp. 1098–1100). Leiden: E. J. Brill & London: Luzac & Co.

Husik, Isaac. (1916). *A history of mediaeval Jewish philosophy*. New York: Macmillan; reprinted New York: Atheneum, 1969.

Idel, Moshe. (1986). Sitre 'Arayot in Maimonides' thought. In Shlomo Pines & Yirmiyahu Yovel (Eds.), *Maimonides and philosophy: Papers Presented at the Sixth Jerusalem Philosophical Encounter*, May 1985, pp. 79–91. Dordrecht, Boston, & Lancaster: Martinus Nijhoff.

———. (1988). *Kabbalah: New perspectives*. New Haven: Yale University Press.

———. (1990). Maimonides and kabbalah. In Isadore Twersky (Ed.), *Studies in Maimonides*, pp. 31–79. Cambridge & London: Harvard University Press.

———. (2004). Maimonides *guide of the perplexed* and the kabbalah. *Jewish History* 18:197–226.

James, William. (1902). *The varieties of religious experience: A study in human nature*. New York: New American Library, 1958.

Jones, Ernest. (1953). *The life and work of Sigmund Freud, Volume 1: The formative years and the great discoveries 1856–1900*. New York: Basic Books.

Kaplan, Aryeh. (1985). *Jewish meditation: A practical guide*. New York: Schocken.

Kellner, Menachem. (2007). *Maimonides' confrontation with mysticism*. Oxford & Portland, OR: Littman Library of Jewish Civilization.

Klein, Dennis B. (1985). *Jewish origins of the psychoanalytic movement*. Chicago: University of Chicago Press.

Klein, Melanie. (1935). A contribution to the psychogenesis of manic-depressive states. Reprinted in *Love, Guilt and Reparation and Other Works. 1921–1945* (pp. 262–289). New York: Delacorte, 1975.

Kraus, Paul. (1943). *Jabir ibn Hayyan: Contribution a L'Histoire des Idées Scientifiques dans l'Islam. Volume 1: Le Corpus des Écrits Jabiriens. Mémoires Presenté a l'Institut d'Egypte* 44.

Krippner, Stanley (Ed.). (1972). The plateau experience: A. H. Maslow and others. *Journal of Transpersonal Psychology* 4:107–120.

Lakoff, George. (1993). The contemporary theory of metaphor. In Andrew Ortony (Ed.), *Metaphor and thought* (2nd ed.). Cambridge: Harvard University Press, pp. 202–251.

Lakoff, George, & Johnson, Mark. (1980). *Metaphors we live by*. Chicago: University of Chicago Press.

———. (1999). *Philosophy in the flesh: The embodied mind and its challenge to Western thought*. New York: Basic Books.

Langer, Susanne K. (1957). *Philosophy in a new key: A study in the symbolism of reason, rite, and art* (3rd ed.). Cambridge: Harvard University Press.

Leary, David E. (Ed.). (1990). *Metaphors in the history of psychology*. Cambridge: Cambridge University Press.

Leatherdale, W. H. (1974). *The role of analogy, model, and metaphor in science*. Amsterdam: North-Holland, & New York: American Elsevier.

Lesher, James H. (1973). The meaning of NOUS in the posterior analytics. *Phronesis* 18(1):44–68.

Linden, Stanton J. (Ed.). (2003). *The alchemy reader: From Hermes Trismegistus to Isaac Newton*. Cambridge: University Library.

Lorand, Sandor. (1957). Dream interpretation in the Talmud (Babylonian and Graeco-Roman period). *International Journal of Psycho-Analysis* 38:92–97.

MacCormac, Earl R. (1976). *Metaphor and myth in science and religion*. Durham: Duke University Press.

MacDonald, Paul S. (2003). *History of the concept of mind: Speculations about soul, mind and spirit from Homer to Hume*. Aldershot, UK: Ashgate.

Maimonides, Abraham. (1927). *The high ways to perfection* (Trans. Samuel Rosenblatt). Reprinted New York: AMS Press, 1966.

———. (1938). *The high ways to perfection*, Vol. II (Trans. Samuel Rosenblatt). Baltimore: Johns Hopkins Press.

Maimonides, Moses. (1904). *The guide for the perplexed* (2nd ed.) (Trans. M. Friedländer). New York: Dover, 1956.

———. (1912). *The eight chapters of Maimonides on ethics (Shemonah Perakim): A psychological and ethical treatise* (Trans. Joseph I. Gorfinkle). New York: Columbia University Press; rpt. New York: AMS Press, 1966.

———. (1937). *Mishneh Torah: The book of knowledge* (Trans. Moses Hyamson). New York: Bloch; reprinted Jerusalem: Feldheim, 1971.

———. (1949). *Mishneh Torah: The book of adoration* (Trans. Moses Hyamson). New York: Bloch; reprinted Jerusalem: Feldheim, 1971.

———. (1963). *The guide of the perplexed* (2 vols.) (Trans. Shlomo Pines). Chicago: University of Chicago Press.

———. (1966). Maimonides on immortality and the principles of Judaism (Trans. Arnold Jacob Wolf). *Judaism* 15:95–101, 211–216, 336–342.

———. (1983). *Maimonides' commentary on Pirkey Avoth: The Mishna of Avoth with the commentary and selected other chapters of Maimonides*. [First edition, 1973, titled *Living Judaism*] (Trans. Paul Forchheimer). Jerusalem & New York: Feldheim.

Maimonides, Obadyah b. Abraham b. Moses. (1981). *The treatise of the pool: Al-Maqala al-Hawdiyya* (Ed. & Trans. Paul Fenton). London: Oxtagon Press.

Maslow, Abraham H. (1964). *Religions, values, and peak experiences.* Rpt. Harmondsworth: Penguin, 1976.

Matt, Daniel C. (1990). *Ayin*: The concept of nothingness in Jewish mysticism. In Robert K. C. Forman (Ed.), *The problem of pure consciousness: Mysticism and philosophy* (pp. 139–145). New York: Oxford University Press.

Merkur, Dan. (1985). The prophecies of Jeremiah. *American Imago* 42/1:1–37.

———. (1994). Freud and Hasidism. *The Psychoanalytic Study of Society* 19 (Ed. L. Bryce Boyer, Ruth M. Boyer, & Howard F. Stein, pp. 335–347. Hillsdale, NJ: Analytic Press.

———. (1999). *Mystical moments and unitive thinking.* Albany: State University of New York Press.

———. (2001a). *The psychedelic sacrament: Manna, meditation, and mystical experience.* Rochester, VT: Park Street Press.

———. (2001b). *Unconscious wisdom: A superego function in dreams, conscience, and inspiration.* Albany: State University of New York Press.

———. (2008). Revelation and the practice of prophecy: With special reference to Rabbi Nachman of Breslov. In J. Harold Ellens (Ed.), *Miracles: God, psychology, and science in 'inexplicable' events*, 3 vols. Westport, CT: Praeger.

———. (2009). The transference onto God. *International Journal for Applied Psychoanalytic Studies* 6/2:146–162.

Merlan, Philip. (1945). Brentano and Freud. *Journal of the History of Ideas* 6:375–77.

———. (1949). Brentano and Freud—A sequel. *Journal of the History of Ideas* 10:451.

———. (1969). *Monopsychism mysticism metaconsciousness: Problems of the soul in the Neoaristotelian and Neoplatonic tradition.* The Hague: Martinus Nijhoff.

Mora, George. (1969). The scrupulosity syndrome. In E. Mansell Pattison (Ed.), *Clinical psychiatry and religion.* International Psychiatry Clinics, Vol. 5, No. 4 (pp. 163–174). Boston: Little Brown.

Nachman of Breslov, Rabbi. (1990). *Likutey Moharan: Volume 3 (Lessons 17–22)* (Trans. Moshe Mykoff, Eds. Moshe Mykoff & Ozer Bergman). Jerusalem & Brooklyn: Breslov Research Institute.

———. (1993). *Likutey Moharan: Volume 10 (Lessons 109–194)* (Trans. Moshe Mykoff, Eds. Moshe Mykoff & Ozer Bergman). Jerusalem & Brooklyn: Breslov Research Institute.

Nanji, Azim. (1985). Towards a hermeneutic of Qur'anic and other narratives in Isma'ili thought. In Richard C. Martin (Ed.), *Approaches to Islam in religious studies* (pp. 164–173, 232–233). Tucson: University of Arizona Press.

Nathan of Nemirov, Rabbi. (1973). *Rabbi Nachman's wisdom: Shevachay Ha Ran, Sichos HaRan* (Trans. R. Aryeh Kaplan). New York: Sepher-Hermon Press.

Netton, Ian Richard. (1992). *Al-Farabi and his school*. London & New York: Routledge.

Oberndorf, C. P. (1953). Autobiography of Josef Breuer (1842–1925). *International Journal of Psycho-Analysis* 34:64–67.

Origen. (1957). *The song of songs, commentary and homilies* (Trans. R. P. Lawson). New York & Ramsey, NJ: Newman Press.

Otto, Rudolf. (1950). *The idea of the holy: An inquiry into the non-rational factor in the idea of the divine and its relation to the rational* (2nd ed.) (Trans. John W. Harvey). London: Oxford University Press.

Paley, William. (1802). *Natural theology; or, evidences of the existence and attributes of the deity, collected from the appearances of nature*. London.

Piaget, Jean. (1951). *Play, dreams and imitation in childhood* (Trans. C. Gattegno & F. M. Hodgson). London: Routledge & Kegan Paul, 1972.

Pines, Shlomo. (1963). Introduction. In Moses Maimonides, *The guide of the perplexed*, 2 vols. (Trans. Shlomo Pines). Chicago: University of Chicago Press.

Plato. (1937). *The dialogues of Plato*, Vol. 2 (Trans. B. Jowett). New York: Random House.

Popkin, Richard H. (1988). Newton and Maimonides. In Ruth Link-Salinger (Ed.), *A Straight Path: Studies in Medieval Philosophy and Culture. Essays in Honor of Arthur Hyman* (pp. 216–229). Washington, DC: Catholic University of America Press, 1988.

———. (1990). Some further comments on Newton and Maimonides. In James E. Force & Richard H. Popkin (Eds.), *Essays on the context, nature and influence of Isaac Newton's theology* (pp. 1–7). Dordrecht & Boston: Kluwer Academic Publishers, 1990.

Pruyser, Paul W. (1983). *The play of imagination: Toward a psychoanalysis of culture*. New York: International Universities Press.

Rahman, Fazlur. (1958). *Prophecy in Islam: Philosophy and orthodoxy*. London: George Allen & Unwin.

Rainey, Rueben McCorkle. (1971). *Freud as student of religion: Perspectives on the background and development of his thought*. Unpublished Ph.D. dissertation, Columbia University. Ann Arbor, MI: Universty Microfilms.

[Rhazes]. (1950). *The spiritual physick of Rhazes* (Trans. Arthur J. Arberry). London: John Murray.

Rice, Emanuel. (1990). *Freud and Moses: The long journey home*. Albany: State University of New York Press.

Roback, Abraham A. (1929). *Jewish influence in modern thought*. Cambridge: Sci-Art Publishers.

———. (1957). *Freudiana*. Cambridge: Sci-Art Publishers.

Robinson, Daniel N. (1989). *Aristotle's psychology*. New York: Columbia University Press.

Rubenstein, Richard L. (1975). *The cunning of history: The Holocaust and the American future*. New York: Harper & Row.

Ryding, Karin Christina. (1990). Alchemy and linguistics: Connections in early Islam. In Z. R. W. M. von Martels (Ed.), *Alchemy revisited: Proceedings of the International Conference on the History of Alchemy at the University of Groningen, 17–19 April 1989* (pp. 117–120). Leiden: E. J. Brill.

Scholem, Gershom G. (1954). *Major trends in Jewish mysticism* (3rd ed.). New York: Schocken, 1961.

——— . (1965). *Jewish gnosticism, Merkabah mysticism and Talmudic tradition* (2nd ed.). New York: Jewish Theological Seminary of America.

——— . (1972). Three types of Jewish piety. In Gilles Quispel & Gershom Scholem, *Eranos Lectures 3: Jewish and gnostic man*. Dallas: Spring Publications.

——— . (1987). *Origins of the Kabbalah* (Trans. Allan Arkush, Ed. R. J. Zwi Werblowsky). Princeton, NJ: Jewish Publication Society—Princeton University Press.

——— . (1991). *On the mystical shape of the godhead: Basic concepts in the Kabbalah* (Trans. J. Neugroschel). New York: Schocken.

Schur, Max. (1966). Some additional "day residues" of "The Specimen Dream of Psychoanalysis. In Rudolph M. Loewenstein, Lottie M. Newman, Max Schur, & Albert J. Solnit (Eds.), *Psychoanalysis—A general psychology: Essays in honor of Heinz Hartmann* (pp. 45–85). New York: International Universities Press.

Sharpe, Ella Freeman. (1950). The technique of psycho-analysis: Seven lectures (Ed. Marjorie Brierley). Reprinted in *Collected Papers on Psycho-Analysis* (pp. 9–106). London: Hogarth Press.

Strauss, Leo. (1963). Introduction. In Moses Maimonides, *The guide of the perplexed*, 2 vols. (Trans. Shlomo Pines). Chicago: University of Chicago Press.

Thalmann, Marianne. (1972). *The literary sign language of German Romanticism* (Trans. Harold A. Basilius). Detroit: Wayne State University Press.

Thomas, Owen. (1969). *Metaphor: And related subjects*. New York: Random House.

Twersky, Isadore. (1967). Some non-halakic aspects of the *Mishneh Torah*. In Alexander Altmann (Ed.), *Jewish Medieval and Renaissance studies* (pp. 95–118). Cambridge: Harvard University Press.

——— . (1980). *Introduction to the Code of Maimonides*. New Haven: Yale University Press.

Verman, Mark. (1996). *The history and varieties of Jewish meditation*. Northvale, NJ: Jason Aronson.

Vickers, Brian. (1990). The discrepancy between *res* and *verba* in Greek alchemy. In Z. R. W. M. von Martels (Ed.), *Alchemy revisited: Proceedings of the International Conference on the History of Alchemy at the University of Groningen, 17–19 April 1989* (pp. 21–33). Leiden: E. J. Brill.

Wasserstrom, Steven M. (1995). *Between Muslim and Jew: The problem of symbiosis under early Islam*. Princeton, NJ: Princeton University Press.

Weisner, Wayne M., & Riffel, Pius Anthony. (1960). Scrupulosity: Religion and obsessive compulsive behavior in children. *American Journal of Psychiatry* 117:314–318.

Weizmann, Fredric, & Weiss, David S. (2005). Obituary: David Bakan (1921–2004). *History of Psychology* 8/3:317–320.

Winnicott, D. W. (1963). The development of the capacity for concern. *Bulletin of the Menninger Clinic* 27:167–176. Reprinted in *The maturational processes and the facilitating environment: Studies in the theory of emotional development* (pp. 73–82). New York: International Universities Press, 1965.

———. (1971). *Playing and reality*. London: Tavistock Publications; reprinted Harmondsworth: Penguin Books Ltd., 1974.

Wolfson, Elliot R. (1994). *Through a speculum that shines: Vision and imagination in medieval Jewish mysticism*. Princeton, NJ: Princeton University Press.

———. (1996). Iconic visualization and the imaginal body of God: The role of intention in the rabbinic conception of prayer. *Modern Theology* 12(2):137–162.

Wolfson, Harry Austryn. (1935a). The internal senses in Latin, Arabic, and Hebrew philosophic texts. *Harvard Theological Review* 28/2:69–133.

———. (1935b). Maimonides on the internal senses. *Jewish Quarterly Review* 25:441–467. Rpt. in *Studies in the history and philosophy of religion* (Eds. Isadore Twersky & George H. Williams) (Vol. 1, pp. 344–370). Cambridge: Harvard University Press, 1973.

Wolpe, Joseph. (1958). *Psychotherapy by reciprocal inhibition*. Stanford: Stanford University Press.

Zilboorg, Gregory & Henry, George W. (1941). *A history of medical psychology*. New York: W. W. Norton.

Index

Abraham ben David, Rabbi, x
Abulafia, Abraham, x, 30, 41–42
Account of the Beginning, 29, 97–98, 99–100, 101, 102–112, 121
Account of the Chariot, 29, 97–98, 99, 100, 101, 102, 114–125
Active Intellect, x, 8–9, 11–12, 22–23, 25, 31, 33, 34–35, 37, 38, 39, 41, 43, 46, 47, 55, 56, 57, 60, 70, 74, 81, 95, 110, 117, 137–138, 140–141, 158, 159
Adam and Eve, 106, 108–109, 110, 112
Afterlife, 79, 81
Akedah (Binding of Isaac), 66–69, 76
Akiva, Rabbi, 89–93, 103
Akrasia, 18–19
Alchemy, 76–77, 95, 100
Alexander, Franz, 46
Al-Farabi, x, 4, 13–15, 23, 38, 50, 53, 54, 55, 57
Altmann, Alexander, ix
Angels, 7, 38, 41, 59, 60, 66, 70, 91, 103, 10–16, 147, 159
Anger of God, 63, 160
Anthropomorphism, 51, 62–63, 105, 114, 118, 124, 125, 160
Apatheia, 4
Aquinas, St. Thomas, 1, 37, 139, 140, 141
Arayot, 97, 100–102
Argument from design, 30–32, 34, 45–46, 47, 88, 127

Aristotelianism, x, 1, 2, 4, 6, 7, 8, 9, 17, 20, 22, 25, 32, 35, 38, 41, 45, 49, 51, 52, 53, 55, 70, 82, 93–94, 105, 109, 110, 154
Aristotle, 2–3, 4, 5, 6, 7, 8, 9, 10, 11, 12, 13, 15, 18, 19, 20, 25, 26, 29, 38, 44, 45, 49, 50, 51, 52, 100, 158, 159, 163
Asceticism, 127–128, 132, 136
Avempace. *See* Ibn Bajjah
Averroes. *See* Ibn Rushd
Avicenna. *See* Ibn Sina

Bahya ibn Paquda, 25–26, 27, 47, 54
Bakan, David, 35–37, 45, 47, 148, 154
Belief, 26–27, 45–47
Biblical citations and commentaries, 6, 7, 8, 10, 17, 19–20, 21, 22, 26, 27, 40, 51, 57, 58, 60, 63–70, 86–87, 92, 103–112, 114–120, 122
Bion, Wilfred R., 58
Blumenthal, David R., x, 33–35, 40
B'nai Brith Society, 142, 149
Book of the Commandments, 1, 26
Brentano, Franz, 9, 39, 140–141, 150, 163
Breuer, Josef, 141–142
Brill, Abraham A., 139
Buber, Martin, 42

Capp, Donald, ix
Client population, 127–136

179

INDEX

Commandments of beliefs and affects, 26–27
Commentary on the Mishnah, x, 1, 9, 53, 75–76, 78, 95, 101, 104
Conflict model, 150–152, 164
Contemplation, 4, 5, 13, 25–26, 32, 40–42, 45, 46, 52, 82
Corbin, Henry, 92
Corrective emotional experiences, 46
Creation out of nothing, 120, 122, 123–124, 125, 147, 159
Cure of souls. *See* Psychotherapy
Curriculum, 27–32

Davidson, Herbert A., 16, 102–103
De Leon, Moshe, x, 30
Denial, 19–20
Desensitization, 16–17
Dream, 55, 56, 58–60, 67, 68, 70, 74
Drob, Sanford L., ix

Eckhart, Meister, 1
Ecstasy, 12, 35, 45, 47, 127
Eight Chapters, 1, 15, 61, 78, 87, 154, 163; European translations of, 139
Elior, Rachel, 101
Epicureanism, 82, 83
Esotericism, 75–78, 90, 95, 98, 100, 105, 144, 158
Ezekiel, 69, 102, 107, 114, 116, 117, 118, 122, 147, 159

Faculties of the soul, 3–5, 13–14, 49; appetitive, 46, 47, 62, 113, 125, 131, 154; nutritive, 62. *See also* imagination, intellect
Fastidiousness, 128–129, 132, 136
Fear of God, 32–33, 45, 47, 69, 70, 75, 89, 127, 132
Fishbane, Michael, 133, 134
Fliess, Wilhelm, 148
Form, 2–3, 6–7, 40, 60–61, 105, 107–109, 109, 110, 112, 125, 147; equivalent to angels, 7, 105–106. *See also* Intelligible
Four Who Entered Paradise, 89–93, 95, 125

Free association, 154–156
French, Thomas M., 46
Freud, Amalia, 138, 139
Freud, Jacob, 137–138, 141, 163
Freud, Sigmund, viii, ix, x, 17, 20, 45, 50, 58, 135–136; ancestry of, 137–138; philosophic studies with Brentano, 140–141; relation to Judaism, 139; religious education, 139–140; self-analysis, 149
Freud's convergences with Maimonides: concept of psychic reality, 157–158; concept of unconscious, 158–160; dream theory and technique, 142–146; identification with Moses, 162–163; sociocultural conflict model, 150–152; theories of pathology and therapy, 152–156; theory of sexuality, 147–150; understanding on one's own, 158; view of Judaism, 160–161

Gemara, 28, 90–91, 97
Ghazali, 54
Glory of the Lord, 70, 115–116, 117, 119
Guide of the Perplexed, vii–viii, x, 1, 29, 30, 41, 42, 49, 50, 51–52, 53, 75–76, 80, 86, 91, 93, 99, 100, 101, 104, 107, 109, 113, 114, 120, 141, 160, 163; European translations of, 139

Ha-Levi, Judah, ix–x
Hammerschlag, Samuel, 140, 141, 142
Hartmann, Eduard von, ix
Hasidei Ashkenaz, 41
Hasidism, 137–138, 163, 164
Hekhalot literature, 92, 93, 95, 121
Heschel, Abraham Joshua, 52
Holiness, 117
Hylé, 109–110
Hysterical symptoms, 20, 21, 23, 127, 154, 164

Ibn Aknin, Joseph, 52, 99, 113
Ibn Bajjah, x, 53, 54
Ibn Daud, Abraham, 54

Ibn Rushd, x, 38, 53, 54, 81, 140
Ibn Sina, x, 4, 38, 53, 54, 55, 57, 100, 140
Ibn Tufail, 54, 93–94
Idel, Moshe, x, 33, 101
Illuminism, 38–39, 57
Image of God, 6, 8
Imagination, 5, 6, 49–50, 55–56, 57, 60–62, 67, 70–71, 121, 124, 125, 135, 137, 143, 154, 157
Inclinations, good and evil, 61–62
Insight, 5, 18, 52
Inspiration, 5, 25, 40, 42, 43, 45, 52, 53, 57, 84
Intellect (rational faculty), 5–6, 10, 11, 55–57, 60, 62, 73, 74, 106, 109, 131, 141, 143, 150, 153, 157, 158; actualization of, 10–12, 13, 25, 37–38, 55–57, 70, 80, 84, 88, 124
Intelligible, 7, 8, 12, 46, 53, 55, 57, 63, 64, 74, 95
Interpretation, 51–52, 62–63, 71, 73, 92–93, 98, 108, 112, 118, 125, 132, 149, 156, 157; of dreams, 142–147, 148, 163; in Hasidism, 138
Intuition, 5, 25
Isaac the Blind, Rabbi, x
Isaiah, 102
Ismailis, 77

Jabir ibn Hayyan, 76–77
Johnson, Mark, 121
Judaism: as natural religion, 74, 135; views of, 160–162

Kabbalah, ix–x, 30, 40, 50, 57, 93, 118, 137, 138, 147–148, 149, 164
Kaplan, Aryeh, 42
Klein, Melanie, 22

Lakoff, George, 121
Langer, Suzanne K., 121
Laws, ceremonial and rational, 130–131, 151–152
Logos, 159
Love of God, 32, 34–35, 45, 69, 70, 75, 88, 127, 132
Luria, Rabbi Isaac, ix

MacDonald, Paul, 38
Maimonides, Abraham, 41
Maimonides' convergences with Freud: concept of psychic reality, 157–158; concept of unconscious, 158–160; dream theory and technique, 142–146; identification with Moses, 162–163; sociocultural conflict model, 150–152; theories of pathology and therapy, 152–156; theory of sexuality, 147–150; understanding on one's own, 158; view of Judaism, 160–161
Maimonides, Moses: familiarity with Greek philosophy, 53–54; writings of, 1
Maimonides, Obadyah, 41
Makhshavah, 94
Malakut, 55–56
Maslow, Abraham, 44
Matter, 105, 107–110, 112, 125, 147
Mean, doctrine of, 4, 14, 15, 16, 23, 46, 129–130, 136
Meditation, 25–26, 27, 32, 40, 42–43, 45–47, 50, 54, 75, 80, 127, 132, 135, 137, 154–156, 164
Mental images, 49–52, 55, 57–58, 71, 92, 93
Merkur, Dan, x, 138
Merlan, Philip, 33
Messianic era, 79, 89
Metaphor, 55, 69, 91–92, 93, 107–108, 110, 113, 118, 120–121, 122, 124, 127, 137, 160
Metaphysics, 29, 102, 112, 117, 124
Microcosm, 26, 119–120
Mishnah, 82, 83, 86, 88, 97, 98, 99, 113, 114
Mishneh Torah, x, 1, 26, 27–29, 41, 53, 79, 88, 101, 104, 106, 131
Mystical death, 87, 88, 89, 92, 93, 127
Mysticism: intellectualist, x, 10, 33–35, 37, 39, 47, 53, 54, 55–57, 74, 80; Islamic, 33, 57, 65, 93, 127; Maimonides' three phases of intellectualist mysticism, 34–35; monistic, 93–95; rational, 35–37, 45, 47, 52,

Mysticism *(continued)*
  82, 83, 84, 87, 88, 127, 132, 164;
  similarity of psychoanalysis to,
  35–37, 156

Negative theology, 51
Neoplatonism. *See* Platonism
Newton, Isaac, 1, 35

Onqelos, 6, 106, 116, 118, 144
Origen, 101
Otto, Rudolf, 32

Parables, 57, 64, 65, 67, 69, 73, 79, 91, 93, 110, 145
Paradise, 89–90
Parmenides, 9
Pedagogical psychology, 13–16, 18, 19, 23
Perek Helek, 78–80, 82–89, 95
Perplexity, 49, 62, 64–65, 73–75, 89–93, 95, 112, 114, 118, 125, 127, 132, 157–158
Pfister, Oskar, 164–165
Philosophical realism, 9–10
Philosophy: competence in, 64, 124
Physics, 29, 102, 105, 112, 124
Piaget, Jean, 57–58
Pines, Shlomo, 34
Plato, 5, 9, 11, 18, 19, 30, 107, 147
Platonism, x, 3–4, 11, 20, 22, 33, 38, 49, 53, 55, 93, 109–110
Plotinus, 38
Practice of the presence of God, 39–44
Prophecies of Abraham, 64–69, 70; of Ezekiel, 69–70; of Moses, 58, 60
Prophecy, 40–41, 47, 52, 54–60, 70–71, 74, 87–88; terror during, 58–59, 65, 86–87
Psychic reality, 157–158
Psychoanalysis, 119, 135–136, 144, 149, 151, 152, 154
Psychotherapy, 2, 12–13, 14–15, 20–21, 25, 45, 47, 50, 51–52, 75, 87, 89, 132–133, 135, 137; behavioral, 15–17, 44; insight-oriented, 5, 52,
164; supportive, 46–47, 132, 136, 149, 164; uncovering, 137
Pythagorean theorem, 38

Rashi, 52
Reason. *See* Intellect
Reik, Theodor, 139
Repentance, 20–22, 44, 154, 156
Repression, 148, 153, 154
Resistance, 21, 45, 47, 135–136, 149
Resurrection, 82, 83, 85–87, 88, 89, 95, 127
Rhazes, 3–4
Roback, Abraham, 139
Robinson, Daniel N., 11

Saadia Gaon, 52
Sabbath, 111–112
Sabianism, 161
Sages, 51, 61, 66, 67, 70, 75, 84, 90, 95, 97, 99, 101, 108, 109, 114, 118, 129, 130, 144, 152
Saintliness, 129–130, 136
Satan, 61, 67, 71
Scholem, Gershom G., ix, x, 89–90, 92, 94, 112, 133
Schur, Max, 148–149
Secrets of the Law, 62, 90–125, 147, 148
Sefer Ha-Bahir, x, 94, 104–105, 111–112
Sefer Shiur Komah, 121
Sefer Yetsirah, 26, 41
Self-actualization, 11
Self-analysis, 149
Sextus Empiricus, 9
Sexuality: manifest, 110, 114, 117–118, 147; metaphoric, 112–114; privileged place of, 147–152, 164; universal, 150. *See also* Arayot, Account of the Beginning, Account of the Chariot
Sharpe, Ella Freeman, 171
Socrates, 13, 17, 18, 19, 22, 26, 152
Strauss, Leo, viii, 106–107
Sublimation, 47, 164–165
Sufis, 25, 33, 57, 65, 93, 127

Talmud, 28–29, 30, 40, 56, 70, 75, 84, 88, 90, 91, 92, 102, 104, 112, 114, 118, 119, 124, 127, 141, 147, 164; definition of, 28–29
Ta'wil, 76–77, 95
Theological method, 31–32, 62, 64, 73–74, 83
Thirteen principles of the Law, 83–89
Treatise on the Resurrection, 76

Unconscious, 11, 50, 55, 57, 137, 158–160
Understanding on one's own, 97–98, 158

Wasserstrom, Steven, 76
Will, 18–21, 32, 44, 50, 61–62, 71, 127, 153
Winnicott, D. W., 11, 22
Wolfson, Elliot, 92
World to come, 78–82, 88, 95, 127

www.ingramcontent.com/pod-product-compliance
Lightning Source LLC
Chambersburg PA
CBHW030654230426
43665CB00011B/1085